THEY FOLLOWED THEIR DREAMS

Books by Michelle Russell

The Deppe and Ganser Families (1790–1987)

Musical Memories: Songs the Gumm Family Sang

The Gumm Family Souvenir Song Book

Sabrina: The Autobiography of a Cat

From Tennessee to Oz: The Amazing Saga of the Gumm Family, Vols. 1 and 2

Children's Books:

A Cat Named Toto

Meet Lily: A Very Little Girl

THEY FOLLOWED THEIR DREAMS

The Story of Three Chicago Families

By
MICHELLE RUSSELL

CATSONG PUBLISHING
Grand Rapids, Minnesota
2017

Copyright © 2017 by Michelle Russell

All rights reserved. No part of this book may be reproduced or utilized in any form or by any means, electronic or mechanical, including photocopying, recording or by any information storage and retrieval system, without written permission in writing from the publisher—except for brief quotations in critical reviews or articles. Inquiries should be addressed to Permissions Department, Catsong Publishing, 33034 Crystal Springs Road, Grand Rapids, MN 55744, or catsong2@netzero.net

Visit: http://www.catsongpublishing.com

Published by
Catsong Publishing
33034 Crystal Springs Road
Grand Rapids, MN 55744
218-326-6056

Russell, Michelle
  They Followed Their Dreams
  Includes bibliographic reference, appendix and index
  ISBN: 978-0-9800642-5-4
Library of Congress Control Number: 2017904662

Cover design: Michelle Russell & Marny K. Parkin
Interior design: Marny K. Parkin
All photos, with the exception of historic works or noted, copyright © Michelle Russell

*To all those who have waited
such a long time for this book*

Contents

Acknowlegements ix
Introduction 1

The Old Country
1 Prüm 7
2 Ancient Times 9
3 Enter Napoleon 19
4 The Deppes 27
5 A New Life in Prüm 37
6 To America 43

The New World
7 Chicago 51
8 Chicago to Richmond 63
9 Back Home—to Chicago 79
10 The Gansers and the Kochs 85
11 Anarchy 93
12 Bakery Life 105
13 1871—The End of the World 115
14 Chicago to Indiana: Success and Tragedy 125
15 The Booming 1880s 143
16 The Deppe Children 159
17 The Deppes in Indiana 169
18 The Early '90s: A Trip, a Fair and Marriage 175

19 A Trip to Prüm	199
20 The Steins	209
21 Bertha	229
22 Joys and Sorrows in the 1890s	243
23 Oscar and Etta	259
24 A New Century	265
25 Love and Scandal	277
26 Golden Days	287
27 No Goodbyes	297
Notes	301
Bibliography	313
Photo Credits	317
Index	319

Acknowlegements

MY HEARTFELT THANKS TO THOSE WHO SO GENEROUSLY HELPED with this history. Beginning with family members who have passed on, deepest gratitude to my grandmother, Rose Victoria Ubil, my mother, Marian Prefontaine, my great aunt, Dorothy Wright, and my cousins, Kay Foxcroft and Tom Wright.

Following in her late husband Gerald Canine's footsteps, Caroline Canine shared the contents of the Ganser/Kirchstein/Canine archives. Without her generous gift, this book would be incomplete. Kathryn Stitt, granddaughter of Kate Deppe Lockwood, has also been a great source of information and photos, as was her cousin, the late Betsy Moen, daughter of Charlotte Lockwood. After her passing, Betsy's widow, Tom Moen, kindly left her scrapbooks with me.

Much appreciation and gratitude to Kay Foxcroft's niece, Kathryn Ringrose, for sharing many rare photos, and to her husband, David Ringrose, for scanning them. Dorothy Wright's daughter, Louise Ghidossi, lent precious family artifacts and pictures to be photographed for the book. Frank Deppe IV and his wife, Frances, opened their home and archives to me, greatly adding to the information on his father, Francis Deppe III; his great grandfather, Edward S. Dreyer; and the Deppe Baking Company.

In memorium, I would like to express my gratitude to LeRoy Schamper, grandson of John Ganser, and to his lovely wife, Elaine, who welcomed me into their home on numerous occasions; also to Isabel Deppe Lippelt, a descendant of both Joseph Deppe and John Ganser. Additional thanks to the Brackens, Josephine Gourley, and Alton Ochsner, Jr., who all gave of their time and knowledge in the early days of my research.

In Germany, I owe many thanks to Monika Rolef, historian of Prüm, and Guntar Reichertz, Standesamt, who helped me over a period of thirty years. Also, appreciation to the following German government offices: Standesamt Trier, Stadtarchiv Trier, Landeshauptarchiv Koblenz, Secret State Archives Foundation in Berlin; State Archive North Rhine-Westphalia; Department of the Rhineland; and the Eifelkreises Bitburg-Prüm Kreisarchiv in Bitburg.

In Chicago, many thanks to researchers: Craig Pfannekuche of Memory Trail, who unearthed information on Deppe property records, and Diane Gonzales, who solved the resulting mysteries! Interestingly, Diane was listed in my 1980s notes as a person to contact; something that finally happened in 2016 by chance!

Many thanks to historians Melanie Appel, Barry Smith of the Lincoln Park Presbyterian Church, Joy Kingsolver of Sinai Temple, and Valerie Deehan of Indiana for going out of their way to look things up and share what they had with me.

And thank you to the many institutions of learning, archives and historical societies which helped me, both in-person and long-distance: The Chicago Public Library, The Chicago Historical Society, the Newberry Library, the Sousa Archives, and the Batavia Historical Society. Finally, much gratitude to my designer, Marny Parkin, without whose knowledge, talent and patience, this book would not exist in this form.

This book is for my family, for Chicagoans, and for all who love the history of America and her people.

Introduction

THE EXISTENCE OF THIS BOOK BEGAN WITH THE STORIES MY GRANDmother told me when I was a child. Engraved in my memory are those summer nights in her Malibu cottage as we three—my grandmother, mother and I—lay in our beds, listening to the pounding surf. It was then that my mother would ask my grandmother, Rose Victoria Ubil, about growing up in Chicago and about the relatives: Uncle Frank, Aunt Anna, Edwin, the Ochsners, Aunt Kate and Uncle Oz. Many nights, I fell asleep wondering about these people, especially "Uncle Oz," who sounded as if he might be related to *The Wizard of Oz*. It all sounded so enchanting.

Yet no matter the story, the subject always came back to "the Deppe Bakery." That was the thing around which family life revolved when my grandmother was a girl. Even as a small child, the stories she told fired my imagination, and as I got older, my curiosity grew, as did my desire to touch to past.

That desire to touch the past took form when I was eleven. One day, I made a family chart with names and dates of birth. Then, I asked each of my grandparents (my mother's parents) to put their signature next to the information. Somehow I knew this would be historic.

By the mid-1980s, with both of my grandparents gone, I decided to preserve all the family history I could. Making my first six-week trip to Chicago to gather information, with the help of my great aunt, Dorothy Wright, I contacted all the relatives in the area. They welcomed me into their homes and shared their stories. Finally, thanks to Owen Deutsch, the owner at that time, I was able to visit that legendary bakery building where it all began and the apartments where the family lived. These rooms were much grander than I had imagined. I wish I had the foresight to photograph those rooms then because by the time of my next visit, the interior of the building had been forever changed.

My research in the mid-1980s resulted in a small self-published, hand-bound book titled, "The Deppe and Ganser Families (1790–1987)." This was merely a genealogy book, but it laid the foundation for the present work, which was originally planned as a "historic novel." Sections of that work are included here; many were written in Chicago at the site where the event took place.

During the passage of the next thirty years, research and writing were done periodically. Meanwhile, trips were taken on more than one occasion to Prüm, Germany, Chicago, Illinois and Hobart, Indiana.

One day, on a travel layover, I visited Old Town and walked down Wells Street, an area where my great, great grandfather Franz Deppe's first bakery had been located. Being there, I hoped to pick up some remnant of the past—some clue as to what my ancestors experienced and who they were. More than one hundred years had passed since they traveled down this street, yet as I sat in a sidewalk café and later walked in their footsteps, I felt great admiration and gratitude. Franz and Catharina Deppe came to this country as strangers with little money. And they succeeded, not only in building a life for themselves, but in helping others as well.

It was then that it hit me—the past is not so far away; it is not gone. To a large degree, I owe who I am to those who came before me. It is because of them—the choices they made, the things they did, their faith and ethics that I am who I am today. I am deeply grateful to them for this. The past is never completely gone. It is still with us today.

Sadly, as often happens, life got in the way of completing this book sooner. In the meantime, many of the people who urged me on and contributed so greatly to this work are gone.

It is 2017 now, and there can be no more waiting. Perhaps someday, someone may discover more, but for now, this the story.

The Old Country

Chapter 1

Prüm

OUR STORY BEGINS LONG AGO IN A PLACE KNOWN AS PRÜM. THERE, amidst the hills of the Moselle Valley, this lovely town lies. Only sixty-six kilometers from Luxemburg, the road to Prüm passes through rolling hills and green pastures, until the rising spires of the ancient basilica reveal themselves.

A slender stream known as the River Prüm flows happily here. Passing along the village borders, its clear waters sparkle as they leap over stones and gravel. The gentle hills form yet another barrier between the village and the outside world.

In spring and autumn, the chill of the evening air causes a warm mist to rise from the hills surrounding the town. The reason for this mysterious veil lies deep beneath the earth's surface. For more than a thousand years now, people have journeyed to Prüm for this—a wealth of healing mineral springs surrounded by beauty. Like the view, Prüm is a simple place, with a wealth of mystery beneath its surface.

San Salvatore Basilica

Chapter 2

Ancient Times

The tiny village of Prüm has always known she was important, for her roots are legendary.

Prüm's existence as a place of note began with a Merovingian Princess. In A.D. 721, Bertrada of Prüm welcomed a group of monks to her large estate along the Moselle River. It was during this visit that the Princess and her son, Charibert, the Count of Laon, signed an agreement with the monks to found the Abbey at Prüm. So eager were the monks to settle there, they began to lay a foundation for the abbey the very next day. In return for the land, the monks took on their first task—praying night and day for the souls of the Princess Bertrada and her son, Count Charibert.

Although the size of the abbey built at this time is unknown, its ruins left a good sized imprint, which today is covered by the present abbey, church, and cemetery.

Historically, there is much more to the story. Princess Bertrada had a granddaughter (Charibert's daughter), who was named for her.* Twenty years after the founding of the Abbey at Prüm, this Bertrada, known as "Bertrada of Laon," married Pepin. Ten years later, in A.D. 751, Pepin would be crowned King of the Franks.†

---

* Sometimes referred to as Heribert.

† Pepin was also known as Pepin the Short, Pepin III and Pippen.

Four years before this event, Pepin and Bertrada had a son, whom they named Charles. Many years later, this same Charles would be known to the world as Charlemagne the Great. In short, Princess Bertrada—founder of the Abbey at Prüm, was the great-grandmother of the legendary Emperor.

During these early years, many tribes roamed the lands which we know today as Europe. Most of these tribes were pagan; people who worshipped multiple gods, mostly gods based on nature. Now, Pepin's great grandfather, Clovis, was a pagan, who had married a Christian Burgundian princess, Clotilde. Clovis allowed Clotilde to baptize their first son, but after the child died, his heart was hardened and he refused to be baptized.

Then, one day, in A.D. 496, Clovis found himself in the midst of a fierce battle. In desperation, he began to pray, promising Jesus that if he won this battle, he would have faith and be baptized. In the midst of what seemed an impossibility, the tide turned; Clovis and his troops won. Keeping his promise, he was baptized and became a Christian. Ultimately, this conversion led to the spread of Christianity throughout Western Europe.

Clovis also had a great deal of admiration for Roman customs. It was his hope that as he conquered Europe, and granted lands to his soldiers and the citizens in various areas, these lands would be turned into Roman-style villas and estates.

Statue of Pepin, San Salvatore Basilica

Pepin and Bertrada's son, Charlemagne, was twenty-nine when he became king. Two years later, the Lombard Desiderius tribes invaded the Papal States. In desperation, Pope Hadrian sent an urgent message asking that Charlemagne give the church his protection. Because of the Pope's request, Charlemagne went to war, captured Pavia, and assumed the crown of a state just north of Italy, Lombardy. Simultaneously, he became the Church's protector.

Charlemagne, San Salvatore Basilica

It is said that Charlemagne's ultimate goal was to unite the warring Germanic tribes into a single, peaceful Christian state. In this, he succeeded.

Among the European invaders were the Saxons, a pagan tribe, which conducted many attacks, including the burning of churches In response to this destruction, when the Emperor conquered members of this tribe, he gave them a choice: become Christian and be baptized or die. Hundreds were killed, but many also became Christian.

During his life, Charlemagne personally led a series of fifty-three campaigns. By the time of his death in 814, he had conquered most of Western Europe. These lands included those in the west, from the Pyrenees of Spain, where he drove back the Muslim Arabs, to the Carpathian Mountains bordering Romania and Ukraine in the east, and from the Mediterranean Sea in the south to the Baltic Sea in the north. As a result, of his campaigns, Charlemagne was crowned Emperor of the Holy Roman Empire.

During the reigns of both Pepin III and Charlemagne, Prüm was considered the Carolingian Dynasty's favorite monastery. Because of this, the Abbey received many special gifts and advantages. On August 13, A.D. 762, King Pepin III gave an order to have the forty-one year old monastery rebuilt and bestowed a wealth of land to the Abbey. During this same period, Assuerus was named Abbott, and brought a group of monks from the city of Meaux, near Paris, to live in the Abbey under his guidance. Thus, the Abbey grew on many levels.

Prüm Abbey Coat of Arms

It was during the reign of Charlemagne, that the Abbey's church was built in the form of a basilica—a long building with double colonnades and a semicircular apse. This form was one used by the Romans, which no doubt pleased Pepin. The monks named the new church San Salvatore, "Our Savior." Built with great care, the Basilica was spacious enough to accommodate several hundred monks now living at the Abbey.

When San Salvatore Basilica was completed in A.D. 799, both Charlemagne and Pope Leo III were present for the consecration. Pope Leo had traveled all the way from Rome. This event reveals the importance Prüm's Abbey held at that time for both king and papacy.

Meanwhile, because of the Abbey's favor with Charlemagne and the kings who followed, many holy relics were brought to San

Salvatore. Most notable of these are a pair of ancient sandals, said to have been the "sandals of Christ." King Pepin personally brought the sandals from Rome, as a gift from the Pope.*

Aside from religious reasons, it seems the Abbey had other uses for the monarchy. In 793, after Charlemagne's illegitimate son, Pepin the Hunchback, failed in his attempt to overthrow his father's throne, Charlemagne had him exiled to the Abbey Prüm, where he remained until his death in A.D. 813.

Charlemagne's grandson, Lothar I, also had a great fondness for Prüm. After years of fighting with his siblings and others over his kingdom, Lothar renounced his title as king, and divided his lands among his sons. On the 23rd of September A.D. 855, he retired to Prüm Abbey to live out his days as a monk. But Lothar was not well. Only six days after his arrival, he passed away. He was buried without ceremony, but in 1860, his grave was found. His remains now rest under one of the altars in San Salvatore.

Although Prüm was a peaceful place, it was not entirely safe from war. At the end of 9th century, the area was over-run twice by Norman invaders. During the first invasion in A.D. 882, the Normans attacked Prüm, but left it intact. During the second invasion in 892, however, the Abbey was pillaged and burnt to the ground.

As the monks attempted to recover from this terrible destruction, they came to the realization that the amount of property owned by the Abbey was far more than they could manage. As a result, they donated some of this land to form a principality. So it was that the village of Prüm was born.

During the eleventh and twelfth centuries, Prüm Abbey held as many as three hundred monks. For the most part, the monks spent their time cultivating the land and growing grapes. The rich soil and the mild, sunny climate of the Moselle Valley made it a perfect place to grow grapes for the making of fine wine.

---

* It is uncertain whether the donor was Pope Zachary or Pope Stephen.

Other members of the Abbey spent their time caring for the poor and the sick. The hot mineral springs nearby were found to be a wonderful means of restoring health. The springs in the midst of the Eifel Mountains contain mineral ingredients which make them healthful, both for drinking and bathing. These same waters exist in Aachen as well, the place where Charlemagne and his father, Pepin, chose to live. It is said that in earlier days, Roman legions pitched their camps in the foothills of the Eifel to take advantage of these healing waters.

During this time, a religious house for ladies of noble birth was founded by head Abbott Gerhard in Neiderprüm, a small village less than a quarter of a mile down the road. This abbey and church were quite large and grand.

For over five-hundred years, the Abbey at Prüm thrived, but after years of peace and prosperity, during the thirteenth and fourteenth centuries trouble brewed amongst the monks in the form of greed and corruption. It was during this time, the Abbey building began to crumble. In fact, the problem became so severe, many monks chose to live outside the Abbey.

The city of Trier, some 60 miles away, was the nearest city to Prüm. It was the northernmost city inhabited by the Romans [30 B.C.–A.D. 316]. It was also the location of the Catholic Archdiocese for the area.

When the Archbishop of Trier learned of Prüm's problems, he decided the best way to take care of the Abbey would be to incorporate it into the Trier Archdiocese. The monks of Prüm, who were used to ruling supreme and who were probably somewhat snobbish about their history, rejected this idea wholeheartedly. They informed the Archbishop that they refused to be a part of the Trier Archdiocese. An argument between the Abbey and the Archdiocese ensued and would continue for the next sixty-three years (1511–1574).

Finally, in 1574, the Abbey had fallen into such a state of disrepair, those remaining had little choice but to submit. Thus, the Archbishop of Trier, with the title "Prince Bishop," took over administration of the Abbey.

Under the direction of the Archbishop of Trier, the Prüm Abbey was restored and began to flourish once again. By 1718, when two French Benediction "antiquarians" visited Prüm Abbey, they declared it to have one of the finest spirits of all the abbeys in Germany.

This great new spirit at the Abbey led to the rebuilding of San Salvatore Church under the plans of Balthasar Neumann. Neumann, an architect from Bohemia, is now considered the foremost master of late Baroque style—a style which fused Austrian, Bohemian, Italian and French design into one.

Yet, despite the great improvements facilitated by the Archdiocese of Trier, the monks of Prüm were very unhappy about being under its control. A Catholic history of rebellion tells the story of troops being sent to fire on the Abbey at Prüm because the monks would not submit to the Archbishop. The monks attempted to fight the soldiers by throwing stones out the windows of the Abbey at them. In the end, however, they were forced to capitulate.

In the early 1700s, Prüm was still a small village with a fairly small population. The Schoden family was one of the oldest families there, having resided in the area between Prüm and Niederprüm, farming the land since at least the 1600s. The Schodens were among those who witnessed the decline of the Abbey and its resurrection.

Joseph Peter Schoden [listed in church records by his Latin name, Joes Petrius] was baptized in Niederprüm around 1728. He married Angelica Pinten of Feverscheill in 1740. Their son, Gerard Schoden, would one day marry Magdalene, and together, they would have six children.

The Schoden's daughter, Anna Marie, born in 1784, was baptized in Niederprüm's St. Bartholomew Church. Eight years later, on July 29th, 1792, Anna Marie and her cousin, Caspar Schoden, were confirmed at St. Bartholomew's. In coming years, Anna Marie would marry another Niederprüm citizen, Johann Ganser.

During the early seventeen hundreds, Prüm grew from a hamlet on the edge of the Abbey, to a busy village of winding lanes. There was a square that included shops, two fine hotels, a building for government business, and some rather wealthy homes. Most villagers nestled their cottages on the hillside facing the Abbey. On a

Prüm hillside, with a view of San Salvatore

little square, halfway up the hill, stood a well, where locals gathered to collect water and exchange news. All in all, Prüm was an idyllic place to live if one ignored the political arguments and the uncertainties of invading Rhineland-Palatinate dukes and French soldiers.

In 1769, the village was nearly destroyed when a great fire swept through town and burned one hundred homes. But working together, the villagers soon rebuilt Prüm. That same year, workers completed a new façade on St. Salvatore Basilica. Not many years later, French troops arrived direct from the Revolution in Paris. Once again, the town was under French rule.

After the initial events of French Revolution and the execution of the monarch, the French army set out to liberate neighboring countries. Their goal was to free the common man from the feudal way of life—that of lord and serf.

Because of their close proximity, it did not take long for soldiers to cross the French border into the low mountains of the Eifel. The French were given a warm welcome by citizens of the Germanic states, who cheered the cause of freedom and equality for all. When news reached Prüm of France's new military leader, Napoleon Bonaparte, the citizens were excited.

Among those living in Prüm during this time were: Michel Darimont, Johann Wellenstein, Stephen Anton Reuland, Johann Moritz Koch and his wife, Barbara Rascop. Barbara's parents, Peter and Margaretha Rascop lived in Niederprüm, as did Johann Peter Ameis and his wife, Anna Christina Keller. The children and grandchildren of these people would all one day play a part in the story about to be told.

"Napoleon Slept Here," Prüm Museum, 1987

Chapter 3

Enter Napoleon

For many years the citizens of Prüm preserved a room where, it was said, Napoleon once slept. When, at the end of WWII, a munitions storage exploded, most of the town was destroyed, including this room. Today, if you ask whether Napoleon was ever there, the response may be, "Who knows?"

THE SOFT LIGHT OF AUTUMN SHOWN DOWN UPON THE TINY VILLAGE that afternoon in October of 1803. Tucked amidst a circle of hills and quiet streams, the citizens of Prüm lived peaceful lives. Still, they were hardly ignorant of turmoil in the outside world. They knew about the revolution in France and the new leader, Napoleon Bonaparte. In fact, the city council had sent him an invitation to visit the town.

That October day in 1803, a young man sat on his stoop, enjoying the afternoon sun and catching a bit of air as he rested from a long morning of baking bread. Then, looking down the lane toward San Salvatore, something drew his gaze. A rather grand horse with a rider dressed in military garb had just galloped into the square.

The young baker rose and hurriedly joined several other men on their way to the area in front of San Salvatore's Basilica. They all wanted to know what the matter was. One thing was clear—the soldier was French.

"Prepare yourselves. First Consul Bonaparte is coming," the uniformed rider stated boldly.

A murmur escaped the group gathered around him. Napoleon was coming to Prüm? Amazing. And he would be there within the hour! Some threw their hats in the air and began to cheer. Others ran home to change into their Sunday best. It did not take long before the square was filled with citizens.

"He will stay at my hotel," said the owner of the Goldenstern.

"My hotel is finer," said the owner of the Gebaur.

"Stop fighting, men. Prepare yourselves."

The town was bustling. Decorations were hastily hung over doors and windows.

Twenty-five year-old Johann Wellenstein peered out of his shop and wondered what the confusion was all about? Just then his wife, Magdalena, appeared. She had been at the well, getting water, when she heard the news.

"Napoleon Bonaparte is coming to Prüm! Napoleon! Ja, it is true," she exclaimed, adding, "The whole town is in an uproar!"

Johann, who had lived in Prüm since his birth in the late 1700s, had never seen such excitement.

One year earlier, the citizens of the area had taken a vote as to whether they were in favor of Napoleon becoming First Consul for life or "Lebenszeit." The results on August 2nd, 1802, showed that 5,077 were in favor, while 66 were not. Two years later, around the time of Napoleon's coronation as Emperor, once again the citizens were given the opportunity to voice their opinion. This time, 6,099 would vote "yes," and only 7 would say "nay."

Down the street, cloth-maker Caspar Darimont was hard at work on his loom. Although of French descent, Caspar had lived all his life in Prüm. After hearing news of Bonaparte's imminent visit, he thought immediately of a fine piece of cloth he'd completed recently. Now, there was no doubt in his mind as to what he would do with it—he would give it to Napoleon as a gift.

Meanwhile, in the next room, Claudia Darimont tried to keep their three children, Susanna, Anna Margaretha and baby Johannes quiet, so as not to disturb their father.

Less than a quarter mile away, in the village of Niederprüm, Johann Ganser had just finished cutting a pile of logs in his saw mill and decided to leave work early. Although it was warm out and probably would be a nice evening, the mist rose so quickly these days, one could never be quite sure about seeing the way home. Besides, Johann had only been married to Anna Marie Schoden for a few months, and he was eager to get home.

Back in Prüm, twenty year-old Georg Anton Koch headed toward the square with a quickened step. Was it true? Was Napoleon Bonaparte really coming to their little town? Would he see the great man with his own eyes? He could scarcely believe his good fortune. Prüm was a small village, but it did not lack for educated people. Georg had an intense interest in politics and the affairs of the world. Even at the age of twenty, he had read as many books as he could procure. His father was a cloth-maker, something Prüm was well-known for, but he would be a merchant.

Within the hour, a crowd had gathered along the road leading into town. There were people waiting impatiently everywhere. Suddenly, someone pointed to the horizon, where faint forms could be seen moving in their direction. A large group of soldiers on horseback soon became visible. Was the figure in the center Napoleon? Indeed, it was he! A cheer went up. As the group moved forward, who could fail to see and feel the intensity of his presence.

What cheering there was as the army arrived, led by the singular figure on a fine black horse. His eyes were dark and, his demeanor serious. One could not mistake his tri-cornered hat with the small plume. His coat was blue, embroidered with fine thread. His pants and waistcoat were white, accentuated by the black leather boots, which went up to his knees.

Those who saw Napoleon up close said that his face looked very Italian with a long, straight nose, eyes of light blue-gray, and a smile that revealed very white teeth. His hair, worn in a pigtail, extended from beneath his black hat, revealing brown hair with a surprising reddish tint. All in all, the majority decided that France's new ruler was a normal person, easy to approach, and the people were pleased.

As the soldiers halted in the square, Napoleon pointed to the Gebaur Inn and, leaning in, whispered something to the officer beside him. Then, after waving to the crowd, he dismounted his horse and entered the Inn. His right-hand man announced that "His Excellency" was tired from the long journey. He would speak to the people tomorrow, after he had rested. He had come to grant the town's request to lay a cornerstone for the new gymnasium.

Early the next morning, Napoleon Bonaparte was present for the grand ceremony, where he laid the cornerstone for the new school in place. What an honor for the citizens of this small town. Then, he spoke to them. Filled with awe and respect, the citizens did not notice that he was a man of only medium height, nor that he hid his left hand in the breast of his coat much of the time. They found no flaw in him. This soon-to-be Emperor did not smile much, but neither did he appear arrogant. Surveying the crowd, he seemed to take everything in. There was a power about him and something a little sad.

Napoleon stayed in Prüm one more night. Any who dared to wander in the darkness and look across the way to his room, would have seen that his candle burned until dawn. There, in the flickering light, Napoleon paced and, then, paused to think. When he left early the next day, many men from Prüm left with him. In the not so distant future, as Emperor, he would lead the French Army north to Russia. Napoleon had not lost a battle and his voracious appetite now led him to try to conquer that unconquerable land. It would be, perhaps, the greatest mistake of his life.

*Napoleon's room at the Gebaur Hotel,
Prüm Museum, 1987*

The people of Prüm were not surprised by the number of young men who left with the French army the following day. Most likely, there were many who wanted to go. Just as likely, there were probably many who did not. For years, this sort of thing had gone on. Prüm was a pawn between France and Rhineland; sometimes belonging to one, and sometimes to the other. Most of the locals spoke a mix of French and German. In fact, there were almost as many French names among the citizens as there were German. Yet the citizens of Prüm took things as they came.

Before Napoleon's visit, French revolutionary troops had come to Prüm in 1794. When they arrived, all lands, including those of the Roman Catholic Church, were declared to belong to the citizens. France had chosen to become a secularized society, and now declared the same for all lands she conquered.

Prüm had seen the completion of the new abbey in 1748, but in 1794, the monastery was closed and the monks evicted. Although many religious returned to their home towns, others were taken in by local citizens. Meanwhile, a good amount of former churches were rented or sold to the public.

For a town which owed its very existence to the church, this was a drastic change. Life would no longer center around religion and its rules. At the time, most of the citizens seemed pleased. At last, they felt they had some control over their destiny; they were moving into "modern times."

In the history of Niederprüm there exists the story of a man named Johann Ganser. Whether this Ganser is the same Ganser in our story or merely a relative has yet to be proven. By the early 1800s, there were a large number of Gansers living in the area, and this man may have been an uncle or cousin of the Ganser in our story.

Our Johann was born in Niederprüm around 1782. When he twelve, he witnessed many changes taking place in his community. As an adult, he was betrothed to Anna Marie Schoden, the daughter of Gerard Schoden. The couple was married in Niederprüm around 1800. Their only known child was Heinrich Ganser.

When revolutionary France took church property, they sold it to local citizens, and shared the profits with those who were hungry and in need. Johann Ganser was one of the people who bought a chapel; in fact, he bought one of the most popular chapels in Niederprüm, the "Wendalinus Kapelle," which he turned it into a store.

For quite a number of years, Ganser was very happy in this spot and built quite a successful business for himself. After 1819, when the Eifel was no longer under French rule, the citizens of the area began to return to their religious customs. They missed going to mass and praying. As a result, they wanted their churches and chapels returned.

Some years later (by some accounts, 1832), the Catholics of the Niederprüm formed a parade to Wendalinus Kapelle and asked that the chapel be returned to them. They even offered Johann Ganser money, but he was unmoved. He let them know he had no intention of giving up his store.

Frustrated, the citizens left, only to return a few days later. This time, they brought a sizeable amount of money with them. At their insistence that the chapel be returned, Johann became very angry. In fact, the exchange between him and the crowd became so intense that finally the citizens threw their money through the doorway and left. Johann picked it up and put it away.

A few days passed without a word. Then, a lawyer showed up and told Johann he had accepted the people's money, now he had to leave. The chapel was a sacred place, built by the hands of their ancestors, and the citizens would not let it go. So, he was forced to accept the citizens' offer.

According to the story, Johann Ganser saved the money and eventually used it to move to America. Again, while there is no proof that the Johann in this history is the same man in our story, this tale clearly reveals something about the events and emotions of the time.

In another marker of the period, the local citizens decided to erect Stations of the Cross on the road leading into Prüm. Johann Ganser joined together with Heinrich Graf, a fellow businessman, to erect the 9th Station—*Jesus Falls the Third Time*. The result was a cross on a pedestal, with the engraved names of both men and the date, 1823. The raising of the cross was a proud moment for the men; a testament to their faith.

Station of the Cross similar to those erected in 1823

Early View of Prüm

Chapter 4

The Deppes

FRIEDRICH CARL DEPPE TRAMPED ALONG THE ROAD FROM BERGweiler with his donkey. He was headed to Prüm, a small town approximately 25 miles away in the Moselle Valley. Although he had traveled longer distances, the road was hilly, so he considered himself lucky to have a donkey. Unlike his father and grandfather, who were carpenters, Friedrich had chosen a new profession. He felt fortunate to be an assistant surveyor. Rhineland was growing, and there was work to be had surveying land, that is if you were smart, young, and willing to travel. He was all of these, and loved the adventure of it all.

On this day, the bright sunlight made the green of the grass and trees against the blue sky appear even more brilliant than usual. Nearby, a stream bubbled over rocks. Friedrich stopped to take a drink of cool, clear water, allowing his donkey, Peter, to take a drink as well. The afternoon sun was warm, and the water felt wonderfully refreshing.

After a short rest under a tree, Friedrich decided to ride Peter for a while. He must be getting close to Prüm now. Crossing a green meadow, they followed the path to the top of the hill where they discovered a small chapel dedicated to the Blessed Mother. A bouquet of wild flowers had been placed there by someone. Friedrich pulled on Peter's reins, jumped down, and said a prayer. Then, passing through a grove of trees, he spied a tiny village in the valley below. It was Prüm. This quaint village had been built on the hillside and in the valley facing the church.

Finding a narrow path of stepping stones leading down into the village, Friedrich led the donkey carefully along the path, wending his way between backyard gardens and cottages. He wished he could pick an apple off one of the garden trees, but he dared not.

At the end of the path, he stopped short; the vision before his eyes erased any thought of food, for there, in the center of a small square stood a lovely young girl, busily pumping water into her bucket. In that moment, without knowing it, his life changed forever.

Friedrich's grandfather, Rudolf Deppe was born in Saarbrücken in the early 1700s. No one is quite sure how long the family resided in this city. They had probably not been there more than twenty years. In the future, Deppe descendants would recount a family history passed down through the generations, though probably some of the facts changed with time. One of these stories states that the Deppes originated in Palermo, Italy. Their name, spelled "Deppeé" (according to the story), meant awkward—one reason for this being that the Deppes were unusually tall. Deppe family members then left Italy and moved to France, where they settled in an area that now bears their name. The place referred to in this recollection may be Dieppe, a town on the northern coast of Normandy.

By the early 1700s, due to political events, the Deppe family feared for their lives and fled France, this time, traveling east to the Rhineland-Palatinate border, where they settled in the capital city, Saarbrücken, in the state of Saarland.

While there is no proof that this story is true, the move to Saarbrücken makes sense on many accounts. To begin with, the journey from Dieppe to Saarbrücken is not exceptionally far. Secondly, Saarbrücken had deep roots in French history, and, at that time, French was spoken fluently by most of the citizens in the area.

Finally, Saarbrücken was rich in natural resources. As a result, the city had a wealth of jobs and was financially quite healthy.

Once a part of the Roman Empire, Saarbrücken was captured by the Franks in the first century A.D., and for hundreds of years after that, France tried to hold on to it. Their desire to hold the state of Saarland stemmed from two logical reasons: Saarland was just across the French border, and her wealth of natural resources, mainly coal, were of great benefit to them.

During the Thirty Years War (1618–1648), Saarland was so devastated by battles and the resulting deprivations, the population of Saarbrücken decreased from 4,500 in 1728 to a mere 70 citizens nine years later.

Following almost immediately after the Thirty Years War was the Franco-Dutch War in 1677. This time, when Louis XIV's troops invaded, they burnt Saarbrücken to the ground, leaving behind only eight homes. Still, because of area's abundant resources in coal, Saarbrücken bounced back quickly. Then, in 1690, a short time before the Deppes moved there, France was forced to let Saarland go.

Rudolf Deppe, an artisan carpenter and cabinet maker, was probably very successful in Saarbrücken. By the mid-1700s, he was married to Maria Magdalena Weiland of Zweibrücken, a town situated 20–30 miles away. Zweibrücken, which literally means "twin bridges," was a Protestant center and contained one of the earliest grammar schools of Protestant faith.

By the late 1700s, Rudolf and Maria Magdalena moved back to Maria's "Heimat" or hometown, where they remained for rest of their lives. Rudolph would pass away on May 3, 1777, and Maria Magdalena, nearly twenty years later, on June 17th, 1794.

Saarbrücken Bridge

The city of Saarbrücken, where the Deppes lived, was equally busy to Zweibrücken, if not more so. Cut in half by the River Saar, the citizens built a stone bridge over the river in 1546, thus joining the two sides. That bridge remains to this day. When the coal mines were nationalized (1741–1768), the area became a highly industrialized, and the citizens reaped the benefits of this prosperity.

During his lifetime, Rudolf Deppe witnessed the raising of numerous grand structures, including Ludwigkirche (Ludwig Church), St. Johann's Basilica, Friedankirche (Peace Church), the grand Saarbrücker Schloss (castle), and the beautiful St. Johannes Market, where farmers and tradesmen sold their goods. Rudolf may have sold items there, but likely had his own shop. Indeed, Saarbrücken was a beautiful city, and those who lived there took great pride in it.

The only known child of Rudolf and Maria Magdalena Deppe is Carl Deppe. Carl grew up under the rule of the Counts of

Nassau-Saarbrücken. As a youth, he took on his father's tradition, working as a carpenter and turner.*

Sometime around 1800, Carl married Katharina Loew, the daughter of a city inn keeper, Johann Mathias Loew. Their son, Friedrich Carl Deppe, was born on March 17, 1804. By then, the state of Saarland was once again under French rule. This time, however, it was revolutionary France that ruled.

As with Prüm, in 1793, French revolutionary troops invaded the city of Saarbrücken. They would remain in control until 1815. It was during this time that the disorganized Germanic states were reorganized, and many of the smaller states combined with larger states. One major difference from the past was, rather than being ruled by the feudal dukes and princes as of yore, under French revolutionary rule, town and state governments were run by the citizens. When French rule ended, a majority of the citizens realized the need for further change. Ultimately, French Revolutionary rule of the Germanic states set into motion changes that would lead to Germany becoming a nation.

To most of Europe, the Germanic states appeared charming, but backward. In addition, their lack of military organization made them easy prey for whomever wished to invade and conquer, something that had occurred repeatedly throughout history. Now, realizing the need for an organized army, much of Germany was consolidated into two large states: Rhineland and Prussia. By 1816, Saarbrücken was a part of Prussia.

There were more changes coming to Prussia, mainly in how their way of life was seen. The old way under local princes and dukes was one of laissez-faire; citizens were pretty much allowed to live as they pleased. Now, the new government of Prussia made it their goal to build up industry, wealth, and power. In the interest of creating this powerful, new nation, the state police began to pay attention as to how their citizens were living. While the grand

---

* A turner works on a lathe, cutting wood into various shapes.

purpose was to encourage production and success, a good many people resented this invasion into their lives.

On March 17, 1826, Friedrich Deppe's father, Carl, died. A short time later, his mother, Catharina, moved to Kiesweiler. Likely, she went there to live with a sibling or child. Without his parents in Saarbrücken, Friedrich no longer had a reason to remain in the city. This, however, may not have been his only reason for leaving. It seems plausible that he may have been among those who resented the government's new regulations. In any case, shortly after his father's passing, he moved to Bergweiler, a small town about 72 miles north of Saarbrücken.

Bergweiler is an ancient village in the Eifel, dating back to the Stone Age. In the 1600s, it became a parish seat. The most important landmark there is Fintenkapell, a field chapel built in the 17th century, which became a place of pilgrimage for those wishing to pray for sick children. The chapel was very small, with a pulpit built on the outside wall, where the priest could stand and preach to the people in the field below.

How long Friedrich Carl Deppe lived in Bergweiler is unknown. As a surveyor's assistant, he was no doubt called to jobs in many areas. One day, he was called to Prüm.

Friedrich entered the tiny square, halfway up the hill from the basilica, and slowly approached the water pump.

The young girl standing there was so intent on her work, she scarcely seemed to notice him. He waited a moment, enjoying the view of her face and gold of her locks. She had pulled back her sleeves to keep them from interfering with her work. Now, she pumped the lever up and down, until the clear water poured into her bucket.

"Excuse me, Fraulein, might I have a dipper of water?" Friedrich asked.

The girl jumped, her soft, blue eyes flashing. She was startled by his presence, but perhaps even more startled to find he was a stranger.

"I am sorry, did I frighten you?"

The girl blushed a bit. "Oh no," she said quickly, looking down at her pail. Then, glancing at him quickly, she smiled and offered him a dipper full of water.

After drinking, he spoke. "Excuse me, Fraulein. I am Friedrich Deppe of Saarbrücken, lately of Bergweiler. I am here on a job. Bitte (please), can you tell me where I might find . . ." He mentioned the man he was to find.

The girl directed him, happy to have some serious task that made their talking official.

"Thank you very much, Fraulein."

Then, turning to go, he asked, "What is your name?"

"Catharina Wellenstein."

"I hope we may meet again soon, Fraulein Catharina.'

In 1828, eighteen year-old Catharina was living at home with her mother, Magdalena Kauffman Wellenstein. Her father, Johann Wellenstein, had died some years earlier. Catharina and her parents were all born in Prüm. Magdalena's parents were from Esch. Only two children have been verified from the marriage of Magdalena and Johann: Susanna, born in 1803, and Maria Catharina, who was born on February 4th, 1810.

Friedrich did see Catharina again. He had not lived long in Bergweiler, though certainly long enough for a record of his residency to be official. It seems, however, that his desire to marry Maria Catharina was reason enough for him to change locations and move to Prüm.

The couple were married at ten o'clock in the morning on January 29, 1829. Magdalena Wellenstein, who went by the name "Helena," was present for her daughter's wedding. As was the tradition, both bride and groom answered questions about the two generations of family before them. This information was duly recorded on their marriage license. And so, for the next five years, Herr and Frau Deppe lived happy, uneventful lives.*

---

* It should be noted in advance that public records of names in Germany sometimes vary. For instance, Friedrich Carl Deppe is also called Carl Friedrich Deppe. In addition, the letters "K" and "C" seem interchangable. While Katharina and Karl are generally spelled with a "K," sometimes for the same person these are changed to "C."

Early 1800s Peasant Home, Prüm History Museum, 1987

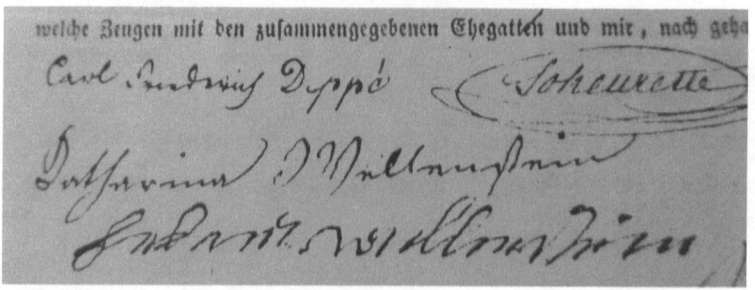

Signatures of Carl Friedrich Deppe and Catharina Wellenstein on their marriage certificate

Chapter 5

A New Life in Prüm

WHEN FRIEDRICH AND CATHARINA MARRIED ON JANUARY 29, 1829, he was 24 and she nearly 19. During the first years of their marriage, Friedrich traveled a great deal on surveying jobs, while Catharina stayed home with her mother and kept house. It would be five years before a child arrived.

On March 8, 1834 at 8:00 a.m., a baby girl arrived. They named their tiny bundle, Susanna Sophia Deppe. Now at last, her parents could celebrate the fact that their family had begun.

It would be two years before another baby arrived. On March 15, 1836 at 4:00 p.m., a son was born. Friedrich and Catharina gave him the grand name, Franz Joseph Ferdinand Deppe. There is no further record of this child, so it appears he must have died in infancy.

A second baby boy followed quickly, arriving just after the Christmas holidays on December 29, 1837. He was baptized Joseph Friedrich Deppe. Joseph was a sturdy child, and the Deppes felt blessed.

It would be three more years before Maria Catharina gave birth again. Once again, the baby was a boy. His parents celebrated by giving him the name of the baby they had lost two years earlier: Franz Joseph Ferdinand Deppe. Franz arrived at 10:00 a.m. on March 25, 1840. As with most of the Deppe children, he was fair, with blond hair and clear, blue eyes.

A fifth child arrived on May 8th, 1842. This time a girl, Friedrich and Catharina named her Anne Marie Deppe. It was not uncommon at the time, for families to lose one or more children at an early age. So it was with Anne Marie. There is no further information about her.

Four years later, with three children at home (Sophia, 10, Joseph, 8, and Franz, 4), Maria Catharina give birth to her sixth child, a son, whom they named Carl Friedrich.* Born on May 20, 1844, at twelve noon, Baby Carl's birth was celebrated, but all was not well in the little home.

Throughout her pregnancies, it seems Catharina may have had trouble, but this last birth had been too much for her. Whether her mother was still alive to help with the house and children is unknown. In many homes of the period, the eldest girl took a great deal of the burden on herself, but as a ten year-old child, it is doubtful Sophia could provide all the help needed. With Catharina so ill, perhaps another relative or neighbor came in to lend a hand.

Then, on November 26, 1844, only three months after Carl's birth, Maria Catharina passed away. She was 34 years old. Besides the baby, she left behind three children between the ages of ten and four.

Friedrich was devastated. For the next two years, he remained alone with the children. What help he received for the care of three month old Carl is unknown. Sophia and the others all helped as they could, but within the next two years, another woman was clearly on the scene. Her name was Katharina Darimont.

The Darimonts were a fine family of cloth makers, who originated in France. Katharina's father, Caspar Darimont had passed away a few years earlier, leaving behind a house full of girls. Perhaps Katharina had been a friend of Maria Catharina's. Though slightly older than her, at thirty-seven, she was the one Friedrich chose. He was happy with her presence, and she filled the need of wife and mother.

---

* This child has sometimes been referred to as Carl Henning Ludwig Deppe. The original birth certificate, however, is difficult to read.

On August 11th, 1847, at three in the afternoon, Carl Friedrich Deppe, now 43, and 38 year old Katharina Darimont were married. The children joining them were now 13, 9, 7, and 2.

Ten months after their marriage, Katharina and Friedrich welcomed a son, Moritz, born at 8 a.m. on July 3rd of 1848. A little over a year later, on December 10th at ten a.m., a little girl arrived. She received the name Katharina Christina. It would be three years before any more babies arrived. Likely, the couple did not expect another child because, by now, Katharina was forty-three years old, but on December 4th, 1852 at eight in the evening, Friedrich and Katharina welcomed another son into their home. He was given the name Friedrich Edmund Deppe.

As can be imagined, at this point, the house was quite full. There were two adults and seven children, including Friedrich's children with Maria Katharina Wellenstein: Sophia, 18; Joseph, 15, Franz, 12, Carl, 8, and the children with Katharina Darimont: Moritz, 4, Katharina Christina, 3, and Baby Edmund.

Although there is no exacting information on this, it seems at some point along the way, the Deppes became involved with the baking profession. Because Friedrich Deppe appears to have remained in his profession, that of assistant surveyor, more information is needed. Many questions regarding this bakery in Prüm remain unanswered. What year was it opened? Did the family go into business with Deppe money and recipes? Or was it the Darimont money and recipes that created it?

During this period, Prüm itself was undergoing changes. The town had a growing population and not much work. Yet despite this, good bread and pastry were always in demand, and, as it turns out, the Deppes came up with many delicious items to sell. Thus, for the time being, the small bakery across the square from San Salvatore church was a success and afforded the family a comfortable life in Prüm.

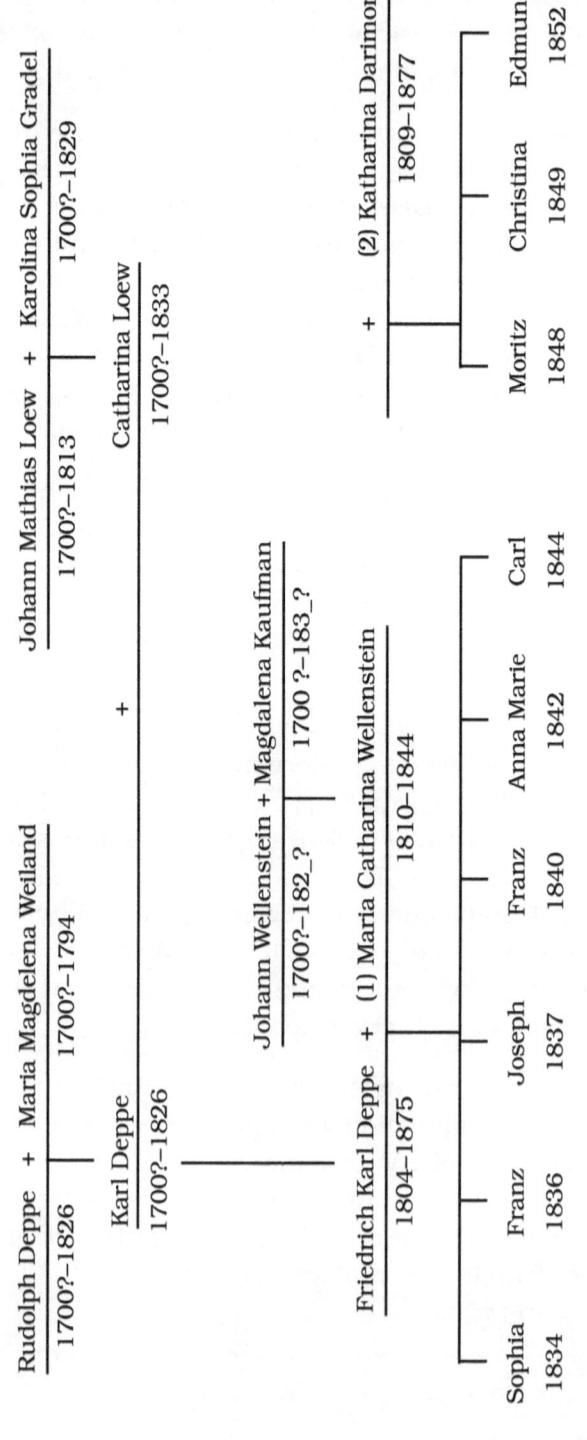

For four to six years, Joseph and Franz attended school at the Prüm Abbey. While higher education was available, it seems unlikely the average person in Prüm attended school beyond the fifth or sixth grade.

By the time, Friedrich Deppe married Katharina Darimont, fifteen year-old Joseph had probably found a job. Perhaps, he worked as a tanner, an important industry in Prüm. Once the bakery opened, it seems likely that Franz and Carl apprenticed there, helping to knead dough and bake bread.

During his school years, Franz served as an altar boy at San Salvatore Basilica. In time, however, he found he did not care for church very much. As a child, he had to go to church every day and kneel on the cold stone floor. Having lost his mother at the age of four, Franz bore wounds, which, for him, were only soothed by nature. Whenever he could, he preferred to run free, climbing the hills to the woods filled with linden trees; sitting at the top of the hill amidst wild flowers, and gazing at the green meadows below; meadows which stretched as far as the eye could see. It was a grand adventure. Even as an adult, Franz would tell his family, he preferred to find God in nature, rather than in a church.

There was another reason for Franz's dislike of the church. It is said the priests at San Salvatore were very strict, and Franz was often punished, even whipped. His resentment for these punishments ran deep. They were wounds he carried his entire life.

Sometimes when Franz and little brother, Carl, were out roaming the hills, they met two little girls from Prüm. Anna Maria and Catharina Ganser were the daughters of Heinrich Ganser, a wealthy ironmonger in town. At ten, Anna Marie was two years younger than Carl. Her little sister, Catharina, was eight. Anna Marie seemed to be a very intelligent child. She loved the hills of the Eifel. Despite their age differences, meeting one another in the beauty of nature, the children formed a friendship that would last long into the future.

Chapter 6
To America

By 1861, the Deppes had seen plenty of trouble. Not only were there uprisings in Europe and the Germanic states, but these uprisings had touched Prüm as well. A large percentage of the citizens were living in poverty with little to eat. The wheat crop had gone bad, raising the price of bread, and like many other towns in Europe, Prüm was no longer able to support its growing population.

During the 1850s and 60s, salesmen were traveling to towns and villages throughout Europe, advertising a land of plenty called America. In America, they said, there were grand cities with jobs of every kind, jobs that would pay enough money to make a man rich. And just beyond these grand cities, lay unlimited farmland. Anyone willing to work hard could live a fine life! These stories, along with the letters that arrived from those who had already crossed the ocean, served to stoke the imagination. "Follow your dreams," the voices said. Those with brave hearts, who were willing to leave the past behind, could live a life better than anything they imagined!

As time progressed, Joseph, Franz, and Carl realized the difficult future they faced. Inheritance laws in Rhineland stated that all property should be divided equally among all descendants. With seven siblings, there simply wasn't enough to go around. Clearly, the Deppe family bakery could never support all of them. So, amongst themselves the older children decided that the bakery should go to Moritz and Edmund.

There was one other matter which spurred them on. The Deppe sons did not want to be drafted into the military and forced to fight one of Europe's ever-rising wars. They saw plenty of soldiers in town; soldiers the citizens were forced to house and feed, a situation adding to their burden of poverty

For some time, Joseph and Franz discussed the possibility of going to the America. Joseph dreamt of owning a farm. Franz wanted to live in a city. The chant, "Go to America. Your dreams can come true!" repeated itself over and over in their thoughts. The brothers were restless and eager for a new life. In the end, it was decided that the two eldest boys would go first. Once they were settled, they would send for Carl.

By 1862, Joseph was 24, Franz, 22, and Carl, 18. Around this time, the family received word from a relative who had already settled in an American city called Chicago. In the letters sent back home, the Deppe brothers learned that Chicago was a big city with many opportunities. It was a place where many immigrants from southern German had settled, and some of these fellow Germans had already made enough money to buy their own little house, with a cow and a garden.

Chicago seemed an unusual name. It was mysterious and exciting. The boys learned that "Chicago" was an Indian name, meaning 'onion field.' Apparently, at one time the land there contained a field where many onion or garlic plants grew.

Founded in 1830, this growing metropolis in the middle of America was just a little over thirty years old. In those thirty years it had grown from a fort on a muddy patch of land along the great Lake Michigan to a thriving city. In fact, the place was growing so swiftly, there were more jobs than could be filled.

Joseph and Franz mapped out plans for their journey. Joseph had been saving for the journey, and he had quite a nest egg. A good deal of money would be needed. Not only would they have to pay for the voyage across the ocean, they would also have to supply the price of train tickets, once they arrived. It was a thousand or more miles from the port of New York to Chicago.

Meanwhile, every day the brothers became more aware of the need to move ahead. As sad as it might be to leave their family and the only home they had ever known, there was no way they could continue to live in Prüm. The Deppe house was too crowded, jobs too scarce, and what jobs there were paid too little money. Although their half-siblings were still young, Moritz, now 14, was working in the bakery. Christina, at thirteen, was nearly a young woman, and Edmund was nine. Their oldest sister, Sophia, twenty-eight, was still unmarried. She would stay at home.

Having six adults under his roof to support could not have been easy for Friedrich, even with their help. Yet, as he saw his eldest sons preparing to leave, it must have been a sad time for him.

In the 1800s, when someone left home for the new world, it was almost certain you would never see them again. No doubt, Friedrich had resigned himself to what was best. For the standard of the time, at fifty-nine, he was an old man, and would not live much longer. Now, rather than complain or worry, he placed himself and his sons in God's hands. His children must look to their future.

By the late 1850s and early 1860s, most major cities in Germany were connected by the railway system. The railway to Prüm, however, was not completed until 1887, though they might have been able to board a train in another place, such as Trier.

The nearest port was Antwerp, Belgium, a 220 kilometer trip (approximately 137 miles). Unable to afford a train, many persons traveled by wagon. Some even walked to reach the seaport. Upon arrival, it was necessary to complete paperwork in order to purchase a ticket. Then, the travelers had to wait for the next ship. This wait might be days, weeks or even months. The ship company was required by the government to watch over those waiting. At most ports, there were private boarding houses or "emigrant hotels," where ship passengers were housed until their ship arrived.

Official ship records for two Deppe brothers traveling together have not been found. It is uncertain as to whether Joseph and Franz traveled to the new world together. It was a common practice for one family member to go ahead, earn money, and send it back home for the next person.

A record for a Joseph Deppe, age 25, is found leaving the port of Antwerp in July of 1863 on the ship, *Neptune*. The listing states that he is a Prussian laborer. Joseph arrived in New York City on August 8th of that year. Surprisingly, he was able to purchase a cabin, rather than being forced to travel in steerage, as the average immigrant did. The price of his ticket was approximately $20, though it is said fares were higher during the Civil War.* An additional $10 would have been needed for food.† Joseph may have saved the extra money needed for this ticket by walking or riding in a wagon from Prüm to Antwerp. Although we have no proof that this is Joseph Deppe of Prüm, all facts in this record match him correctly.

In later years, official U.S. records for both Franz and Joseph declare that they came to America in 1863. These sworn statements must be true, for they are in line with the record of work the two men performed in Chicago. Still the question remains, how did Franz come to America? Was he somehow missed on the ship record? Did he work his way across or enter the country some other way?

Joseph was fortunate to have a cabin. The voyage across the Atlantic was difficult enough. To be out on the ocean for days without seeing land was part of the experience. The sea, beautiful and calm one hour, might change without warning. Churning

---

* $20 = approximately $462 in 2014.

† $10 = $226.00—2014

waters with swells as high as the ship, strong winds, and blinding rain could make one fear for one's life. A voyage across the ocean in the 1800s was not for the faint of heart. Many lost their lives.

After seven days at sea, Joseph and Franz would meet a city the size of which they had never seen. There were sights, sounds, smells, and sensations they were innocent of, having spent all of their lives in a tiny, protected village. After arriving in New York, they made their way to the train station, walking through crowds with people of every nationality. At the station, for $5.00,* they purchased train tickets and boarded a huge steam engine, which carried them across country to Chicago. Some twenty-four hours later, they arrived. A new life was about to begin.

---

* $5.00 = $113.00 in 2014.

The New World

Chapter 7

Chicago

IN THE 1800s, CHICAGO WAS ONE AMERICAN CITY WHERE A LARGE number of German immigrants chose to settle. In fact, of all nationalities coming to Chicago, their numbers were the greatest. While some only remained for a short time before moving on, a greater number of German immigrants decided to stay and use their ingenuity to succeed. Chicago was a tough city, but the Germans were up to it. As a result, they brought to the city something that set it apart from other places. Between 1860 and 1870, the German population in Chicago grew from 22,230 to 59,299; a quarter of the city's population.

On the North side of the Chicago River, German immigrants basically created their own town. In the early days, this area was known as the "cabbage patch," a place of cottages, gardens, churches, and schools. There were also German clubs, theatres, and newspapers. On Sundays, the beer gardens provided entertainment with music from the homeland, dancing, and food. While the new citizens carried on traditions of the past, they also made the city uniquely theirs. Then, and in the future, their style of decorative architecture made Chicago unlike any other city.

Shortly after arriving in Chicago, Joseph Deppe found a job working for Eliel & Co. as a tanner. The business, located at 115 Kinzie, was owned by two brothers, Gustav and Louis Eliel. The tannery where Joseph worked was further north, at the northwest corner of North Branch and Hawthorne Avenues. Joseph found a room in a boarding house at 54 Wesson, only a few blocks away from his new job.*

The job of tanner was not an easy one. The term "tanning" comes from "tannin," a German word for oak or fir trees and the substance that comes from them. The tanning process is one that involves treating the skins and hides of dead animals in order to turn them into leather, a much desired durable and weatherproof material.

As a tanner, Joseph spent long hours working on the skins. To begin the process, the hides had to be warm. Then, they were either salted and pressed into packs for 30 days or agitated in heavily salted water for 16 hours. Following this, they were soaked, limed, cleaned of extraneous skin or hair, then de-limed and further treated. After that, the skins were soaked in water to remove all salt. Finally, tannins or other extremely astringent chemicals were applied.

As one might guess, this process is a dirty, smelly, and difficult job, which requires long hours and a great deal of skill. The average laborer of the period worked 10 to 14 hours a day. Continuous exposure to the chemicals used to preserve the hides over a long period of time, may cause health problems to the tanner. Meanwhile, Joseph was happy to have a good job, especially one that left him enough cash to send to his brothers and father back home.

Since a record of Franz Deppe's departure from Germany and his arrival in America has yet to be found, we can only imagine how it occurred. The following is a fictional account, written in Chicago some years ago. The facts, gleaned from numerous immigrants' written experiences, may tell something of what life was like for Franz when he arrived in 1863.

---

* Wesson Street was changed to Cambridge in 1909.

Chicago

I

The train whistle pierced the air with a shrill scream, and the big engines slowed. It had been a long trip. They had passed mountains, rivers, and flat prairies. Franz had never seen so much flat land. Now, they were entering a huge city on the edge of a lake, a lake so large it seemed like an ocean. This was Chicago? Franz looked out the window at the buildings. He had arrived! This was the place he had dreamt of—the place he would seek his fortune!

"CHI–CA–GO!" yelled the conductor as the train ground to a screeching halt. Men began throwing their travel bags over their shoulders, while the women grabbed their whining children by the hand. All of them strained their heads towards the huge city before them.

Franz blinked as he stepped off the train. He could not believe the sight that lay before him. Rising from the flat earth, standing against the gray sky, there were buildings of every size and shape as far as the eye could see. Beyond that, puffs of black smoke were filling the air.

"Smell that?" asked the conductor, as he passed Franz, whose face must have been awe-struck, "That is success." In all his dreams, Franz could never have imagined a city like this.

"Room sir?" one man asked, jostling his shoulder.

"Jobs for men willing to work," yelled another. Voices in different languages and accents accosted him right and left; a pushing mass of humanity, odors, tightness of bodies, the sound of boards being hammered, squeaking wheels, horses neighing, and every now and then, a burst of wind off the great Lake Michigan, which lay just beyond the tracks.

There were no rounded hills in sight, no green, no warm and friendly faces . . . only noise and roughness. In the air were pungent odors, not of fresh green grass and bread baking as in Prüm, but the odor of smoke, sweat, cattle, and worse.

Franz shook his head and moved on. He could not remember when he had ever felt as tired as he did now. He ached from the long, bumpy ride on the train, but this was no time to be tired. His youthful enthusiasm for life and the feel of the city's energy pulling him forward into the thick of things prevailed.

Wide paved boulevards with buildings like palaces rose up block after block. There was not just one church, but many. There were also trees, carriages, streetlamps and finely dress men and women parading along the avenues. The number of shops boggled the mind; shops selling every kind of item imaginable, everything from pianofortes to wool. Along the way, a policeman, dressed in a blue frock coat and grey pants with a dark stripe down the sides, sauntered down the avenue, swinging his baton.

Franz couldn't help noticing how everyone went on their way at a quick pace, as if on an important mission. To Franz, this was a miraculous city. So amazed was he by the new sights and sounds, and the myriad of people, he had walked several blocks before he remembered to pull out the address written on the small, carefully folded piece of paper in his satchel.

He had been directed to go north to the German area and ask for "Wells Street." He looked for someone who might speak German, and asked for instructions to this place where, hopefully, a job awaited him.

"Excuse me, sir. Bitte, wo ist Vells Strasse?" He asked several persons before an old man directed him in German to an area a few blocks away.

Franz felt grateful that a friend had given him this connection in the new world. He would not need to depend on strangers. He had been warned of the tricks sometimes played on unsuspecting immigrants, who were put in jobs as indentured servants or had their money and belongings stolen.

It was necessary to cross over the river to reach his destination. At the end of the street stood a large bridge, an amazing bridge.

It had just turned sideways to let a ship with tall masts pass through. Then it turned back again, forming an arch that allowed foot passengers to cross the river. A trail of wagons and men stood waiting to get across. What an adventure to walk over this bridge!

The river below was a muddy looking brown and, as Franz crossed, he knew why. It smelt of sewage and rotting garbage. The air was so foul, he held his breath as long as he could while he walked across.

Heading further north, the city thinned. Although there were a number of houses, the prairie was visible beyond. Dotted here and there were a few trees, and to the right, the lake.

Franz quickened his pace. He had brought with him very little in the way of luggage; only his cloth satchel and the clothes on his back. He was eager to move on to a new life. He had been given the name of a family who would help him; they were persons from the Eifel.

The street ahead was not paved the entire way; there were only wooden sidewalks to walk on. It reminded him a bit of home. The familiar tongue of his homeland was being spoken; he recognized the dialect. That was a comfort. The street, however, was broader than any street at home. Many of the residents were selling produce from their gardens right in front of the houses. Carrots, potatoes, cabbage and berries. Not all of Chicago was city.

At last, Franz approached a small bakery. He entered, asked for Herr Becker, and announced his name to the woman behind the counter. Her cheeks turned pink as she hurried into the next room, calling "Peter!" with such excitement. A man of middle age came running out, followed by two little ones. To meet someone who had just come from the old country and had news of his dear brother, Georg, was a special treat. After Bettie served him warm soup with a hot roll, the couple plied him with questions about home.

"Jah, Jah," Peter said, responding to Franz's query about work. He could use some help with the baking and deliveries around town. They would have a place for him to stay as well. So, all was set.

He started work the next day. Chicagoans worked hard, not in the leisurely fashion of Prüm. It seemed that everyone had an important job to do here. The city was growing by the day, and opportunity abounded for the men and woman who were willing to do labor in this once, not long before, primitive city on the lake. All it took was the desire and ability to succeed. Yes, *follow your dreams*. Franz was happy to be here, and soon was caught up in the Chicago pattern of life.

Rising at four in the morning, he began baking bread for the day; including hard rolls and loaves. Everything had to be ready when the shop opened. There was plenty of bread needed in this city. For new arrivals with little money, bread was a godsend. People from Europe were used to living simply; bread and cheese or bread and gruel were all that was needed. Meanwhile, Franz was learning the baking business.

After a morning of hard work, he might be called to deliver the rolls and loafs around town, sometimes selling directly off the wagon. His days were full of new experiences. He learned his way around Chicago, learned her manners and customs, and a new language, English. He liked this new world, so full of energy and life. The pay he received was not a lot, but certainly more than at home. And so the days passed.

II

There came a day when Franz met his brother, Joseph, in this new world for the first time. The excitement Joseph felt as he saw Franz's face cannot be expressed. Unmindful of the crowds around them, the brothers embraced.

"You are here! Really here in Chicago! " Joseph said as he watched his brother gaze at the city around him. Franz saw many changes in Joseph. To begin with, he was dressed like other men from the new world. How strange to see his brother so at home in this city of Chicago.

"At first, it will seem difficult after the quiet of Prüm and the ways of Prüm," Joseph explained, "but then, wait and see. You will discover how exciting it is to be in this fast-growing city!"

Often after a long day of kneading dough and putting loaves in the hot stone oven, Franz went to the local German tavern and listened to the stories of fellow Germans, some of whom had lived there for many years and had watched her rise.

"You see how tings are now," asked Hans, a man of about 35 years. "When I came ten years ago, there was nothing here! No train. No grain elevator. The prairie came right up to our doors!"

"That is nothing," chimed in an old man. "When I came, this place was a swamp! Indians roamed the land. We never knew from one day to the other. . . Now over one hundret trains go through Chicago every day. They bring lumber, food, and more people."

"Yes, and more people means the need for more houses, food, and more jobs," chimed in his friend. "This city will be the greatest city in the world! Smell that smoke. It is alive with power! Success! The future!"

Franz said little, he only listened, but as he listened, he thought to himself, "If I could get enough money, I could have my own bakery."

That was his dream. In Germany, he had no birthright, but here, he was sure he could build a future.

All that the men said was true. Chicago had grown by leaps and bounds. In 1846, the population was a mere 14,000. By 1854, it had grown to 75,000. The year 1848 saw the building of a canal.

That meant sugar and other produce coming up the Mississippi by boat could reach Lake Michigan, be reloaded in Chicago, and from there, shipped to Buffalo, New York. Ultimately, Chicago was now linked to the Atlantic Ocean and the Gulf of Mexico. As one historian wrote, Chicago owed its very existence to that canal. In the meantime, as it grew, the small settlement on the lake extended further and further. Chicago had spread itself out into the flat plains of the prairie, further than anyone dreamed possible.

In 1847, there was no railway to Chicago. By 1857, Chicago was the rail center of America. William Ogden, who built the first railroad—the Galena & Chicago Union—was hailed as the railroad king of the west. The following year, 1858, saw the arrival of the first telegraph. The telegraph made it possible for Chicagoans to communicate with the rest of the America and the world! That same year, the Illinois and Michigan Canal allowed for the arrival of the first ocean-going steamer in Lake Michigan.

Cyrus McCormick, inventor of the first mechanical reaper, a harvesting machine, moved to Chicago from the Shenandoah Valley in Pennsylvania in 1847, and built his factory there. The factory put out 10,000 reapers in a year. The Chicago Board of Trade was established the next year, and giant grain elevators soon stood along the Chicago River. The list of progress in this great city seemed endless.

Life was so full in Chicago, the homesickness Franz sometimes felt, soon grew less and less. On Sundays, he and Joseph met. The long work days, ten to fourteen hours a day, six days a week, did not allow for much socializing. But on Sundays, life was good.

When the Deppe brothers were together, they often read letters received from home, discussing every point. They also worked on a response. When they were able, the brothers put their money together and sent it back home. It was not possible for their parents to come to the city, but brother Carl was eager to make the trip. Soon, even Moritz was considering it. Their older sister, Sophia, who was nearly forty, said she would like to see America one day as well. Of course, Sophia would never leave home while their father was still alive.

What excitement there was in Prüm the day their first letter arrived. The boys had made it safely to Chicago. They had met other German families, and now had good paying jobs. The letters of Joseph and Franz would be shared with others in town. The one thing Friedrich and Katharina likely did not share with the neighbors was the fact that the boys had sent them money.

Their letters included stories about Chicago, a huge city one hundred times or more the size of Prüm. Later, they would describe the winters, and the bitterly cold winds coming in off the lake. All these things would have seemed like a fairytale to those far away in Prüm.

Although the city directories clearly show that Joseph Deppe was a resident of Chicago from 1863 to 1865, there is no record of Franz Deppe. Later, on his citizenship papers, Franz would declare that he also arrived in Chicago in 1863. In 1865, when Franz joined the military, unlike many, he registered as a resident of Chicago. By then, he spoke English and knew his way around the city. Clearly, he had been there for a while.

III

As time went by, Franz found he was not completely satisfied with life as it was. The winter had been brutal, far worse than anything either he or Joseph had ever known. When the wind blew in off the lake, it went right through their clothes, as if they had nothing on at all. Sometimes, it even seemed as though the rickety wooden houses would not withstand the winds off Lake Michigan, nor the snow that slammed up against the walls. A man could easily be hurtled across the street by its blast. Hands and faces were red and cracked from the dry, bitter cold.

To survive the Chicago winters, men greased themselves with pig fat and covered themselves in animal fur skins, which were often sold at a premium. If one did not protect oneself from the cold, frostbite might easily set in. But Franz was dissatisfied with more than the weather.

"Joseph," Franz told his brother one day, "The reason I came here was because we did not inherit the bakery. My dream is to own my own bakery. I must find a way to do so."

"Don't worry, Franz. We are doing that. It will happen. You are too impatient!"

Franz had scouted further north in the city. Already, new communities were being built there. Just above North Avenue, then considered the "city limits," many Germans were building new homes and businesses around St. Michael's Church. If he had money, this would be the perfect place to start a bakery.

Meanwhile, the United States, to which they had immigrated, was in the midst of a Civil War.

Richmond, Virginia

Chapter 8
Chicago to Richmond

Using historic facts, some dramatic license has been taken to tell the story.

CHICAGO HAD BEEN A GREAT SUPPORTER OF PRESIDENT LINCOLN from the beginning. In fact, his nomination for President took place at "the Wigwam," an old dilapidated warehouse on the edge of the Chicago River. This event occurred only two years prior to Joseph and Franz's arrival.

When the war broke out, the citizens of Chicago supported the Union Army. This support continued throughout the war. There was a Federal draft in effect, but it wasn't needed in Illinois. Volunteers were so plentiful, their numbers far exceeded the numbers called for by the draft. In addition, the city provided a huge portion of the food and supplies needed by the Union Army.

Camp Douglas served as the local training camp, but soon became one of the main prisoner-of-war camps for Confederate soldiers. Conditions, however, were deplorable. As a result, during the second year of the war, thousands died in this camp. The following year, improvements were made and other recruitment camps, like Camp Fry, were opened to alleviate the strain.

In March of 1865, Lieutenant Colonel Samuel Simison rode into town on an important mission. Simison, a thirty-six year old carpenter, had just joined the army the previous year. Now, he was commander of the Battalion *23rd Illinois Volunteer Infantry Regiment*, which included ten companies consisting of four hundred and forty men.

Working for headquarters, Simison was on his way back from Virginia with an order to bring in new companies of recruits—an assignment handed down to him from Governor Yates. The 23rd Illinois Infantry had suffered great losses in the battles of 1863, but the desire for new blood was about more than replacing fallen soldiers. The war had gone on for four years now, costing the loss of thousands of lives. At the start of 1865, a new goal was set by President Lincoln.

Standing before the officers at Camp Fry that March day of 1865, Simison passed on the message:

'On the request of President Lincoln, I have been asked by the Governor for more troops. We are accepting men for five new companies. The news is to be spread. Men who enlist for one year will receive a bounty!"

The news went out. It was posted on walls, outside saloons, and in the Chicago newspapers.

One afternoon, Franz Deppe was walking down State Street, when he noticed a man passing out handbills, and a group of men scrambling for them. He walked over and picked up a handbill that had fallen to the ground.

> *'President Lincoln is asking for men who can help finish this war to preserve the Union. Join the Army for one year and receive a $400 bounty for signing up.'*

Franz was excited. $400! That was more than he could make in a year, and besides, he would have no expenses.

Later that day, Franz met Joseph at the local pub. His brain had been burning all day with dreams of adventure and money. He was tired of this noisy, bustling city. He would travel, help save the Union, be a hero, and in the end, he would have money.

Even before Franz spoke, Joseph could see the change in him.

"Joseph, my brother, I have found the solution!"

"The solution for what?"

"To start the bakery. I am going to sign up for the army!"

"Sign up for the army?!" exclaimed Joseph. "You left Germany because you didn't want to fight."

"That was different. I will be paid $400 for only one year in the United States Army. That is all it will be. Besides, they say the war is almost over."

"Are you sure you want to do this?" asked Joseph.

"Yes. This is the opportunity I have waited for. When I return we will have enough money to open the bakery together. The Deppe Baking Company!"

Joseph said nothing. After all, Franz knew his own mind. He was always ready for adventure.

"Do you want to go too?" asked Franz.

"Franz," replied Joseph, "I will wait for you."

The brothers hugged, but Joseph was worried.

"God bless you, Franz. You must come back."

"I will be fine. Don't worry."

Franz was determined. With a wave of his hand, he was on his way to a new adventure. His life had begun the day he left Prüm. This was only the next step.

II

Prior to the day Franz Deppe signed up, several of Company K's new recruits fell ill and died at Camp Douglas. Whether Franz was ever at Camp Douglas is unknown. Camp Fry would have been safer and closer to home.

It was a cold and rainy April day when Franz found his way just north of the city to Camp Fry. The camp was located where Diversey and Clark Streets crossed. He carried with him a sack packed with nearly all his worldly possessions. Like many other enlisting that day, he was ready to go.

"Name" said the gruff officer seated at the table, his red face, rugged against the blue wool of his uniform with gold buttons on the front.

"Franz Deppe."

"Francis Deppe" repeated the man. "Age?"

"Twenty-five."

They measured him and took note of his appearance.

"5'5", light hair, blue eyes, light complexion."

It did not matter that he was not a citizen.

"Living?" Franz stared at the man not understanding.

"What is your profession?"

"I am a baker."

"What do you make?"

"I make breads, Kuchen . . . cake and other things."

"Good. We can use you."

Franz stood on line with the other men and waited to be examined by a doctor. Eyes, ears, teeth, heart, lungs, and other matters he was not used to.

Then, he stood on a long line with the other men and waited to be called. He heard his name.

"Francis Deppe! You pass muster."

It was Monday, April 3, 1865. He had passed. He felt excited, then, suddenly fearful. But the deed was done. He would not back out.

III

Camp Fry was not a bad place, certainly better than Camp Douglas, but they would not be there long. A few more men were needed. Then, they would leave for the South.

Franz was a soldier now—a member of the Illinois Infantry, 23rd Regiment, Company K. He received an ill-fitting uniform, which included a grey pullover shirt of rough wool with three buttons, blue baggy trousers with pockets, and a navy jacket. There was also a slightly darker overcoat that went to the knee. It had a single row of eight gold buttons with eagles, the same as his jacket. Not to be forgotten was the forage cap with floppy crown that all privates wore.

Besides his accoutrements, Franz received a loose canvas sack in which to carry his belongings, and a canteen for water, which all the soldiers slung over their shoulders. The sack contents usually included a plate, eating implements, clean socks and anything else of personal importance. Some carried Bibles along with letters from home and the picture of a loved one. The soldiers also carried a tin cup and a wooden rifle more than 3 feet in length with ammunition. Added to that was a wool blanket, which they carried on their backs.

The army recruiter had listed Franz as "Francis Deppie," but his commanding officer told him, "We'll just call you Frank."

Army life was rough. During the day the men marched and learned the tools of war. At night, they slept in tents and froze, often with rain or snow coming down. Within the first five days at Camp Fry, three recruits grew ill and died. Another fellow was transferred to the Navy, and still another was rejected.

When Franz wasn't busy training, he worked in the kitchen. He was young and eager; nothing felt like a problem. In a year, he would be out of the Army. Then he could have his bakery and get rich. After that, he would get married.

The new recruits of Company K were to be commanded by Captain Henry Siegel of Chemung, Illinois. Siegel, a native of Norway, mustered into the army two days after Franz. He stood 5'10" with dark hair and dark eyes, and seemed a capable enough soldier to handle the job. His aides were First Lieutenant Daniel Morgan, a sailor by profession, and Second Lieutenant Giles Slocum of Cook County. There were four sergeants from Chicago beneath them: John A. Montgomery, Frederik Aagaard, Jacob H. Jackson, and Henry Syvertson; and eight corporals, all from Chicago: Arrent Olson, Peter N. Green, Gus W. Roe, Christian Midell, Lars P. Christianson, Benjamin Johnston, John Stephens, and William H. Haviland. The company also included two musicians: forty-four year old Loton L. Aiken and twenty-two year old August H. Pfund, a farmer from Switzerland. They played fife and drum.

Franz was one of seventy-eight privates. In addition, there were forty-nine unassigned recruits, thirty-four of which joined in Chicago. Like Franz, many of the new recruits were immigrants. Most of the men who mustered in in March and April of 1865 were around his same age, twenty-five. While a good number were Irish, the company also included immigrants from Sweden, Norway, Switzerland, and Germany.

On Friday, five days after mustering in, Franz learned they would be leaving within the next forty-eight hours. They would march several miles to the train station near the stockyards, where they would board flatbed cars. Some were eager to go, but as the hour of departure grew closer, others seemed anxious.

Word was the fighting in Virginia was intense, and that was where they were headed. The Union had taken Richmond, the capitol of the Confederacy, but the war was not over yet. Franz noticed that Private Thomas Dorsey, a tall, dark-haired twenty-one year old Irish laborer, seemed timid and uncertain. The captain yelled at him, and when it was time for dinner, he was gone. The next morning, his friend, Charles Kelly, a tinsmith from Ohio, had disappeared as well. Another eight men had already deserted before Franz signed up. Whether they simply wanted the bounty or were frightened and felt they could not withstand the army, they left.

After boarding the train, Franz and his fellow soldiers had their first stop in Pittsburgh, Pennsylvania. The train, powered by a steam engine, was primitive, uncomfortable and unhealthy—without seats, windows or facilities. After approximately nine hours on the train, the men disembarked to stretch their legs, breathe fresh air, and eat. The following day, they arrived in Morrisburg, Pennsylvania, and the day after that, in Baltimore, Maryland, only forty miles north of Washington, D.C.

Down in Virginia, the war was quickly coming to an end. On April 3rd, Mrs. Robert E. Lee, wife of the Confederate Army commander, arrived in Richmond. Guards were posted at the door for her protection. President Lincoln and his son Tad traveled on a gunboat, the *Malvern*, up the St. James River to the St. James docks. Walking through the city amidst cheering crowds, the President entered, one of the few buildings left standing—the Confederate White House, which was now Union Headquarters. Outside, crowds of former slaves lined the road to see the great man who had freed them.

It is said that upon seeing President Lincoln, one old black man, a former slave, fell to his knees and cried out, "Bless the Lord! Here is the great Messiah." In response, Lincoln told him, "Don't kneel to me. You must kneel to God only. Thank Him for your freedom."

Lincoln walked a mile down the road to greet and shake hands with the cheering African-American men and woman reaching out to touch him.

Between April 3rd and 9th, soldiers of the Illinois Infantry, 23rd Regiment, who had been in the war since the beginning, were in Virginia, hot on the trail of General Lee. They followed him to the end and were convened outside the Appomattox Courthouse when Lee surrendered.

On the 9th, General Lee waited at Appomattox for the Union Commander, General Ulysses S. Grant to arrive. During their meeting, General Grant promised Lee that the soldiers of the Confederacy would not be treated badly. There was great celebration for the Union that day, but many a Southern boy still held hate in his heart. All these events Private 'Francis Deppie' missed, but in the coming weeks, he would hear about them from the men who had lived them.

Company K did not arrive in Richmond until the 11th of April. Entering the once beautiful city was like marching into a city of hell. One week earlier, realizing the Union was about to take their capitol, the Confederates set the city on fire to prevent the Yankees from having anything.

The new recruits were not prepared for the conditions they witnessed. Aside from the Capitol and a few other buildings, by the time they arrived, most of the city was a mere shell; a pile of burnt rubble, with only the white skeletons of formerly grand buildings rising from the charred earth. The vision was something none of the soldiers, including Franz, would ever forget.

Marching down the streets of Richmond, there were blue uniforms everywhere. Scores of Union soldiers were hard at work, clearing the smoldering ruins. Others set up feeding stations, where they helped pass food out to starving residents. But the largest and most continuous job for the men was guard duty.

Officially, the war was over, but to bring order to the war-torn city, martial law was declared. Richmond's citizens were told to stay off the streets. In addition, Union soldiers were commanded not to use any insulting language or gestures towards Richmond's citizens. Meanwhile, there were Confederates who couldn't accept the loss of the war, and who would have liked to start it up again. Now and then, the sound of shots were heard, shaking the nerves of those who had lived through horrific battles.

Civil War reenactment, Richmond, VA 1989

Franz had seen very few black people in his life. Here, there were persons of color everywhere, many of them in rags. The situation became urgent as hundreds of former slaves descended upon the city, looking for food and shelter. They were like people in the Bible who had been taken from their land and had nothing left. They built huts, and looked for food and clothing to survive.

Franz also was surprised to see that there were a large group of black soldiers in Union uniform as well.

But the blacks were not the only poor people. Many of the whites were in almost as bad a situation. Although he knew they had been wrong in their cause, Franz couldn't help feeling sorry for some of the Southern citizens, especially the women and children. Women, who obviously had been well-off only a week earlier, now walked the streets, veiled in black, their clothing in tatters. One woman even wore a dress made of Union flags. Many of these women seemed weak and lost as they walked through the streets filled with rubble. Not only had they lost their men, they had lost their homes, the servants they depended on, and—with the city in ruins—even a sense of where they were.

The soldiers of Company K were told where to pitch their tents. They were also informed that food was scarce; so they should guard it with their lives. "It takes a long time to get a supply, so watch it." The men soon learned not to be surprised by either white or black persons coming to beg or steal. Indeed the cost of basic items had gone up. A bushel of wheat, which would have cost $2.00 in 1862, was now $65.60. The Union bakery was turning out thousands of loaves a day. This was the only thing most people had to eat.

The soldiers warded off hunger with hard tack, a bread made of unleavened wheat and water. They also kept suspended pots over the fire to make coffee. Some meals were made of dried beef and pork, but fresh food was scarce to non-existent here.

The authorities estimated that there were approximately 20,000 men, woman and children—both white and black—who were without food or money. It would later be estimated that between April 2rd and April 21, approximately 128,132 issues of rations had been distributed. A makeshift hospital held 6,000 beds, all filled. Added to these numbers were mobs of men roaming the streets, many of them convicts freed from the state penitentiary. One thousand prisoners were taken into custody, and five thousand

Confederates, wounded and in need of treatment, sought shelter within the city boundaries. Adding these figures and aspects together can give the reader an idea of what the Union soldiers faced as they guarded the city of Richmond.

One item of interest was noted at this time. Alcohol was strictly forbidden by all. The Provost Marshall General of Virginia stated that anyone found selling an alcoholic beverage to a Union Soldier would be tried and punished. As part of organizing the city, four districts were set up with a Provost Marshall for each. In these districts, the Provost Marshall had the duty of preserving order, registering residents, and administering Oaths of Allegiance to the United States of America for those who wish to take them.

After a few of days in Richmond, the men of Company K were given orders to march to City Point, Virginia. Located on the Appomattox River, City Point had been General Grant's headquarters during the St. Petersburg Campaign. Company K arrived there on Friday, the 14th of April.

The following day, the terrible news reached them. President Lincoln was dead, shot the night before at Ford's Theater by a Confederate assassin. Many men cried openly at the news, while others bowed their heads, too grief-stricken to speak. The sorrow of the soldiers over the loss of this beloved President was great. Now, they must carry on the work begun. How Franz Deppe felt during this time is unknown. He had been thrust into the midst of American history; a stranger, who now felt on a much deeper level—this was his country.

On Wednesday, April 20th, it was time to move again. This time the 23rd Regiment was sent marching to Petersburg, the city which had lived through the longest siege of any in the country, from June 9th, 1864 to March 24, 1865.

In the final days of the war, mobs had plundered the stores of Petersburg in search of anything to help them survive. Fires spread to the arsenal and explosions rocked the city. Conditions there were even worse than Richmond. Although the most dire events had occurred on April 2rd, things were not much better when the Union Army arrived and raised the United States flag on the capital building. Even then, the residents seemed as barren of hope as their streets.

On the twenty-first of April, an article was published in the newspaper stating that the War Department was offering a $1000 reward for the capture of President Lincoln's assassin. Twelve days after Lincoln was shot, John Wilkes Booth was discovered hiding in a barn in Virginia and killed.

Nothing further of note occurred until May 15, 1865, when orders came down for an inspection by Lt. E.H. Bierer, Brigadier. That day, "every available officer and man" was ordered to line up for inspection. Col. Camden was to make a preparation inspection to see that items and "accoutrements" were in proper condition. The order went on to say:

> "clothing clean, both on the person and in the knapsacks . . . the knapsacks properly packed."

Just because the war was over, the men were not to become lax; in fact, just the opposite was true. They were informed of the fact that from 8:00–9:00 a.m. and from 4:00–5:00 p.m.:

> "daily there will be inspection and drill. No drill on Saturday afternoon or on Sunday. Immediately on the call, each company will fall in line. Each company will be held in strict compliance of the above order."—Lt. Simison

Private Deppe, like the other men, fell in line and followed orders. There had been more death in this war from illness than from bullets. They were deep in the south now, a hot humid climate; cleanliness was necessary and to be strictly followed. Besides, they represented the United States government. The day after this order was given, Company K marched north, back to Richmond.

III

Although it was only mid-May when Company K settled in Richmond, it was hot—hotter than anything Franz had ever known. In the morning, the sky was a beautiful, clear blue, but by afternoon the air was hazy with humidity, and as hot as a baker's oven. Sometimes Franz felt as if someone had placed him in a stew pot and put the lid on. The sun was direct, and burned like fire. Water poured from his head, his armpits, and every joint in his body. The uniforms, which were wool, didn't help. They were supposed to keep you cool in summer, but instead, with the heat they were itchy and hot. Homespun long johns were the only thing that helped this condition. Franz's one advantage was the fact that he was a baker, and used to working in the heat. Richmond felt not too different than an oven, and the soldiers rationed their canteens, staying in the shade as best they could.

Marching back to Richmond, the men came upon streams where one could get a drink. There were sloping hills and beautiful trees with leaves that hung from high branches all the way to the ground, but in the meadows, the grasses were already turning a wheat-bleached tan. As hot as the days were, the nights were no cooler after dark. The moisture in the air seemed to make the heat all the more intense. The citizens of Richmond were on curfew at nightfall, and at night, the Federal bands played for the soldiers' entertainment.

It seems possible, at least during this time of duty, that Franz helped with the baking of bread. On their return to Richmond, the soldiers of Company K found the city much more orderly, though still in need of a great deal of work. One difference was the distribution of bread to those in need. On April 24th, the U.S. Army Commissaries began the daily issue of an eighteen ounce loaf of bread to each citizen for "six and a quarter cents." In addition, residents were encouraged to fish in the James River, and three hundred women were hired to sew clothing.

After cooking and marching all day and evening in the heavy, wet heat, Frank sat under the stars and dreamt of his future. He also thought of his father and family in Prüm. He could barely imagine that he had once lived in a village so peaceful. But as difficult as this time seemed, now that the war was over, he knew it would not be long before he returned to Chicago. So, the days pushed on, one after another.

One day, walking through Richmond, Frank was surprised to see some "Negros" wearing simple clothing decorated with gold, diamonds and sapphires. Passing a humble log cabin, he spied fine furniture inside, sitting on a dirt floor. The woman standing at the door looked at him sternly. Then, turning to her daughter, a child of about ten, she said, "Kahisha, you close that door." But Franz didn't care. Later, when speaking to another young man in his troop, Franz told him what he had seen.

"Oh, yes, when the war was ending, before the Confederates surrendered, many of the Southerners ran out of town to the woods, afraid of what the Union soldiers might do to them. Of course, the black folks had heard we were there to free them, so they had little fear."

Some of the other boys, who were seated nearby, joined in the conversation.

"I never in my life will forget what happened when we came here. We came up from Petersburg. It was a sure thing. Richmond was already beaten. Lee had been giving us a beating . . . but we cut them in two on April 2nd. By the time we got here the next day, we could hear the church bells ringing from the distance, Anyway, when we got here, it was night. One Negro told me they had started running out, thousands of people in the late afternoon. Even the guards in the penitentiary fled. And those prisoners, you know what they did? They burned their way out of that prison.

Anyway, they must have all been in a frenzy. The Rebs started burning homes, so we couldn't get to them. Someone set off a gunpowder magazine and when that thing blew up, they say windows for two miles were blown out of houses."

Franz had never heard of anything like this before, but one thing was clear, war changes everything. He was glad he had not joined sooner.

By now his English was greatly improved. In fact, being in the Army had helped him to learn English more quickly and fully than he might have otherwise. Now, he hung on every word that the soldiers were saying.

"You know, folks loaded up wagons with food and everything, they and were just running for it. Those who weren't leaving formed a mob and they took over Main Street. The troops got pretty wild when we got here. I mean it'd been a long hard fight and here we were in the capital of the South and we won. . . . We were triumphant. The men were yelling and brandishing their swords; all this in the night with only the light of the moon and, then, the fire.

"Then, the colored troops started singing "John Brown's Body" . . . but some of them just went wild breaking into homes and stores. By one p.m. the next day, a wind came up and flames spread throughout the city.

"General Wenzel did his best to gather the troops and we started fighting the fire. I think the entire city would have gone up, had we not fought that fire. We were beating the flames down, and passing water. Later, the Army was ordered to start blowing up buildings to stop the spread of the flames."

At this point, another man joined in, taking everyone's attention.

"The next day, we had the biggest surprise of all. An ambulance carriage drives up with all the windows closed and the door opens and there is Abe Lincoln standing as sure as day. Before my mouth could drop open, we were hooting and hollering. . . . He had his little boy, Tad, with him and all the colored folks and kids gathered around and wanted to shake his hand and talk to him. I just couldn't believe he was here. Now, I can't believe he's gone."

The conversation paused for a moment, as they all sat, reflecting on the sad events which followed. Then, the man continued,

"After Mr. Lincoln came here, things got better. They got the Christian Commission and Relief Association up here. We all saw these people as our enemies. They were suffering, but they still wouldn't give up."

For a few moments, the men went on to speak of the terrible straights everyone was in, and their sorrow over Mr. Lincoln's death. Then, the talk turned to home, and then there was silence as each man thought of the life he had left behind and the people he was hoping to see very soon.

On May 25th, two Corporals and eight Privates were ordered on Picket duty for a week. Acting as a guard could be tiresome, but at least they didn't have to fear for their lives.

Returning from "Darley Duty," on July 16th, a good portion of Company K was told they were being relieved to go home. The men on this list included: F. Deppe, F. Rosenfeld, J. Beames, T. Johnson, F. Kishner, and C. Johnson. The 16th was a Sunday, which barely meant anything these days, except for the fact that the church bells rang and folks walked in groups on their way to church. Nonetheless, Franz bowed his head and thanked God. He had survived and he was going back to Chicago. Home.

On Monday, July 24th, Franz Deppe was mustered out of the Army. A little less than five months after he joined, he was free to go. That day, Lt. Horton signed the papers for him along with approximately 159 of the remaining soldiers and officers in Company K. The men got on a train traveling north. Some got off sooner, but most returned to Chicago. What a happy ride it was. The war was over and all was peace. The many long nights of sleeping on the damp, hard ground had left Franz with aching joints, but he was glad just to be alive. [For State of Illinois Certificate, see Notes page 303.]

Chapter 9

Back Home—to Chicago

WHEN FRANZ STEPPED OFF THE TRAIN IN CHICAGO THAT LATE July of 1865, he was truly coming home. He had had his adventure and made his money. Now, he was ready to fulfil his dream. On their first meeting, Joseph embraced his brother joyfully. "You look tired, Franz."

It was true, he was tired. The sight of destruction and suffering; the odors of a burning city, rotting flesh, and unsanitary conditions; the strange accents of black and white southerners, and the army sergeants of various nationalities all filled his mind and sense of being. It would not be long, however, until the new "Frank" was ready to set to work.

Franz Deppe

Chicago was thriving. Changes had taken place, even in the short time he was gone. North Town had grown with new houses and businesses along Wells Street. His old neighborhood had gaslight lamps on the street! Even further north, the fields where cows once grazed were being replaced with homes and businesses.

How wonderful to be back, to sit in the beer garden with friends and acquaintances from the homeland. Even more wonderful was having a clean soft bed to sleep in and good food to eat. No more cold nights on the ground. No more days marching in the burning sun or worrying that he might be shot. With the money he received for his service, Franz began to make plans for his bakery.

Upon his return, there was another surprise for the Franz. The Deppe's twenty-two year-old brother, Carl, had arrived from Prüm. By the end of the year, he was followed by their seventeen year-old brother, Moritz. Recently found in a 1953 Eifel magazine was this reference:

> Moritz Deppe, born July 3, 1848, son of the assistant surveyor Friedrich Deppe, went to America in 1865, and "entered into the household of his four siblings based in Chicago."*

Now Franz rented a small house for he and his brothers at 477 N. Wells Street. Located on the east side of the street between Goethe and Siegel Streets, the house was only a few blocks from Lake Michigan and just south of North Avenue. As in the past, the location was in a German neighborhood with plenty of activity. Likely the money Franz made in the service made this possible. Now his bakery business was begun.

Although Franz knew about baking before the war, he may have learned some important new recipes while in the Army. All of his past experience was now the foundation for his new business. And with Carl and Moritz helping, the business was all the more fun and exciting. They could all become successful together. Once the bakery opened, it did not take long for it to thrive.

Things with the family, however, did not go quite as planned. Moritz is found in only one *Chicago City Directory*. Where he went and what happened to him after this is unknown. Perhaps he returned home.† Carl, listed as "Charles," remained in Chicago for at least two years.

---

* Moritz made four. No other sibbling living in Chicago at this time is known. The spelling of their name was then Deppeé.

† A Moritz Deppe is found in St. Clair, Illinois, 1874.

During this time, Joseph Deppe met the woman he wanted to marry. Her name was Helena Weckman. Born in Germany in 1847, Helena and her sister, Barbara, came to America with plans to work, make money, and return home, but that plan changed when Helena got sick crossing the Atlantic Ocean. In fact, she got so sick, she said she would never step foot on a ship again. Joseph and "Lena," as she liked to be called, were married in Chicago sometime around 1867.

After Moritz Deppe left Chicago sometime in 1866, Joseph, who was now working as a currier and still living at 54 Wesson, left his job and joined Franz in the bakery business. By 1867, to save money, he and Lena had moved in with Franz.

In need of more room, Franz found a nice two-story building a few blocks above North Street at 570 Sedgwick, an area known as North Town. The brothers were able to have their baking business downstairs and their living quarters upstairs. For Joseph and his wife, this was a much nicer area to live. Meanwhile, Franz was intent on finding a nice German girl for himself.

Since leaving home, Joseph and Franz had kept in close touch with family members back home and, as with most people living in a small town, their parents and siblings kept them informed regarding events in the old neighborhood. During the years 1865 and 1866, the letters from home were filled with news about the Ganser family.

Once looked upon with admiration, the Gansers had fallen on hard times. In fact, due to the political climate in Prüm, it seems the family had found it necessary to flee Prüm in fear for their lives. By 1867, they were destitute, and Mrs. Ganser was hoping to find some way for her two eldest daughters, Anna Maria and Katharina, to come to the United States, where they could begin new lives.

Exactly what occurred at this point is unknown. Anna Maria's family believed that an uncle brought the two girls to Chicago, however, no ship manifest has been found to verify this. In fact, no manifest has been found that shows either girl coming to America during this time period.

Many questions remain. Were the Franz and Catharina friends in Prüm? Did they hope to marry one day? When Franz left home, Catharina was fifteen, a pretty girl walking happily down the street, her brown braids wrapped around her head, and a sweet smile on her face. How the girls came to America can only be guessed.

It seems likely Catharina Ganser came to the United States as the fiancée of Franz Deppe. Certainly, the idea of marrying someone from home must have been appealing. Whatever the story of Franz Deppe and Catharina Ganser, there is a much larger story to be told.

*An upper-middle class home in Prüm circa 1850.
Prüm History Museum 1987.*

Chapter 10

The Gansers and the Kochs

During their early years in Prüm, Anna Marie and Catharina Ganser had a good life. They lived in a beautiful home with servants. Their maternal grandfather, Georg Anton Koch was an elected official, which meant that the family was well-respected. At the time, no one could have dreamt how things would change.

Anna Marie and Catharina's father was Heinrich Ganser, the son of Johann Ganser and Anna Marie Schoden. Heinrich had been born in Niederprüm on September 17, 1819. He grew to be a lively, handsome lad, eventually following in his father's footsteps as tradesman-merchant. This led him to the profession of "Eisenhandler," or ironmonger—one who sells hardware made of metal, such as nails and tools. At the time, this may have included household tools and utensils.

Like his father before him, during his teens, there were many changes in the community. As a youth, Heinrich was keenly aware of the struggle going on as the Germanic states attempted to rise from a feudal way of life—a life ruled by lords and princes—to a life of equality and advancement for those of every social status.

When it came time for him to marry, the handsome Heinrich probably found much to be fascinated by in the young, dark-haired Katharina Koch. But aside from any attraction or friendship, most likely theirs was a marriage arranged by two wealthy merchant fathers, who wished to ensure the successful future of their children.

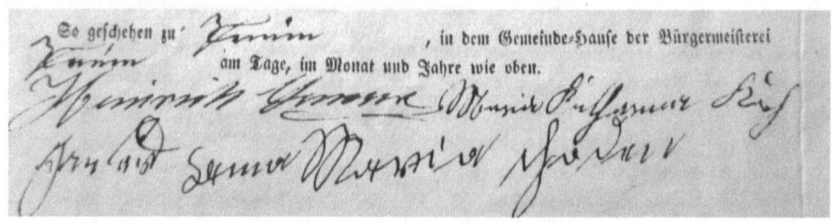

Signatures of Heinrich Ganser (left) and Maria Katharina Koch (right) on their Marriage License

Heinrich and Katharina were married on January 21, 1846, just three days after the bride's 24th birthday. The groom was twenty-seven. The parents of both bride and groom were present for the wedding, something not that common in a society where many had already passed on by the age of 30 or 40. The groom's parents were 64 and 62. The bride's parents were both 63.

Heinrich's new wife came from one of Prüm's well-respected families. The Koch family had lived in the town of Prüm, at least as far back as 1700. Katharina's grandfather, Johann Moritz Koch, was part of the cloth-making industry, something the town was well-known for. In fact, many persons in Prüm kept looms in their homes and worked to create fine fabrics.

Herr Koch and his wife, Barbara Rascop, had at least eight children. Katharina's father, Georg Anton Koch, was the eldest. Born in 1783, he became a merchant, a profession in which he was quite successful. Katharina's mother, Maria Katharina Ameis, was born in Prüm in 1788, and like many citizens in town, was of French descent.

The Koch's daughter, Maria Katharina, was born on January 18, 1822, seventeen years after Napoleon's visit. She had dark hair, dark eyes, and was probably a great deal more light-hearted in youth than later in life. It is said she spoke French. This information confirms an oft repeated family comment, that "Prüm changed hands so many times during this period, the citizens scarcely knew if they were French or German."

In 1847, the year his granddaughter, Anna Maria Ganser, was a year old, Georg Koch was one of twelve officials elected to the city council. Over the years, Koch, who was destined to live a long life, would continue to serve his community in many ways.

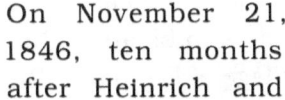

Maria Katharina Ameis Koch

On November 21, 1846, ten months after Heinrich and Katharina's wedding, their first child, Anna Maria, arrived at 7:00 in the evening. Two years later, on November 4th, 1848, a second girl, Maria Katharina arrived at 5 o'clock in the morning. Two years after that, on November 20, 1850, the first son, Johann Peter Ganser was born, at 5 o'clock in the evening.

It is interesting to note that the Ganser babies arrived regularly every two years in November. Barbara, who was named for her great grandmother Rascop, was slightly off schedule, arriving on 7th of October, 1852, at 1:00 in the morning. This leads to the question of whether Heinrich, due to his business as an ironmonger, was only home during the winter months.

The birth of the Gansers' fifth child, Elizabeth, broke the mold when she arrived three years later, on the morning of September 2, 1855. Their second son, Gerhard, also surprised the family, by arriving at 3 a.m. on January 18th, 1857. His birth certificate was signed that same day by the mayor of Prüm, Johann Hass.

By now, the Ganser home was quite full, but that was not a problem because there was plenty of money to care for all of the children. By town standards, the Gansers lived quite well. The year Gerhard was born, there were six children at home: Anna Maria, 10, Maria Katharina, 8, Johann Peter, 6, Barbara, 4, and Elizabeth, 1.

The Gansers were a handsome family; the eldest two taking after their father in appearance. Anna Maria was tall and slender with wavy, blonde hair and blue eyes. Her sister, Catharina, although more rounded in figure, had a handsome face, framed by straight, brown hair and light, blue eyes.

All of the Ganser children attended school in the village. The eldest, Anna Maria, was found by her teachers to be a shy, but bright and sensitive child. She loved the village of Prüm and the wooded hills surrounding it. Later in life, she would say of her childhood that she was happy living in this beautiful village and surrounding forests, adding, "Nowhere in the whole world are there so many beech trees."*

When Anna Maria was eight, she learned about poetry. One day, her teacher, Miss Agnes Gondermann, asked each child in the class to write a poem. Anna, whose heart was already filled with romantic ideas about life and the beauty of nature, wrote her first poem to the "Virgin Maria," for whom she was named. Miss Gondermann was impressed by her work, and encouraged the little girl to keep writing. In the future, Anna would write many poems

---

* Early interview with Anna Kirchstein reprinted by "Club Bulletin."

The Ganser Family Tree

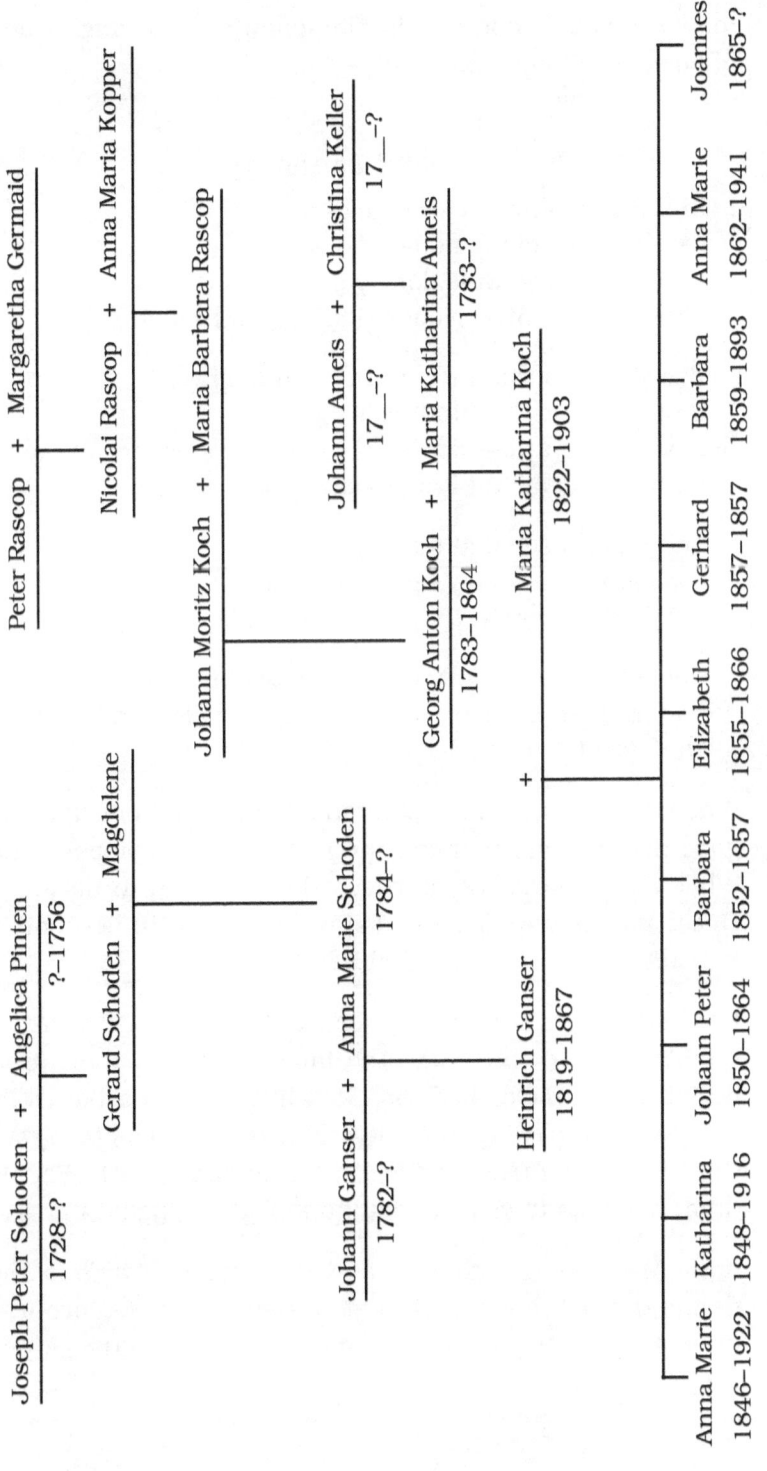

to her "Heimat" (homeland). The following is a rough translation of one poem "Eifellandschaft":

Eifel Landscape

In hard clays, in so strange blue,
I see the sky of my homeland wide;
I see it in those wide, lonely pages,
This Eifel country, gloomy-looking and rough.

The slate mountains stand parted in gray,
Projecting castles, that ages ago
Saw through their doors, in the riding splendor of the hunt,
A thousand valiant knights and noble women.

And more, I see that as deep eyes
Looked mysteriously up to the sun
They knew worlds, they have the riddle to proclaim.

How eerily quiet! Only damp breezes breathe,
And ordinary rushes, herbs and gray willow nod,
As if ghosts come and go.

When the Ganser sisters weren't busy at school, they spent a good deal of time roaming the woods and hillsides of the Eifel. While Anna Maria was particularly interested in nature, Catharina seems to have preferred staying home with her mother, and helping with the younger children.

Life had always been happy for the Gansers, but shortly before Anna's eleventh birthday, the family suffered their first great heartbreak. On October 15, 1857, little sister Barbara, who was only four years old, grew sick and died. As sad as the grown-ups were, they were used to the idea of an early death. For the children, however, it was a difficult and frightening loss to accept.

Anna Maria sought comfort by singing church hymns and wandering through the beautiful monastery gardens. Encouraged by her teacher, she wrote poems about the roses in the garden, and she prayed. Certainly, little Barbara was with the angels now. Mother Mary and Jesus would take care of her.

Mother was still very sad. Elizabeth, who was only two, could not understand. Peter, six, and Catharina, eight, understood better. To relieve their sadness, the children climbed the hills and ran in the green pastures with their friends.

Blessed Mary, San Salvatore Church

Only two weeks after her sister's death, Catharina turned nine. Although there is no memory recorded, it seems possible Catharina and Franz Deppe, who was now seventeen, could have met and spoken during this. Prüm was a very small village, and everyone knew everyone. Having lost his mother as a child, Franz understood loss, though not, perhaps, the loss of a sibling so close in age to oneself.

Yet, despite sorrow, life continues. So it was that at midnight on May 14, 1859, Katharina Koch Ganser, age thirty-seven, gave birth to her seventh child. The baby, a girl, was given the name, Barbara, in honor of the child they had lost.

Two years later, in 1861, Katharina gave birth to another little girl. This baby was named after her eldest daughter, Anna Maria. In the early years, this little girl was known as "Maria." Later, she would be known simply as "Annie." Like most of her siblings, Annie was born in November, on the first day of the month.

Sometime after Maria's birth, Heinrich Ganser went to live in Trier, where, once again, he held the profession of ironmonger. The reason for his move had nothing to do with a marital separation. Rather, it was related to the problems arising from his political beliefs and actions. The family's financial situation may also have weighed into the move, for Trier was a large and very busy city where Heinrich might better earn the money needed to support his family.

Along with their father's departure, there were rumblings in the air that the children could hardly have understood. In fact, it would be many years before they were able to fully comprehend the significance of what had taken place in Prüm with their father. In those days, it was customary to keep unpleasant matters from children. What the Ganser children did understand, however, was that day by day there was less money. Soon, they would barely have enough to eat, let alone to stay in the lovely home to which they were accustomed.

Being the oldest, Anna Maria was the most sensitive to the events occurring around her. She would not forget the day her father departed. Nor would she forget her mother's tears, and the tragedies to follow.

Chapter II
Anarchy

WHEN FRANZ DEPPE WAS EIGHT YEARS OLD, A SHOCKING EVENT occurred in Prüm. On the night of May 18, 1849, the local headquarters for the military—the "Armory"—was attacked, pillaged, and burned. The investigation immediately after revealed that the attack had been carried out by a group of revolutionaries aimed at overthrowing the government. More than one hundred men had taken part.

In time, half of the men involved in the uprising were found to be citizens of Prüm. The rest came from nearby towns. Further investigation revealed that there were three significant persons leading the revolt. First on the authority's list was Dr. Carl Grün, a philosopher from Trier. The other two were Peter Imandt, a representative of the workers' movement in Trier, and Victor Schily, a government lawyer, also living in Trier.

Dr. Carl Grün

Soon after the attack, many of the men involved were arrested. While Dr. Grün had not been present for the storming of the arsenal, he was considered guilty for "intellectual responsibility," and jailed. Victor Schily, however, remained on the move, fighting alongside Peter Imandt in the Palatinate-Baden uprising later that month. When this uprising ended in defeat, both men escaped to

Switzerland. Meanwhile, in the process of investigation, one thing was clear—these men were planning similar attacks on other towns.

The trial was set for the beginning of 1850 in Trier, the judicial center for the region. During the eight months between the terror attack and the trial, an intense search took place for additional conspirators and witnesses, and during that search one name came up again and again: Heinrich Ganser.

According to witnesses, the iron wrench used to break into the Armory came from Heinrich's store. It was also rumored that he had been present during the break-in. Now, more rumors began to circulate. If Ganser had given the wrench to one of the conspirators and had been seen at the uprising, maybe he was one of them. Although the sympathies of the townspeople were not on the side of the government, they were frightened. This uprising against the state was a serious crime punishable by prison, or even possibly death. Further investigation soon led to a subpoena for Heinrich Ganser to appear in court.

During the previous forty-five years, huge changes had taken place in the Germanic states. At the time Napoleon came to power, Germany consisted of thirty-nine states. By 1845, for the most part, there were two: Rhineland and Prussia. When Napoleon lost power (1814–1815), and the French left, the Germanic princes attempted to take back their power. This meant returning the vast majority to a feudal way of life. Citizens of the Germanic states, however, were not willing to give up their new-found freedoms and rights of equality that had come to them under revolutionary France.

In 1843, a wave of uprisings in Europe began with riots in Poland. These led to violence against the Polish nobles. Five years later, in 1848, the people's revolutionary demonstrations broke out in Paris with such intensity, King Louis Phillipe, fearing for his life, abdicated the throne. That same year, students in Vienna took to the streets in protest. Ultimately, these protests helped to overturn Prince Metternich's government. Even though these bursts of revolution and violence did not last, the effects were powerful enough to shake the royals up.

In the Germanic states, there was a large liberal culture among the students at the universities, as well as the intellectual middle class. By the late 1840s, these two groups were stirred to action; they wrote pamphlets, news articles and, generally, set out to educate others by word of mouth.

It was during this time that the crops failed in Germany, resulting in a shortage of wheat. Prices rose so high, many people could not even afford a loaf of bread. As a result of these occurrences, homes and farmland were lost, with a large percentage of the population going hungry.

Like the citizens of other states, the people Prüm suffered from these events. An added factor to the unrest was the Armory. The Prussians had taken over and, as one historian noted, the citizens of the area were not suited to this kind or iron-handed ruling. Even with the hardships of the time, the Prussian government forced families in Prüm to house and feed soldiers stationed at the Armory. The citizens suffered in silence, but there was a sense of tension in the air, that was quickly moving to the breaking point.

Victor Schily, who was seen as the leader of the revolt, was born in Prüm in 1811, and attended grammar school there. In high school, he moved to Luxemburg, and after that to the Reheinische Friedrich-Wilhelms-Universitat in Bonn, where he studied law and attended lectures given by Schlegel. Schily then moved to Trier, where he served as an attorney for the government court. He became a deputy member of the Prussian National Assembly, and, in 1848, was elected President of the first Congress of Rhineland.

The trial in Trier, titled *Criminal-Procedure Against Dr. C. Grün and 22 Companions for High Treason resp. Looting the Armory at Prüm*, began on January 7, 1850.

Public interest in the trial was so great, by 8:00 o'clock that morning, the entrance to the courthouse was filled with people waiting to get in. For safety purposes, a military force equaling half the size of the crowd was sent to stand guard and protect against a riot.

At the opening of the trial, the defendants were seated with their counsels. Thirty-four potential jurymen were also there. After a thorough questioning, fourteen men were chosen to serve as a jury. The judge then ordered the courtroom opened to the public until all seats were taken.

Altogether more than forty men were subpoenaed to court, each man being listed with the following information:

1. **Victor Schily,** 34, lawyer, born in Prüm, resides in Trier
2. **Carl Grün,** 31, Doctor of Philosophy and journalist, resides in Trier
3. **Peter Imandt,** 26, literary figure, born at Wadern, resides in Trier;
4. Christoph Thubeauville, 29, writer, born and resides in Prüm;
5. Adolph Delahane, 20, businessman, born and resides in Trier;
6. Joseph Nels, 24, Oeconom, born and resides in Bitburg;
7. Hugo Hensch, 33, born and resides in Wittlich;
8. Andreas Klein, 29, laborer, born and resides in Wittlich;
9. Benedict Bach, 19, no profession, born and resides in Prüm;
10. Nicolas Lacquinot, 48, merchant and innkeeper, born in Neuilly, France, resident of Prüm (and his son below);
11. Martin Lacquinot, 2, baker, born and resides in Prüm;
12. Anton Forster, 35, baker, born and resides in Prüm;
13. Augustin Spaniards, 36, laborer, born and resides in Prüm;
14. Bernhard Varain (Barain), 25, tobacco spinners, born and resides Trier;

15. Sebastian Seibel, 26, trimmer, born in Limburg, resides in Trier;

16. Ludwig Vallat (Ballat), 30, cloth dyeing, born Luxemburg, resides Trier;

17. Gotthard Diedenhofen, 31, brewer, born and residing in Wittlich;

18. August Schröder, 21, merchant, born and resides in Wittlich;

19. Heinrich Wilhelm Deuster, 23, gunsmith, born and resides Wittlich;

20. Matthias Briss, 27, Rothgerber, born, and residing in Wittlich;

21. Peter Niles, 43, Drechsler, born and residing in Wittlich;

22. Johann Baptist Warweiler, 33, dryer, born and residing in Bitburg;

23. Hubert Clemens, 23, baker, born and resides in Bitburg;

24. Nicholas Schneider, 29, soap maker, born and residing in Bitburg;

25. Hubert Hoffmann, 22, laborer, born and residing in Bitburg;

26. Peter Hamann, 20, laborer, born and residing in Wittlich;

27. Peter Sprinkling, 20, laborer, born and residing in Wittlich;

28. Peter Henry, 29, locksmith, Born in Briedel, residing in Wittlich;

29. John Neustadter, 30, writer, born in Trier, resides in Wittlich;

30. Nicholas Thiel, 49, city council, born and resides in Bernkastel;

31. Christopher Hall, 20, baker, born and resides in Bitburg;

32. Liborius Schloßmacher, 57, laborer, born in Wesel, resides in Prüm;

33. Gotthard Schlossmacher, 32, laborer, born Weinheimer, resides Prüm;

34. Franz Jacob Käs, 33, locksmith, born and resides in Rachtig;

35. August Wellenstein, 30, gold worker, born and resides in Prüm;

36. John Dillenburg, 28, laborer, born and resides in Wittlich;

37. Andreas Göbel, 22, gardener, born and resides in Bitburg;

38. Bernhard Reissen, 28, laborer, born in Bitburg, resides in Prüm;

39. William Joseph Collman, 32, Mason, born and resides in Bernkastel;

40. Bernard Anton, 40, carpenter, born and resides in Bernkastel;

41. Michael Heintz, 57, innkeeper and brewer, born/resides in Bernkastel;

42. Wilhelm Albert Siebert, 22, cigarette maker, born in Potsdam, resides in Bernkastel;

43. Michael Stoll, 24, Shoemaker, born and resides in Bitburg;

44. Matthias Foehr, 38, carpenter, born and resides in Wittlich;

45. Gotthard Mehs, 33, laborer, born and resides in Wittlich;

46. Gotthard Nauert, 26, day laborer, born and resides in Wittlich;

47. Jacob Krieschel, 18, laborer, born and resides in Wittlich;

48. Stephan Becker, 33, carpenter, born and resides in Wittlich;

49. Jacob Clemens, 22, carpenter, born and resides in Bitburg;

50. John Daubach, 25, bookbinder, born in Bitburg, resides in Wittlich.

The accused were found namely to be: I. Victor Schily, Carl Grün, Peter Imandt, Hugo Henschleben, Johann Neustächter and Nicholas Thiel. The charges, stated officially, were that 'on May 13, 1849, these men, "conspirators," joined in a plot to overthrow the royal government and to incite the citizens to rise up in armed violence against the royals.'

The trial confirmed that Victor Schily had been placed in charge of the plot to plunder the "Landwehr Armory" in Prüm. This armed "gang," as they were described, consisted of more than twenty persons. The Armory was looted and a number of persons were hurt in the violence that followed. In addition to the damages, a large number of military weapons and uniforms were also stolen.

The officials all agreed that the event had been well planned. It had been scheduled to take place on the day of Prüm's annual festival, a day when more than 100 persons from outside the town came to join in the celebration. Because of the high volume of visitors expected that day, the planners of the attack were able to bring a large number of people into town without causing attention. In addition, it seemed clear the perpetrators had hoped to incite persons in town for the festival to join them in the uprising.

In the midst of the trial, someone stated that the servant of ironmonger Ganser had brought a hoist to help them gain entrance though a window to the Armory. Another stated that Ganser himself had raised an iron crowbar, not once but twice to break a window.

When it came time for his testimony, Heinrich Ganser admitted that Schily had visited his house and asked to borrow a horse. Franz Kas, the locksmith, was also witness to this fact. He added that a crowbar had been taken on that day as well. This testimony took place on the 14th of January 1850.

Some weeks later, in response to the accusations made about him, Heinrich Ganser swore before the court that he had not been the one to break the window, nor had he been involved. In the end, he was exonerated.

Victor Schily, although absent, was condemned to death. As a lawyer serving in an official capacity for the Landwehr government, by taking part in an uprising against the government, Schily was considered a traitor, a crime punishable by death. During his career, he would be condemned to death twice. Both times, however, he escaped—this time to Switzerland, and later to Paris, France.

Peter Imandt was also condemned to death, but like Schily, he was in Switzerland. In the future, Imandt would go to London, where he would collaborate with Karl Marx and Friedrich Engels.

A few of the men involved in the attack were soldiers stationed at the Armory, who had turned tailcoat. Their help had made entry into the Armory possible. The penalties for these men were severe. Six were condemned to death; others given life sentences.

While it is unknown how much Heinrich Ganser had to do with these men, the knowledge of their association brings understanding as to how serious this situation and any involvement with it was.

After the trial ended, for a time things in Prüm were calm, and the Gansers went back to their everyday lives. Heinrich Ganser had always traveled on business, often spending long periods of time away from home. His profession as a merchant ironmonger made this acceptable and unquestioned. In addition, he was

Heinrich Ganser's Signature

wealthy and generally respected, as was his entire family. These facts seem to have allowed the restoration of people's good faith him. Soon, his reputation was restored, and his good name above suspicion.

Time, however, would reveal that many persons involved in this revolutionary cause were upper-middle class. The uprising in Prüm and the succeeding trial in Trier seem only to have been a first step in the eventual destruction of Herr Ganser and the entire Ganser family.

Meanwhile, Heinrich continued to travel and to be absent from Prüm for long periods. His wife, Katharina Koch, along with their servants, took care of the home and the children. Although Franz Deppe was too young to understand the meaning of these things at the time, much later he may have pondered what he knew.

As the years passed, Katharina Koch carried a weight of worry on her shoulders, watching their relatively luxurious lifestyle disintegrate. Although the full details may never be known, it seems Heinrich Ganser was becoming increasingly involved in the cause of revolution, and, in time, it would catch up with him. It would be at least another ten years, however, before the full effect of this was felt.

In 1862, there were seven children at home: Anna Maria, 16; Maria Catharina, 14; Johann Peter, 11; Elizabeth 6; Gerhard, 5;

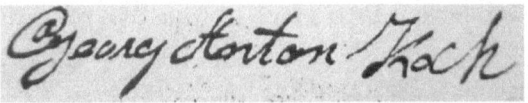

Georg Anton Koch's signature

Barbara, 2, and the baby, Maria. Frau Maria Katharina's father, Georg Anton Koch, who it seems was still a member of the City Council, may have given the family some financial assistance. Yet despite any help the family received, life was exceedingly difficult, both physically and mentally. Then, on July 4, 1864, Katharina's beloved father Georg Anton Koch passed away at the age of eighty-one.

From this point on, the Gansers descended from a respected, upper-middle class family to poverty and social disgrace. Sometime around this period, Heinrich Ganser found it necessary to leave Prüm. Then, on August 23rd, a little over a month after the death of Georg Koch, the eldest Ganser son, thirteen year-old Johan Peter became ill and died. Heinrich may have been able to come home during this time. Coupled with other events in their lives, this loss was almost too much to bear.

The following year, on November 30th, 1865, the Ganser's Katharina gave birth to her ninth child. The baby, a boy, was named Joannes. Katharina was attended to by the local midwife, seventy year-old Magdalen Franz, wife of the late Peter Steilen. As mid-wife, Magdalene was given the job of explaining the whereabouts of the father to the registrar or mayor. The information, as recorded on the birth certificate, states that forty-four year old Catharina Koch was a resident of Prüm, but Heinrich Ganser, age forty-six, was now a resident of Trier and without profession. There is some indication that Heinrich had "escaped" Trier and returned to Prüm at the time of the baby's birth—either because he was running from the authorities or simply to be there for the birth of his child. Officially, he was not listed as a resident of Prüm or Trier.

When Herr Ganser left Prüm for Trier, he moved to a city approximately thirty-three miles away. Trier is considered to be Germany's oldest city. Founded by the Romans in 16 B.C, the city shines with the results of their work. The Porta Nigra, a huge city wall four miles long, still stands today. Rome's legacy in Trier includes roads, aqueducts, imperial baths, and an amphitheater. The French added their own touch to the city in the 1790s, by building a grand, pink palace edged in gold.

By 1867, Trier was a city with centuries of churches and marketplaces built upon winding streets, paved with cobblestones. It was a city full of people and industry, a progressive and liberal place to live. One major source of wealth was Trier's thriving wine business and the Moselle River, the means of a healthy commerce. Thousands lived within Trier's walls; men and women of every type. Trier was the city where Karl Marx, the father of socialism grew up.

But at home in Prüm, tragedy was never far from the Ganser family. On September 2nd, 1866, middle sister, eleven year old Elizabeth, was the next member of the family to die suddenly. Mrs. Ganser was grief-stricken and greatly frightened. How were they to survive? Who would be taken next?

The day came when the family fled Prüm. Although the exact details are unknown, family legend has it that they had to leave Prüm to save their lives. In some stories, Anna Maria herself was in trouble, having spoken out politically. Many years later, in an interview with a German paper she would simply say, "We lost everything."

The family settled in Trier for a time. Besides the problems in Prüm, there may have been more serious personal issues at hand for on May 1, 1867, at the age of forty-seven, Heinrich Ganser died. The cause of his death and the sad circumstances of his life still remain under question. Was he ill? Had he been in prison? Or was he executed?

The cause of Heinrich Ganser's death remains suspect for at least one reason. The witnesses on his death certificate appear to be official men of the state, possibly associated with a prison in Trier. In 2016, after reviewing the case, German officials were unable to verify whether he died in prison, but neither could they eliminate that possibility.

Without money or husband, Katharina and the children must have suffered greatly. According to family stories, the situation eventually was so dire, it became urgent that the two oldest girls leave the country.

In later years, Catharina would state that she arrived in the United States in 1867. Anna Maria said she arrived in 1868. These statements indicate that, despite family stories, each girl likely came to the United States by herself, possibly with a marriage pre-arranged.

We can only imagine the turmoil and sadness mixed with hope that Catharina carried with her as she traveled across the ocean. She would have traveled on a ship from Antwerp, leaving behind all she knew. Possibly, the journey was taken with a relative, using their last name on the passenger list.

What a new world young Catharina journeyed to. She crossed the ocean, possibly by herself—not at all normal for a young woman at that time. Then, by train, she traveled across a country she did not know. Finally arriving in Chicago, Franz Deppe's familiar and friendly face was there at the station to greet her. Upon arrival, the pair rode in the bakery wagon to the Cook County Clerk's office, where they acquired a marriage license. They were married on October 29, 1867.*

---

* It should be noted that in Germany, Catharina Ganser's name was spelt with a "K." From here on, however, she would spell it with a "C."

Catharina Ganser Deppe

Chapter 12

Bakery Life

FRANZ BROUGHT CATHARINA HOME TO THE SMALL COTTAGE JUST north of Menomonee, at 570 Sedgewick Street, where he had been living for the last year. Downstairs was the bakery. Upstairs, there was a small apartment with several rooms. This was a property Franz had been renting, but around this time, he was able to obtain a mortgage from the owner, John Miller. What happy days these were. Franz was not alone anymore. Together, he and Catharina would make a new life.

Catharina was a pretty girl; well-rounded and glowing. Franz had trouble taking his eyes off her. Her lively personality shown in her face. She smiled when he looked at her. He was the same Franz she had known in Prüm, but now he was a part of this new world she had joined.

For Franz, being married to Catharina was amazing. Before, he had spent so much time working, he barely thought of marriage. Now, here was a young girl from his own town; they had a childhood in common. He had someone who had met his family, who had climbed the beautiful hills surrounding their village; someone who had the same customs. Both had dreams and ambitions as well. They worked hard all week, but on Sundays they relaxed and had fun, walking through the German part of town, visiting the beer garden for music and dancing. The musicians played the songs they sang and danced to back home. How they laughed. Life was good in Chicago.

Catharina loved to talk. She had so much to tell Franz. She hadn't seen him in four years. He, in turn, had much to tell her. The sights, sounds, and ways of Chicago must have been a great shock to her, a girl from a small town. This new world was bold and brassy; loud, quick, and busy. Everyone was in a hurry, but she kept up. She was young and full of energy, and just as anxious to make a new life as Franz had been. Like him, things did not bother her much. She knew Franz would protect her.

A little over a year after Catharina's arrival in Chicago, her sister, Anna Marie arrived. Anna, like her sister, was probably engaged to be married before she arrived in the new world because she was married almost immediately after setting foot in Chicago. It seems possible the search for a husband was aided by Anna's new brother-in-law, Franz Deppe. As a baker, he knew many people, and one thing was clear—the Gansers simply could not stay in Germany.

Anna Marie's new husband was Andrew Reutlinger, a German immigrant, seven years older than her. Andrew first appears in the *Chicago City Directory* of 1864, where he is listed as a bartender with Daniel Schafter, and boarding at 254 Randolph Street. By 1867, Andrew had his own saloon at Wells and Quincy, then listed as 227 Wells.

At the time Anna and Andrew were married, Andrew was living at the tavern, only a few blocks south of Franz Deppe's old bakery.* Not wanting his wife to live at the tavern, or "German saloon," as a relative termed it, Andrew found a small apartment a few blocks away, at 282 Wells.

It seems Andrew was a good husband, one who treated Anna with respect. The couple enjoyed a good life together. Among her treasured mementos, Anna kept a ticket to the Germania Club's

---

* Street numbers were changed in 1909, but the numbers for Wells do not translate in the Street Renumbering book for Wells & Quincy. They are pre-fire.

Andrew Reutliner and Anna Marie Ganser

Fancy Dress Ball at the Crosby Opera House, dated March 3rd, 1868.

The Crosby Opera House was a lavish five story theatre palace, built in 1865. Many of the greatest opera stars from around the world appeared there. The cost of Anna's ticket to this event was $10. Today, the price of this ticket would equal somewhere between $153 and $172, quite a hefty sum for a bartender. Perhaps this event was Anna's wedding gift. Andrew certainly wanted her to enjoy the finest things in life.

Now that both Anna Marie and Catharina were married and living in Chicago, life was even better. Joseph and Lena Deppe saw the arrival of their first child on September 29th in 1868—a little girl they named Josephine. So the two sisters were excited when, in 1869, they learned that they were each expecting. Catharina was the first to give birth, on March 4th. The baby, a girl, was named Katharina. Possibly, she was given this name in honor of both of her grandmothers. Anna's child did not arrive until October 21st. This baby, also a girl, was named Ottilie.

Around this time, the Reutlingers changed their home address again, this time moving to 232 Monroe, approximately two blocks from Andrew's saloon. (According to pre-Chicago Fire addresses, this site today may be 301 W. Monroe near No. Franklin.)

Meanwhile, with Franz and Andrew both doing well in their respective businesses, it seems they may have helped pay the passage for their mother-in-law, Katharina Koch Ganser, and the four Ganser children still in Trier.

That June of 1869, the Ganser family traveled to Antwerp, Belgium, where they boarded *The City of Limerick*, and sailed for the new world.

The City of Limerick was built in 1863 as a passenger ship for voyages between England and South America. Constructed by Smith of Glasgow, Scotland, the ship measured 281 feet x 34 feet, and weighed 1,529 tons. It had three masts and a single funnel smoke stack. It was not a large or sturdy ship in the way of ships today,

The City of Limerick, *etching circa 1867*

but it did have an iron hull. In 1875, six years after the Ganser family's journey, and twelve years after her first voyage, the ship, having been bought by another company and re-named, was lost at sea with forty-three aboard.

On boarding the ship, Maria Katharina did not use her married name, "Ganser." Instead, she gave her maiden name, "Kath Koch." In turn, the children were all listed under the "Koch" name: Gerard, 11; Barb, 9; Maria, 7, and little Joannes, listed as one year. In truth, Johannes would have been three and a half. Perhaps he was small for his age, and the price was less for a one year-old child.

Like thousands of others who crossed the ocean to America, the Ganser family found it necessary to travel by galley. There was simply not enough money for Katharina Ganser and her five children to travel any other way.

Traveling in the galley was dark and rough; a journey lasting at least two weeks, possibly longer. There was no privacy, nor was it sanitary. Everyone slept in one unventilated space with chamber pots, the air was foul. Often, under these poor conditions, persons grew sick and died. It has been said that a journey by galley scarred one for life. The Ganser family arrived in New York City on June 12, 1869.

There are still several mysteries concerning the Gansers' entrance into the United States. While it was customary for German women to use their maiden names after marriage, particularly after being widowed, still, considering Katharina's situation, one cannot help but wonder if the use of her maiden name was a sign of how much she wished to distance herself from her husband's past. This leads to the question: were Heinrich Ganser's connections so scandalous, his acts so terrible, that she feared being discovered? Did she think that she and her family might be stopped from entering the United States were these things known?*

---

* Although the events in Germany were known by members in the family, the sense of shame and scandal about Heinrich Ganser continued for over

Although the children would continue to use the name "Ganser" in their adult life, it should be noted that Katharina never again used her married name. For the next thirty-six years, she would be known only as Kath or Katie Koch. Sudden poverty and the loss of three children were enough to hold on to bitterness for a lifetime. Aside from custom, perhaps she did want to distance herself from this painful past.

Another equally important and puzzling question persists: After leaving the ship in New York, where did Kath Koch and her children go? No further record has been found for her anywhere until 1900. Brother Gerhard (who later changed his name to John), Annie, and Barbara are found in Chicago in 1880. But where the family resided for eleven years after their arrival has yet to be discovered.

A third question remains unanswered. What happened to little Joannes? The ship record is the last one known to exist for him. Did he die at sea? Or perhaps, in early childhood?

In 1870, Joseph and Carl Deppe left Chicago. Why they left and where they went is unknown. Perhaps there was a disagreement, or they simply wished to live in another location like Indiana.

After Joseph and Carl left, Franz hired two immigrant men to work for him. These men would remain with the bakery for some years. Henry Lowenstein was a twenty year-old from Wurttemberg, who Franz hired to do the baking. Appoleon May, also twenty, was a Prussian laborer, who was hired as a driver for the bakery's delivery wagon.

Each day before dawn, Franz rose and went to work with Henry. Together, the two men mixed the dough, kneaded it, and laid it

---

one hundred years. When this writer began work on the family history in the mid-1980s, a conversation was overheard by my mother between two grandchildren of Catharina Ganser, discussing the question of whether I should be told "the truth." Unfortunately, in the end, they never told me.

out in long pieces. Once it had risen, the dough was formed on long, flat spatulas, and placed in the stone ovens, where it was baked to a golden brown. Franz and Henry produced hard rolls and bread. It was demanding work.

When she was able, Catharina stood behind the front counter, filling orders and placing the money in the new, cast iron cash register. Sometimes, she helped to make the apple strudel and other special pastries. When Baby Kate was small, Catharina kept her in a basket behind the counter. Business was good at the Deppe bakery, and the family was happy in their small but rapidly expanding neighborhood.

Although Franz had reservations about the Catholic Church, Catharina, was a devout Catholic. She arranged to take little Kate to St. Michael's Church, just a few blocks south, to have her baptized. As she grew, Kate was a happy little girl.

These days, Franz smiled as he went about his work. Not only did he have the most beautiful wife, he had the most beautiful daughter. Little Katherina had her grandmother, Katherina Koch's dark hair and her father's beautiful blue eyes. As she grew older, the little girl showed herself to be a sweet child, who loved to sing and laugh. Clearly, she was Franz's pride and joy.

Catharina had turned their simple living quarters into a cozy German home. From the moment she rose in the morning until the sun set at night, Catharina's energy seemed boundless. She had the house scrubbed, breakfast on the table and was off ready to help Franz with the bakery by mid-morning. Lace curtains hung in the front windows, making their abode feel like a home in Prüm. Meanwhile, downstairs, the bakery business was thriving.

On November 12th, 1870, Catharina gave birth to her second child, another daughter. Catharina named the baby for her sister, Anna Marie. The baby was baptized at St. Michael's church on December 18th of that year. Then, in August of 1871, Baby Anna fell ill and died. She was nine months old.

South of the Chicago River, Anna was living happily with husband, Andrew Reutlinger, and their child. Andrew seems to have been a man everyone liked. He was tall with a dark beard; a very strong, kind man. He was also well-educated and knew a lot of people. During this time, Anna Marie was content with life. Little Ottilie, with her brown hair and blue eyes, brought much happiness into their home.

The city of Chicago felt secure in itself during 1870 and 1871. Indeed, these years were busy ones. The stockyard opened. There was far more traffic in town, more business, more money, more jobs, and more immigrants to fill those jobs. Despite the increased pollution, one couldn't complain. Chicago had no need to fear a recession. It was growth all the way.

Chapter 13

1871—The End of the World

IT HAD BEEN HOT FOR MONTHS. EVEN THOUGH SUMMER WAS OVER, there had not been a drop of rain, nor had the weather cooled. The city was in a drought. In fact, no one could recall a year this bad. In this city of hastily erected wooden houses, barns, piles of garbage, dry grass and hay, fires broke out easily. Things were so bad that summer, there was a fire nearly every week.

"It's a wonder the entire town doesn't go up in flames," said Franz, speaking to Catharina one evening.

When autumn arrived, the situation wasn't any better. Still no rain. Then, on October 7th, a huge fire broke out on Canal near Van Buren Street. It took until 3:30 in the morning for the firemen to put the flames out. Yet, despite their efforts, the fire completely destroyed four blocks of homes and businesses.

After a long night of fighting flames in the already hot and humid air, the firemen dragged themselves home, stopping along the way for a beer. Black with smoke and exhausted, each one arrived home and fell into a fitful sleep.

Sunday, October 8th was quiet, but the heat continued throughout the day. Then, sometime around 9 p.m., a new fire broke out only blocks from the fire of the night before. It started in an area of dry shanty buildings, where there were barns and sheds filled with hay and feed for the animals. The people here owned cows, pigs, and chickens. There were also piles of refuse—plenty to feed a fire.

It was said the fire began in Mrs. O'Leary's barn. There was a great deal of prejudice against the Irish at this time, and in the days following the fire, word was spread that Mrs. O'Leary had been milking her cow, when it kicked over her lantern and set the tragic turn of events into motion. The only thing was, Mrs. O'Leary was nowhere near the barn at that hour of the night.

The fire spread quickly. Someone tried to call the fire house, dialing a number on the fire box at the corner. The call was not answered right away. The firefighters were still tired from the night before. When they finally did answer, they were confused about where they were to go. By the time they arrived, Mrs. O'Leary's fire was raging. Already it had taken down several buildings.

Meanwhile, the wind from Lake Michigan started picking up, which didn't help. Loose materials were flying through the air, landing on buildings and piles of flammable refuse, setting them ablaze too. Since everything was dry, this progression of events seemed to occur easily, and once it started, it seemed nothing could stop it.

In the ensuing hours, men and women retiring for the night noticed that the sky was bright. 'Another fire,' they thought, but those who remained awake soon realized this fire was not being put out— it was getting bigger.

"Ah Franz," Catharina said, as she laid the baby down and prepared to go to bed. "More fire. I hope it is not near Anna and Andrew. Rain must come soon."

Franz glanced at the window and thought he might stay up a bit longer. Catharina's sister, Anna and little Ottilie were living southwest of the river. Silently, he hoped they were all right.

South of the Chicago River, the wind increased, lifting flaming debris and sending it through the air to land on a building a block or so away. Those who thought they were safe soon realized no one could predict where this fire would go.

Sunday night, the Reutlinger saloon, now located at 227 Fifth Ave., was open. Men came in for a drink and to discuss what was going on south of them. Then, someone came in and asked if anyone could help move their belongings to a safe place. Soon, more came. People wanted carriages and horses, and men to help fight the fire. Although the blaze seemed safely distant, before long Andrew and the others realized they were not safe. The fire was advancing.

As the blaze ballooned in size, Andrew's worry grew. Where were Anna Marie and Ottilie? The streets were filling with people, many of whom had obtained carts and horses, and were trying to escape with their most precious belongings.

Although the Reutliner's new residence at 282 Fifth Avenue was not far, much seems uncertain, including Andrew's whereabouts. Perhaps he had gone to help someone. The fire was moving swiftly now; the flames were burning furiously, consuming everything in their path. According to family stories, by the time Anna realized how quickly the fire was moving, she only had time to throw a few of her most precious belongings in a bag. Then, wrapping two year-old Ottilie in a blanket, she ran for her life. Heading north, toward the Chicago River, she joined hundreds of souls just as desperate as she. Surely, the fire would not cross the river.

One could barely hear voices above the roar of the fire, and the heat was so intense, one's flesh felt burnt as it approached. Looking behind her, Anna felt as if she were in a Bible story. A huge wall of flame, a hundred feet or more in the air, was coming after them. People ran, screaming. Some had carts piled high with belongings, and in their hurry many of these carts broke, spilling the contents into the street. In the confusion, people were run over. Finally, the precious belongings men and women had worked so hard to save were abandoned as they realized in order to save themselves, they must let everything else go.

Lost in the sea of humanity, Anna did not go to Andrew's bar but was caught up and carried along with everyone else. Having crossed the river, she prayed she was safe, but it would not be long before a cry went up. The fire had crossed the river and was now burning intensely on the west side, repeating the pattern it had followed south of the river. Where would it end?

The street was a wild mass of people, running. It seemed as if the fire was everywhere. Where could they run to for safety? Anna was one of the last people to cross the bridge. Before long, the timbers of the bridge caught fire and went crashing into the river. This scenario repeated itself as the fire crossed the Chicago River on the north side.

By midnight, flames were raining down from the sky. Men and women were running, trying to carry whatever they could in wagons, by buggy or by hand. The air was growing hotter and hotter, while from the sky a rain of sparks and ash followed them. Someone ran down the street shouting, "The end is coming! . . .The waterworks are on fire!"

Joseph and Lena Deppe went south. It is thought they were living below the fire at this time. There was no other way for them to go. The wind's direction seemed to blow the fire north, then south, and, finally, east. The Deppes traveled with scores of people out to the flat prairie, where there was very little left to burn.

As the night continued on, the residents of Chicago hoped and prayed things would slow or that even a greater miracle would occur—rain. But the fire continued to grow and spread.

After midnight, the wind intensified, and the flames grew bigger until a wall of red, yellow and orange flame 100 feet high shown against the night sky. For those in the distance, the flames seemed to reach the heavens. The night was not night at all; the fire lit the sky as if it were day.

The men and women who were so unfortunate as to be in the downtown area, appeared black with soot as they hurried from home to business and home again, trying to save what they could. Buildings said to be fireproof—like the grand Crosby Opera House, the City Hall and Palmer House—all joined the conflagration, going up in flame as quickly and surely as the tinderbox houses of wood.

Franz Deppe did not sleep much that night. He watched the wall of flame in the distance as it grew closer and closer. Then, he ventured out of doors with his neighbors, hypnotized by this frightening but amazing sight. The idea that they were safe on the north side of the river soon proved false. The fire would not be stopped.

When the morning sun rose, there, barely discernable through the thick haze of smoke, was a distant outline—the remnant shards of Chicago pointing to the sky; the city was gone. By mid-morning, the bells of St. Michael's began to toll their warning. Another hot, dry day was in store and the fire continued.

In the morning, Catharina sold bread to persons hungry after a long and sleepless night. By noon, the Deppes simply gave away what was left. Then the wind began to pick up again, and soon flaming debris was igniting buildings on the north side—the largest being the grain elevators, which soon became towering infernos. It was clear their time was limited.

Then, the warning came. They had to go. Franz had been busy all morning. He had taken items from inside their home and buried them in the yard outside. He chose to bury something at each corner of the building so that their property was marked. Two heavy picture frames and another more delicate, gold oval frame with the picture of a lady that had hung on the wall of their parlor were buried.

The flames were igniting clapboard houses on all sides. When the wooden houses caught the flames, they withered within seconds. The ocean of flame was a mile wide, leaping 200 feet in the air. Explosions were heard. It seemed as if the world was ending.

When Catharina looked out the front door, she saw the flames shooting up in an arch across the sky. As frightened as she was, there was something she would not leave behind.

"Oh, mein Gotte!" she cried, as she ran inside. "Franz, Franz, the baby! Where will we go?"

The fire was only two blocks away. When Catharina ran out the door, her apron was full with all the money they had earned in the last few days. Franz followed with little Kate in his arms.

Down to the lake they went, along with the entire neighborhood. This land, once a cemetery, had recently had the bodies removed, in view of creating a park. Desperate to escape the flames, the citizens sought safety by wading out on the edge of the lake. Looking back, some may have seen St. Michael's steeple as it burned. It did not take long for the huge bell to fall to the ground with an earth-shaking thud. The heat of the fire was so intense, in a short time, it had melted the tower bell into a formless mass of metal. The heat was beyond imagination.

Men, women, and children waited in the cemetery, hoping and praying that the nightmare would soon be over. By 9:00 p.m., the fire had reached Fullerton Avenue. Here, it began to fade. The wind died down, and in the sudden quiet, many fell to their knees in prayer. Then came the sweetest moment of all as raindrops began to fall, on their faces, hands, and arms. They were saved!

The crowds waited by the lake throughout the night. And as the smoldering fires slowly died, they prayed in thanks to God. It was over. They had lost everything, but they were alive!

When the fire finally went down, the devastation was beyond anything anyone had imagined possible. According to a news story at that time, 2,600 acres were burned, and 80,000 were homeless. The city of Chicago was destroyed from De Koven Street in the south to the area just above Fullerton. The burnt area was four miles long and a mile wide. In the process, about three hundred people were killed—a small number in relation to the size of the inferno. The fire had not favored the rich with their grand homes, hotels and banks, or the poor. All were equally devastated. The heat from the fire had been so intense, it melted metal and glass, but Chicagoans were not defeated.

In the future, when people spoke of Chicago, they spoke with wonder of her citizens' resilience during those terrible days. Despite the great devastation, on the day following this tragedy, the men and women of the Chicago picked themselves up, built shelters, and began to ply their trades. Until they were able to clear the fire's rubble, the citizens set up their shops in the vacant fields with hand painted signs. Nothing would get them down. As a result of the fire and the great spirit of the people, help in the form of money, came from all over the United States.

Example of a Fire Relief Shanty at Menomonee and Sedgwick near the Deppe Bakery. The Chicago Relief & Aid Society provided $50 worth of materials to build temporary housing. After the fire, about 35,000–40,000 people resided in these homes.

As for the Deppes, some family stories state that after the fire, the family stayed in Indiana for a while. Although this may have been true of the women and children, it seems most likely that the Deppe men, like the rest of Chicago, went back to work immediately, building a new Deppe bakery. After all, they needed to make money, and people needed to eat. In the following weeks, Joseph, Lena and Baby Josephine, moved in with Franz and Catharina again. Franz offered Joseph a job working in the bakery and Joseph accepted. During this same time, a George Deppe moved in with Frank and Joseph. Although his relation to the family is unknown, it seems likely he was a cousin.

Sample of Post Fire house. The new Deppe Bakery/residence on Sedgwick likely looked something like this. A wood house like this was only allowed the first four years after the fire.

In North Town, the residents wasted little time returning to work. With their sense of industry, soon wooden huts dotted the landscape around the ruins of the St. Michael's Church. That "ruin," of course, would be only temporary.

On Sunday, October 15th, Father Peter Zimmer, pastor of St. Michael's, said mass in a private home. By the following week, a 90 foot shanty was erected against the old stone wall of the parish garden. If the Deppes were in town, they likely attended this service, thanking God they and their loved ones had survived this terrible fire. Soon, the lower floors of the church were rebuilt. For a time, this area would be used as a school. It would be two years before the church rose again to its full height, a glorious red brick building whose bells could be heard throughout North Town. The new St. Michael's was dedicated on October 12, 1872.

In later years, these three terrible days would be remembered as "The Great Chicago Fire," and for many years, there was a museum dedicated to the memory of the fire. It included burnt remnants and a horse car site-seeing tour of the fire area.

St. Michael's Church

Much changed in Chicago after this event. The formerly rich residential areas near Michigan and Wabash became areas of trade. The rich moved north, along the lake, and servants changed positions to become salesman. It was truly a new beginning for the city on all levels.

A few months after the fire, Catharina found that she was once again with child. The baby, a girl, was born on September 11, 1872. They named her Sophia after Franz's oldest sister. On December 1st, Franz and Catharina took her to be baptized in the newly built St. Michael's Church. Sophia, a tiny baby with exquisite features, would soon reveal herself to be a blonde-haired, blue-eyed beauty. Interestingly, although the church noted the 30th as her date of birth and the state noted it as the 11th, Sophia always celebrated her birthday on September 10th. And in the future, she would go by "Sophie."

Chapter 14

Chicago to Indiana: Success and Tragedy

AFTER THE FIRE, LIFE CHANGED. LIVING UNDER ONE ROOF AGAIN, this time Franz and Catharina, Joseph and Lena, all grateful to be alive, truly became a family. Lena was just a few years younger than Catharina, and the two women got along well. Their daughters, Kate and "Josie" were both three years of age, and the two little girls loved playing together.

In the months following the tragic events of 1871, the bakery business bounced back quickly. The Deppes soon had enough money to purchase the property they'd been renting at 570 Sedgwick. Franz obtained a mortgage from the owner, John Miller, (this may have occurred before the fire—but all records would have been burnt). By March 12, 1872, Franz had paid off the mortgage balance and was officially released of all obligation. At last he was a landowner. As noted on the deed, Franz was now officially using the name "Frank Deppe." It sounded more American.

The Deppe property stood between Menomonee and Wisconsin going north on the left-hand side of the street. It was a good location. The building they raised after the fire was a long and narrow two-story wood frame structure with stables and outhouses in the back. It had more room than the previous place and included several apartments upstairs that could be rented out. Now they were set.* With business going well, Franz began saving money toward some new plans he had in mind.

Joseph had plans of his own. Shortly after the fire, he became aware of a vast amount of land for sale just outside the city, in Indiana. City life was not for him; he missed the simplicity of Prüm. He and Helena wanted something different for their children. By working at the bakery and living with Franz, the couple figured they would be able to save enough money in a few years to buy a farm.

During this period, Joseph's profession, as listed in the City Directory, was that of "hostler," a position defined as one who looks after horses for people staying at an inn. George Deppe, who had been living with the brothers for a while, moved to 436 No. Wells Street (now 1243), a little ways south of North Ave. His profession was listed as "clerk."

Meanwhile, because all previous records had been destroyed in the fire, on February 14th, 1873, Joseph and Helena went down to the Chicago City Hall and got married a second time. One reason for this action may have been that the couple planned to buy property in Indiana and wanted legal proof of their marriage.

The following year, on April 2nd, 1874 the couple welcomed their second daughter into the world, naming her Catharina. Two weeks after her birth, on April 19th, she was baptized at St. Michael's Church.

Around this same time, Catharina Deppe was also with child. Sadly, according to the Cook County records, the baby girl Catharina gave birth to was listed as being born and dying on the same day—October 2nd, 1874. Although the baby was not baptized in the church, her parents named her Maria, and buried her in an unknown location, possibly the back yard.

---

* This property (after 1909 changed to 1816) was razed in the second half of the 20th Century.

Meanwhile, the Deppe Bakery business continued to grow. Each morning, Franz and several other workers, rose early to prepare the dough and bake the bread. On some days, Joseph took the wagon and went around town, delivering baked goods.

There were new buildings going up everywhere, and in accordance with the new city building ordinances, these structures were made of brick and other non-flammable materials. Seeing the amount of building going on in Chicago, Franz began to dream of a bigger and better bakery building.

Joseph Deppe was not the only one in the family to have an eye on land in Indiana. Franz was interested as well. On December 15th, 1874, Franz met with Alle Cornelsche Vink and his wife, along with Geert Wieringa, a widower, and paid them $3,720* for two lots in Lake County, Indiana. These two properties totaled 120 acres. One lot contained 80 acres and the other next to it, 40 acres. The parties involved in the exchange met in Cook County before Notary Public, Cornelius Hilligonds.†

The 120 acres of land which Frank bought had been given by the United States to the State of Indiana on January 24th of 1844. This land, according to the Abstract Title, was approved by the Treasury Department in pursuance of Sec. 1 of Act of Congress entitled:

> "An Act to confirm to the State of Indiana the lands selected by her for that portion of the Wabash and Erie Canal which lies between the mouth of the Tippecanoe River and Terre Haute and for other purposes . . ."

Three years later, on July 31, 1877, the State of Indiana gave the land to the Board of Trustees of the Wabash and Erie Canal in order to "aid in the construction" of the Erie Canal. Obviously,

---

* $3,720 = approximately $84,545.45 in 2015.

† Lake County, Indiana, Book No. 110, Page 510

the land was not used for that purpose because on October 15, 1855, the Board divided it into the two parcels, one of 40 acres and another of 80. The Board then sold the 40 acre parcel to Peter Schillo, and the eighty acre parcel to Charles Walton.

For the next twenty years, these lands passed through a number of hands. Then, sometime in the 1860s, one of the owners is said to have built a large, brick mansion on the property. The identity of this owner has yet to be discovered, however, by studying property sale prices, we might be able to guess the answer.

When John Schroeder brought the property from Peter and Margareth Schillo in 1857, he paid $1,212.00. When he sold it 1861 to John Erlinger, the amount paid was $2,000. Again, in 1870, when John and Margareth Schroeder sold the property to George Hiller, a warranty deed was obtained for $3,000. This increase in price may point a significant new structure or structures on the property.

Although neither house nor barn is mentioned in the deed papers, Lake County records state that the house on Liverpool Road was built in 1865. The home was a grand brick mansion, which clearly was built by an experienced city architect with a fine education and advanced knowledge of structure and design.

Structurally, the two story home had walls approximately two feet thick, built with bricks laid in two directors for added strength. The floors were laid with thick wooden planks. A single chimney and a grand red marble fireplace graced the huge living room. The second story had four large bedrooms. The house also included a large basement and attic. The attic was actually a grand ballroom. From the dormer windows at each end, the residents had an unobstructed view of the entire valley.

The property Franz purchased lay just outside a small town known as Hobart. George Earle, an English architect, founded the town back in the early 1800s. At the time, Earle owned 3000 acres of land in an area which now includes Gary, Lake Station, and Hobart.

Deppe Farm House, Hobart, Indiana, circa 1931

In purchasing this property, Franz Deppe may have had plans to start a farm of his own, one where he could grow his own grain for the bakery. One family story suggests that the purchase of this property took place because of Joseph Deppe's interest in farming. Meanwhile, his ownership of the farm in Indiana meant Franz Deppe was no longer just a Chicago baker. Clearly, his status had changed.

Catharina's sister, Anna, and her husband, Andrew Reutlinger, were not having an easy time. Andrew's business and everything he had worked for, had been lost in the Great Chicago Fire. While some money from the Emergency Cottage Relief Fund may have been available, whatever Andrew received could not replace what he had lost.

During the years 1872 and 1873, Reutlinger struggled and, possibly, even borrowed money to get his business back on its feet. The old saloon at Wells and Quincy had been a popular place, but new ordinances put out by the City Planning Commission ensured that downtown Chicago would to be a different place. In 1871, the city blocks were filled with small shanties of every type. These were structures that definitely had helped fuel the fire. That type of building would no longer be allowed.

Due to the new ordinances and planning by the commissioners, the area where Andrew's saloon once stood was now filled with large buildings, some taking nearly an entire city block. Even if there was a place to rent, Andrew could not have afforded it. Instead, he was forced to look outside the city center. Eventually, he found a place to rent on the south side of Chicago at 177 Blue Island Avenue (now 1010). This location, across the river and southwest of the city center, was quite distant from where he had been.

Six months after procuring his new place of business, Andrew Reutlinger purchased a new home at 537 Sedgwick (now 1739). Listed as Lot 1, it was sold by Nicholas Kranz, and stood only a couple of blocks from Anna's sister and brother-in-law, Catharina and Franz Deppe.

For a time, the Reutlingers were a happy family. Anna kept house and took care of little Ottilie, who was a joy to both her parents. Meanwhile, the shock of the fire and the trauma experienced on that terrible night, continued to affect Andrew. He was not the same man he had been, and Anna worried about him.

Andrew Reutlinger's situation was not unusual. Many persons who seemed to be in good health prior to the fire, died within a few years after it. The terrible shock of what they experienced that night and the black smoke which filled their lungs had grave effects in the long run.

For the next two years, all seemed well. Then, disaster struck again in the form of another fire. Reutlinger's tavern on Blue Island Avenue caught fire and was completely destroyed. This time, the financial and emotional loss was too much for Andrew. Around this time, he wrote a will which stated:

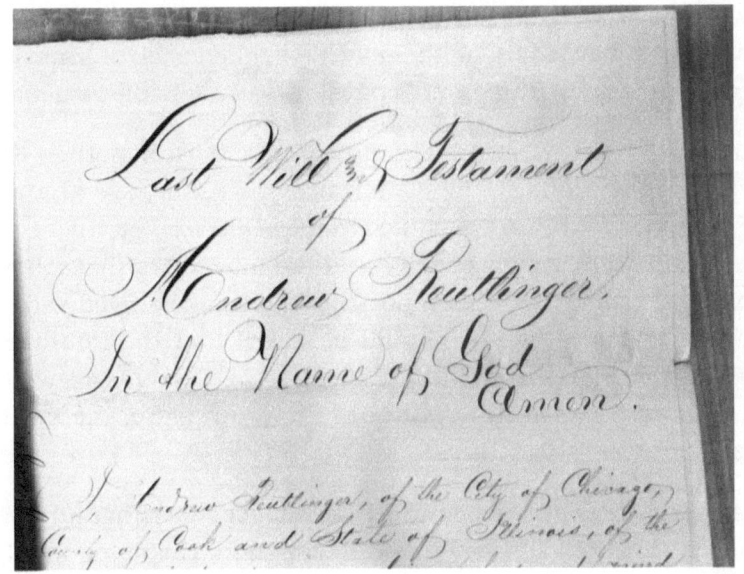

. . . at the age of thirty-six years, being of sound mind and memory, and considering the uncertainty of this frail and transitory life do publish and declare this to be my last will and testament.

That's to say, first after all my lawful debts are paid and discharged, the residence of proprietary, real and personal, I give, bequeath and dispose of as follows:

To my beloved wife, Anna Maria Reutlinger for her lifetime, and after her death to my legal heirs . . ."

Witnesses were Henry Geldermann, George Schert and L. Watry.

On July 14, 1875, Andrew Reutlinger died of a heart attack, leaving behind his twenty-nine year-old wife and six year-old daughter. Andrew was laid to rest on the north side of Chicago at Graceland Cemetery. The plot Anna bought had multiple spaces, and it would continue to be used by the family for more than fifty years.

How Anna survived at this point is not known. Andrew may have had some money saved, or she may have taken a job of some kind. Needless to say, her husband's passing was a terrible loss for her.

In the meantime, the whereabouts of Anna Marie's mother, Katie Koch, and her siblings, John, Barbara and Annie, are unknown. They are not found in the *Chicago City Directory* or the census. Where they were during the fire and the nine years that followed remains a mystery. It seems possible the Gansers lived with the Reutlingers for a time. It should be noted that the Reutlingers were also missing from the 1870 Federal Census, as well as the *Chicago City Directory* put out after the fire. So, the mystery persists.

Less than two years after Andrew Reutlinger's passing, Anna met a man with whom she had much in common. His name was Hermann Kirchstein, and he lived in North Town at 102 Schiller Street, not far from the Sedgwick. Born in Demmin, Prussia in 1840, Hermann came to America via Hamburg, on the *Teutonia*, in June of 1867. Six years later, on November 1, 1876, he renounced his allegiance to the Emperor of Germany, and proudly took an oath to support the Constitution of the United States as an American citizen.

Hermann Kirchstein

Equally, or even more important than his German heritage was the fact that Herman was a bookbinder, a profession he held in Germany as well. Along with a great love for books, Hermann was tall and handsome with thick dark hair and—as was the fashion of the time—a beard.

Hermann seemed to be a very kind man. He certainly showed great love for Anna and her daughter, Ottilie. Although it appears he never adopted Ottilie legally, in every other way, he treated her as his own child.

Anna and Herman were married by a Justice of the Peace, Mr. R.C. Hamuceill, on May 9, 1878. It appears that Hermann was Lutheran, and, at a later date, Anna Marie may have joined his church, St. Paul's.

After the marriage, Herman moved into the Reutlinger home. This made financial sense because the home was paid for. It also made good sense for Anna and Ottilie because this was their home, the place in which they were comfortable.

At the end of 1875, Franz and Joseph Deppe learned that their father, Friedrich Carl Deppe had died on October 11th. Although they knew when they left Prüm, that they would probably never see him again, the news of his passing made this all the more real. It was a sad time for them. Two years later, news came that their step-mother, Katharina Darimont Deppe, had passed away on July 20, 1877. It was truly the end of an era.

Three years after the loss of Baby Maria, Catharina gave birth to another baby girl. The child was born on December 1, 1877, and they named her Maria Louisa. Perhaps because of extremely cold weather, Louisa was not baptized until February 17, 1878. The baptismal certificate at St. Michael's Church recorded the Latin names of the babies, just as the churches in Germany did. Louisa's name on the certificate was *Maria Ludovica*.

Guests visiting the Deppes at this time remarked on the healthy, chubby little girl with the curly blonde hair and bright blue eyes, commenting that she looked a great deal like her mother. Louisa was the Deppe's fifth girl. By now, having lost three children, and

feeling her childbearing years dwindling, Catharina wondered if she would ever have a boy.

By the following year, Catharina was once again with child. On July 7th, 1878, she gave birth to another baby girl. This time, she named the baby for her little sister, Barbara, and on July 23rd, the family went down to St. Michael's to see the baby baptized. Five months later, on December 19th, Barbara suddenly became ill with "spasms" and died. In an era before advanced medical practices, her death was not unusual, but that did not make her passing any less painful.

After Barbara's death, Franz purchased a plot at St. Boniface Cemetery on North Clark Street. Barbara was laid to rest there on December 20th. Around this same time, Barbara's sister, Maria, whom Franz may have previously buried in the back yard, was moved to St. Boniface. Now, the two babies would lie together in peace.

Catharina, Franz, and the children were very sad after little Barbara's passing. Forever after, family members would continue to visit the graves of these beloved babies, who had not survived. Deppe granddaughter, Dorothy Stein, recalled that as a child, her mother, Sophie, often took her to visit the graves of her infant siblings.

In 1879, the Deppes were surprised to learn that Franz's older sister, Susanna Sophia, had decided to leave Germany and settle in Chicago. Following the death of their father and step-mother, Sophia felt it was time for her to follow her brothers to America. The old home really belonged her younger brother and his family. Now that her parents were gone, there was nothing more for her to do there. Having made her decision, Sophia packed her bags and set out for the new world.

Aunt Sophia Deppe

Like Franz, Joseph, Carl, and Moritz, Sophia traveled to Antwerp, Belgium, where she was able to obtain passage on the *Belgenland*. She arrived in Philadelphia on September 11, 1879. At the time, she was 45 years old. Sophia probably had little money, but she was not afraid to work. A position had been arranged for her as a servant in another Deppe home.

The 1880 Federal Census reveals that Sophia was living with the Carl Deppe family on North Avenue and Sedgwick, just six blocks south of her brother's residence. Living in the home were Carl Deppe, 48, a baker; his wife, Catharina Stich, 42; and their six children, all born in Illinois: Frederick, 14; Louise, 12; Johann, 11; Lena, 7; Carl, 4; and Elise, 2.

Sophia, now forty-six, was listed as a "servant." With so many children in the house, Mrs. Deppe was probably in need of a great deal of help, so Sophia was kept quite busy. She would remain in the home at 357 North Avenue for quite a number of years.*

The relation of Carl Deppe to Franz, Joseph, and Sophia—as of now—is still unknown. While it was once thought Carl was Franz's younger brother, this has been proven not to be the case. Voting records reveal that this Carl Deppe arrived in Chicago back in the late 1850s, and was quite a bit older than Franz and Joseph's brother.

In the meantime, a short time after the birth of their second child, Joseph and Lena Deppe moved to Ross Township, Lake County, Indiana. This move would have occurred sometime between 1876 and 1878. Ross Township had been formed by Indiana pioneer, William Ross, only thirty years earlier, in 1848. The Deppe family settled in a farm house about 50 miles away from the hub-bub of Chicago. Now, at last, it was Joseph's turn to make his dreams come true.

One question remains and, as yet, has not been solved. Did Joseph purchase his own property in Lake County, or was the land he lived on part of the farm his brother Franz had purchased in 1874? If so, this farm of 120 acres was the one he oversaw. The main portion of the farm was planted with corn and grains like wheat and rye—grains which could have been used for the bakery. The rest of the farm included an orchard with apples and pears.

Joseph and Lena found the land in Lake County to be fertile, and the community, peaceful and friendly. Lake County, which included the towns of Merriville and Crown Point, was about five miles from the local train station, which ran directly to Chicago. From there, the Deppes could easily visit relatives in Chicago, and relatives could visit them. Although nothing is known about the visits between the two families, it is known that Joseph and Franz were quite close. During these years, there were likely quite a few train trips taken by family members between Chicago and Hobart.

---

* 340 West North Ave.

In 1879, four years after the birth of Kitty, the couple welcomed a son into their family. They named him in honor of his uncle. Frank William Deppe was born on March 15th. A little over a month later, he would have a cousin, also named Frank Deppe, and the two Deppe brothers would finally be able to share the joy of each having a son.

In June of 1880, the census taker found Joseph Deppe's family living quite happily on the farm. Joseph, 42, was listed as a farmer, while Lena, 32, was keeping house. The children were listed as: Josephine, 11, Kittie, 4, and Frank, 1. They were a happy family. Little could they realize how short-lived this happiness would be.

It was an unseasonably warm November day when Joseph told his wife, "Lena, I'm off to the courthouse at Crown Point." The children ran across the yard, waving as he rode out on his wagon, his two youngest horses hitched up. He had decided to take them rather than old Sal. She was slow.

"It will give them some new experience, and they won't tire from the long drive," he thought to himself.

As he headed to Crown Point, Joseph could not help but note the lovely, autumn day. It would take several hours to reach his destination, but it was a ride he enjoyed.

Traveling down the dirt road, he glanced to see how the new neighbors were faring. The preparations for winter had been completed with numerous bales of hay stacked in the field. Down the road were the harvested fields of dirt and straw, waiting for snow. Joseph though happily of what a great crop they would have next year.

After a couple of hours, the wagon reached a crossroads, and he turned the team left to the south. They were riding steady and behaving well.

"Good boys. Come on."

He snapped the reins a bit and set the horses at a faster clip. From here, the road rose slightly, then curved around the bend. He passed the neighboring farms, remembering that they were ripe with corn and wheat the last time he had come this way. He thought about the friends he would see, and about the election.

Joseph was officially an American citizen now, and he intended to use his new privilege to vote. John Keliner, a Democrat, was running against the incumbent Republican, William Heilman, for United States Representative. James Garfield was running against Winfield Scott Hancock for President. It was an exciting day.

Coming over the hill, Joseph could see the top of the red courthouse. Crown Point had been built around the town square, where now a proud courthouse of tremendous size stood. Graceful trees were planted on the lawn surrounding the grand building. There were many wagons in town and groups of men; a lot of hub-bub was going on in the Square. A crowd had gathered to vote and discuss the various candidates. That was something to look forward to, especially when you lived on a farm.

Crown Point Courthouse, built in 1878

Joseph clicked the reins and turned the team toward the front of the square, where many of the farmers had hitched their horses. The horses seemed a bit skittish. They weren't used to all these crowds. As he drove up to the post, one of the horses reared up and whinnied. That set the other one off.

"Whoa, boy. Steady! Steady," he said, but without warning, the pair reared again, pushed back and began to run. The screams of the crowd did not help. Joseph pulled the reins with all his might . . .

It was late now, and Lena put the children to bed. Kitty asked her, "When will Papa be home?"

"Tomorrow, baby," said Lena, trying to sooth her. Joseph had said he'd stay with a friend that night. No need to worry.

Early the next morning, Lena heard someone driving up to the house. Was Joseph back already? Looking out, she saw two men with a wagon and Jospeh's two horses hitched behind. But where was Joseph? Then, before she could have time to think, she realized there was a pine box in the back of the wagon. . .

As the men approached the door, her heart stopped. She could not speak.

"Mrs. Deppe?"

"Yes."

"I'm sorry . . . ," said one man, hat in hand.

How could she get that moment out of her mind, or the moment when Joseph said goodbye. She could not have dreamed it would be the last time she saw him. The shock of it was almost too much to bear. How would she tell her children that their beloved papa was not coming home?

The news reached Franz and Catharina by telegram. They were in shock. Joseph was gone? It could not be. He was just beginning to fulfill his dream. He had little children. Poor Lena.

Franz offered Lena a home in Chicago, but she insisted she would stay on the farm. She and Joseph had their life there. This was what he had wanted for the children. Somehow they would survive.

For a while, she kept thinking he would come home. It was all a terrible mistake. One day he'd come walking through that door, and she'd run to his arms with tears of joy.

They buried him in the Catholic cemetery, Saints Peter and Paul Cemetery of Merrillville. A simple stone was laid in place.

Lena never remarried. Later, when she died, the old stone, perhaps damaged, was replaced by a marker with both their names. They got Joseph's date of death wrong.

Franz and Catharina Deppe

Chapter 15

The Booming 1880s

THE 1880s BEGAN WITH A GRAND SURPRISE. ON JANUARY 28TH, thirty-one year old Catharina gave birth to her sixth child. This time it was a boy! He was a hardy little fellow with blonde hair and blue eyes. His parents gave him the name Franz Deppe, Jr. Later, he would simply be known as Frank, Jr.

By now, thirty-nine year-old Franz had built a grand baking business, yet of late he had despaired of ever having a son. Now, at last, there was someone to succeed him. His son would never know the struggles he had known; he would live in grand style.

As Franz and Catherine watched the Frank Deppe Baking Company grow, they were proud to have money and live well. But of equal joy to them was the fact that they were able help others. During the succeeding years, relatives often came to live under the Deppe roof, a place where they found help and the encouragement. It is also true that after working for Franz Deppe, many started businesses of their own.

The Deppe home in 1880 was full of children and relatives. Living with them at 570 Sedgwick were Catharina's twenty-two year old brother John, twenty year-old sister, Barbara, and little sister Maria, now called Anna, who was just eighteen. In the 1880 Federal Census, Anna's profession is listed as "servant." Likely she helped care for the house and the children. Barbara worked as a clerk in the bakery, and John is described as a "laborer." While it's unknown exactly what he did, we assume he worked for the bakery in some capacity because it was here that he learned his future profession—baker.

While the family lived quite nicely in their upstairs apartment, there were also an array of persons listed in the census, who were living in the various other apartments above the bakery. In particular, were three young men from Germany, all bakers, and all about 20 years of age: Charles Kesker, Casper Steck, and August Biewer, a relative who came to America from Prüm.

By 1880, Chicago was no longer a frontier town. The city had become a force to reckon with, one that rivaled New York. Chicago was a mainstay of the United States economy; a wheel in the financial hub that kept the economy growing. Men came to Chicago with dreams, and frequently those dreams became a reality. Here new ideas took root, real estate was developed, and scientific creations became a part of everyday life. In Chicago, artistic creations and architecture changed form and became innovations that made their mark on America as a whole. Chicago, the prairie city, was continuing to grow with new people and new ideas. It *was* America.

Like the city itself, the Deppe bakery was continuing to expand. It was not just a local mom and pop store anymore. Franz bought delivery wagons and hired a man to paint "F. Deppe Bakery" on the side. These wagons delivered bread, rolls, and pastries around town. The F. Deppe Company had a growing reputation, and Franz was very particular about his help. Only the best and most trustworthy were hired.

Meanwhile, Franz had new plans for the business. A large piece of land, one block down and across the street was for sale. Franz decided he wanted to buy it. Business was good, and he had some money saved, though it was not nearly enough for the plan he had in mind.

On August 6, 1880, in a move often used to obtain cash, Franz "sold" his 120 acres of Indiana farmland to Peter Stich for the sum of $4,000 in cash*. Then, on the same day, Catharine Deppe

---

* $4,000 in 1880 = approximately $93,023 in 2015.

bought the property back for the same amount ($4,000), subject to "taxes or encumbrances" on said land.*

This exchange was probably a mortgage of some kind. In addition, the value of the property appears to have increased, so the Deppes were able to receive a greater amount of cash than they originally invested. With this transaction, Franz had a good portion of the money needed to fulfill a grand dream. He hired an architect, and plans were drawn up for a three-story brick building.

As stated previously, following the Great Chicago Fire of 1871, the city passed new building codes, requiring all buildings to be constructed of fireproof materials. Although a few wooden structures were allowed to remain in North Town, by now all construction used stone, brick, terracotta, or marble. For the bakery, nothing but brick would do. The new Deppe building would have stone ovens in the basement, a large store on the main floor, and a number of apartments upstairs.

On April 3, 1881, in *The Chicago Tribune*'s published list of building permits, there is one for F. Deppe. The information listed states that a four-story building with basement, store, and dwelling space would be built at 545 and 547 Sedgwick, with measurements 37x75 feet. The projected cost was $14,000.† Obviously, this was not going to be an ordinary building.

According to record, the Deppe building was completed in 1881, and proudly displayed at the top of the building, just under the eaves, was "F. Deppe 1881." This name remains there to this day.

What excitement there was the day family members toured the new building. One entered the store through a center door with plate glass windows on either side through which the freshly baked bread, rolls, and pastries could be viewed by passersby. Over the glass door was a hand-painted sign in fancy letters stating: "F. Deppe Baking Company."

---

* Abstract Titles, for Lake County, Indiana, Book No. 29, Page 155 & 156.

† $14,000 in 1881 = $310,467 in 2016, http://www.in2013dollars.com

The Deppe Bakery

The new building was all so grand, the family breathed "oohs" and "aahs" as they walked from room to room. Franz glowed with pride as he happily showed off the new glass cases for pastries and the stone ovens in the basement, with one oven on the north side of the building and one on the south. This was all his. Who could have dreamed when he left Prüm as a young man with no money that he would come to such success! In a neighborhood of smaller structures, Franz Deppe's building stood tall—a proud monument to what one man, an emigrant from Germany, could achieve in less than 20 years.

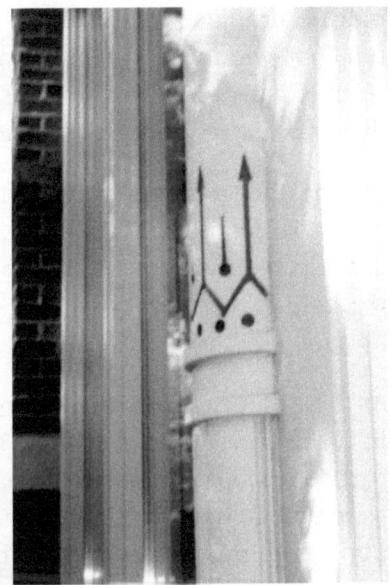

Residential entrance and column design

To the left of the store, was a separate, discreet entrance for the apartments above. That entrance led to a wide hallway with a stairway to the 1st floor. A lovely glass lantern hung on a long chain from the ceiling, lighting the way up the dim stairs. This side of the building had no windows and required lamplight both day and night.

With all his success and his growing family, it is not surprising Franz Deppe wanted a better home for his children. At the time the bakery building was completed, the Deppe children included: Kate, age 12, Sophie, 9, Louise, 6, and Baby Frank, age 1. Little Frank, a serious chap with blond hair and blue eyes, was his father's pride and joy. Of course, he was generally recognized as the heir to the Deppe Baking Company.

The new family apartment was not a humble abode. It opened into a spacious room with twelve foot ceilings and a grand, green marble fireplace to the right. Opposite the entry door were two ten foot windows, through which the afternoon sun streamed. Unlike many city dwellers, in summer and winter, the Deppe family would have plenty of sunlight and ventilation.

Behind the spacious front parlor, there was a large sitting–dining room. This space, when open, made a wonderful area for family gatherings and parties. When the family wished, however, with the help of two floor-to-ceiling sliding "pocket doors," it could just as easily be made into two spaces.

As their name suggests, when pushed, the "pocket doors" retreated into the recesses of the wall. Then, when pulling them out, they turned a single room into two. In this way, Franz and Catharina were able to have quiet time or guests, leaving the children to play and sleep in the back of the apartment.

In addition to the sitting/dining room, the family's apartment also included three small bedrooms, and a kitchen. There was one other unique feature—a bathroom with a round tub.

There were at least five more apartments in this grand new building, two per floor. On the same floor with the family, there was a small apartment, which looked out on the back of the building at the garden and stables behind. These stables housed the horses that pulled the F. Deppe Company wagons. On an interesting note, the back of the building had a soft area which seemed to sink over the years, no matter how many times it was filled. This situation continued even into the 1980s.

The back apartment was obviously less grand than the Deppe apartment, and the view of the stables and alley, much less nice. It would be a place family members, like Catharina's mother, stayed when they came to visit. The other apartments upstairs were rented out to family members, bakery workers, and distant relatives.

Meanwhile, on June 25th, Franz purchased another property around the corner, this time from Louis Letterman and his

Sophie Deppe

Louise Deppe

Frank Deppe, Jr.

children, George and Carrie. The property stood on Tell Court (now Willow), just three lots east of Sedgewick. Deed records describe it as "a three story brick building with attic and basement." Similar in description to the bakery building, not much more is known about this property. The next lot over, described as 'four lots east of Sedgwick on Tell Court,' was another property owned by Franz Deppe—a one story brick barn with loft.

One block south of the new bakery building, at 537 Sedgwick Street, Tante (aunt) Anna and her new husband, Hermann Kirchstein, were happily settled. Herman was a wonderful husband for Anna. As a bookbinder with a love for literature and intellectual subjects, he was a great supporter of her literary interests. He also introduced her to other like-minded persons. During this time, Anna continued to work on her poetry, writing odes to her German homeland, as well as about life, its joys and sorrows.

Anna's eleven year-old daughter, Ottilie, loved her home. She also loved being able to visit her cousins frequently. The Deppes were like the siblings she never had. "Tillie," as everyone called her, attended school with Kate Deppe, and the two became best friends. That year, Kate wrote Tillie a little poem in her book. Whether it was of her own device or the quote of another author is unknown.

> "Love is the blossom of an hour,
> Friendship is the everlasting flower."
> Katie Deppe
> January 30, 1881

Although Herr Kirchstein's new address was slightly north of his previous abode, around this time, the old horse-drawn streetcars were being replaced by electric streetcars and trains. Herman may have had a little further to travel for work, but this residence, so close to Anna's sisters and family, was a fine tradeoff. Not only was it paid for, seeing the joy and comfort it brought Anna to be close to her family, brought him happiness as well.

With the Ganser brother and sisters all living in such close proximity, there were probably quite a number of happy get-togethers during these years.

During the 1880s, the city of Chicago was changing by leaps and bounds. In 1882, the Loop, a train of ten small cars, went into service. In what seemed an amazing modern convenience, this local train traveled from Marshall Fields on State Street down to

Twenty-First Street, some four miles south. Within the next five years, another line was built along the Lake. This line ran all the way to Hyde Park, a distance of nearly eight miles.

As the number of train lines increased, segments of the crowded downtown population found their way to the outer country villages. This new means of transportation meant that Chicago's residents could easily experience country living while keeping their city jobs. The mingling of citizens from different areas further served to mix and meld the various nationalities. So it was that in late 1880 or early 1881, Barbara Ganser met a young man, who showed great interest in her.

Not much is known about "J. Matt Evert," as he was listed in the city directory that year. Both of his parents were born and raised in Luxemburg. Matt, however, was born in August of 1857 in Rosehill, a small community in the northern part of Chicago. The U.S. Census during this period does not show a listing for his parents. Perhaps, because they were farmers, they were missed by the census taker.

During his early years, "Matt" used a number of different first names, including: Math, Mathias, and Martin. This may be one reason for the confusion regarding his early life. Eventually, Mr. Evert took after his father, using the name "Math," both legally and personally. In the future, his gravestone would reveal what is perhaps his true name: Mathias.

Following in his parent's footsteps, Math Evert began his career as a farmer. Sometime later he became a grocer. It was likely one of these professions which led him to Franz Deppe, the bakery, and, ultimately, Barbara. At the time they met, he was twenty-four, and she was twenty-two.

Math and Barbara were married in Cook County on November 17th, 1881. The clerk listed Barbara's last name as "Gancer," indicating how she pronounced it. After the wedding, Barbara gave up her position as bakery clerk, and settled with her husband in

Rosehill.* In 1892, this address was listed as 1907 Clark Street (now 3478).

Eventually Math would be quite successful financially. In fact, in the 1910 Federal Census under "profession," he states "own money." This meant that he was either living on invested funds or had retired with enough money and did not have to work.

Despite the fact that 1881 was a successful year, it was a time of mourning for Franz. The loss of his brother, Joseph, hit him hard. The two brothers had been through much together. Because the whereabouts of Carl and Moritz Deppe are unknown, it seems possible these two brothers may have passed on as well.

The final months of 1881 were difficult ones for the nation as a whole. Now, fifteen years after the assassination of President Lincoln, another president was assassinated. It was a tragedy no one saw coming.

On March 4th, President James A. Garfield was inaugurated into office. Four months later, on July 2nd, the President was shot at point blank range by a man believed to be insane. The assassin, Charles J. Guiteau, said that Garfield had promised him a job. Not receiving it, he took his revenge. After the shooting, Guiteau was quickly captured, tried, and found guilty.

Meanwhile, for the next two and a half months, President Garfield lingered, fading bit by bit. Finally, on September 19th, due to faulty care and the inability to remove one of the bullets, President Garfield succumbed from the infection.

The country was shaken by his loss. The day after the President died, Chester A. Arthur was inaugurated at his New York home, then boarded a train for Washington, D.C. On June 30th, 1882, a little less than a year after the President was shot, Charles Guiteau was executed.

---

* GS Film 1030120, Image 484

Law and Order showed itself in other ways during the decade. In July of 1881, famed outlaw Billy the Kid was killed. Less than a year later, on April 3rd, Jesse James was also shot and killed.

On the bright side, the Brooklyn Bridge in New York City was completed in May of 1883. This beautiful and astounding feat made people proud of their country. In 1886, Americans would have greater reason for celebration and pride as the Statue of Liberty, a gift from France, was finally assembled on a newly completed pedestal in New York Harbor.

On the literary end, in 1884, Mark Twain published his book *The Adventures of Huckleberry Finn*. Although the book was controversial, it became a huge American hit, and everyone wanted to read it.

Chicago, a big supporter of the Union Army in the Civil War, went into deep mourning on July 23, 1885, with the death of former President and Union General Ulysses S. Grant.

As with many families in the new world, the Deppes and Ganser relatives remained close. Franz's sister, known to the children simply as "Tante Sophia," came to visit often. Although she lived and worked outside the family circle, the children knew her well. Her photo was among the treasured items in their home.

In 1885, Aunt Sophia left her employment as a servant in the home of Carl Deppe and started her own business. She was fifty-one at the time. Following in her brother, Franz's footsteps, she took the money she had saved and invested it in a new business, hoping that it would lead to a much easier life.

The Chicago Business Directory that year reveals that Sophia was living at 921 Lincoln Avenue in Lakeview, an area just north of Fullerton Avenue.* Her name appears under "Bakeries," with the respectable title "Mrs. Sophia Deppe."

---

* According to the change of house number, which took place in 1909, by then 921 Lincoln Avenue was gone; 923 would be 3014 today.

Anna and Catharina's brother, John Ganser, had moved to Lakeview as well. His name also appears under "Bakeries," but John had a more expensive advertisement, with large letters. His address is listed as 582 Racine Avenue.*

Like his sister, Barbara, John married in 1881. His new wife, nineteen year-old Elisabeth Wolf (sometimes spelled "Eliesabeta"), was the daughter of Jacob Wolf. She had been born in St. John, Indiana, not far from the farm, on February 9, 1862. After their marriage, John and Eliesabeta settled happily in Lakeview, which was for them an ideal place—a quickly growing community out of the thick of Chicago life.

On the 28th of February 1882, Elizabeth gave birth to a child, who was either still-born or died at birth. The baby boy was unnamed. Anna Kirchstein gave the couple a place for the little grave in her plot at Graceland Cemetery. The baby was buried the following day—March 1st.

Death records reveal that John and Eliesabeta had a number of babies who died in infancy during the first ten years of their marriage: Sherbart, Eleanore, Bernard, and Henry. Bernard was born on May 10, 1884, and Henry on June 5, 1885. The loss of these babies in the early years of their marriage must have been terribly difficult for the couple.

Annie Ganser

Meanwhile, twenty-four year-old Annie, the youngest Ganser sister, was still living and working at the Deppe Bakery. By the mid-1880s, Annie had become acquainted with a young baker

---

* Today 582 is now 2837 Racine.

there named Christian Von Essen. Christian, who was born in Germany in 1858, had arrived in New York in the autumn of 1881. He was twenty-three at the time. Now twenty-eight, Christian was a hardworking, affable fellow. The couple grew quite fond of one another, and it was not long before they decided to wed. The marriage took place on the 22nd of January, 1886.

Having learned the baking business from Franz Deppe, by 1887, the Von Essens were ready to strike out on their own. They moved north to 3165 Archer Avenue, where Von Essen (or Essen as he soon called himself) opened his own bakery.

By 1889, Christian and Annie had joined John Ganser and his family, moving to 1335 George Street (1025 today) in Lakeview. That same year, their first child, a little girl was born. They named her Kathcrine, likely for Annie's mother, who must have been living nearby.

Meanwhile, on February 25, 1887, John Ganser and Eliesabeta Wolfe (as she was listed on the birth certificate) saw the birth of their first well baby, a boy. They named the child Gerard, a close spelling to John's German name, Gerhard. Two years later, "Elizabeth" gave birth to a little girl, Julia Anna, who was born in February of 1889.

By 1887, "Miss Sophia Deppe" had moved to 972 Lincoln Avenue, just down the block from her former shop.* This year, the City Directory reveals she was selling "notions." The following year, Sophia moved again, just a few doors down to 951 Lincoln Avenue.† Once again, she had changed her specialty, this time to "confectionary"—the making of sweets. In 1889, her listing was under "Confectionary and Ice Cream."

---

* Now 3068 Lincoln Ave.

† Now 3046 Lincoln Ave.

On August 22nd, 1888, Sophia Deppe was suddenly taken ill. A doctor was called and diagnosed her condition as "apoplexia cerebri"—a stroke. She was taken to 354 North Avenue at Sedgwick, across the street from the Carl Deppe family.* This address may have been a clinic or a place where she could be cared for. Two days later, on August 24, 1888, Sophia passed away. She was fifty-three years old, had lived thirteen years in the United States, and had never been married. With her passing, another tie to Franz's childhood and the old country was severed. Sophia was laid to rest at St. Boniface Cemetery, in the plot of her old employer, Carl Deppe. This seems to point to the fact that Carl was likely a relative. How they were related is still unknown.

The city of Chicago had always been a rough place; Chicagoans were accustomed to a certain amount of violence. Yet, by the mid-1880s, the city had more reason to fear. Not only was there an intense combination of wealth and poverty—a situation know to increase crime—but in recent years, something new had entered the mix.

Socialism had been taking hold in Europe for some time. Now, the influx of European immigrants, who brought this new political philosophy with them, meant the beginnings of an anarchist movement among workers in America.

On May 4, 1886, just west of downtown Chicago in Haymarket Square, a demonstration of workers striking for an eight-hour workday took place. At the same time, hundreds of citizens congregated in the square in response to the death of several of their colleagues—persons who had been killed by police the day before.

Then, as the police attempted to disperse the crowd, someone threw a dynamite bomb. The blast and the gunfire which followed killed seven policemen and at least four bystanders, but it is believed there were many more. The true number will never be

---

* 401 West North Ave.

known because people feared they might be accused of a crime if it was known they were there. Instead, the wounded and dead were removed without ever being reported.

In the end, fifteen men were rounded up and put on trial. Even though the person who threw the bomb was never discovered, seven men were sentenced to death by hanging for facilitating the bomb. Four were hung, one committed suicide in jail, and the others eventually were pardoned. The Haymarket Riot had a huge effect on the city, and although it did not affect the Deppes directly, like most of Chicago, they were shaken by the riot and its results. As for the Gansers, this event likely brought back memories of things they wished to forget.

Anna, Louise and Frank

Chapter 16

The Deppe Children

THE DEPPE'S ELDEST DAUGHTER, KATE, WAS A STYLISH YOUNG GIRL with dark hair, blue eyes, and perfect manners. In fact, she was the only Deppe child with dark hair, taking after her Ganser grandmother. As the eldest, she was also the apple of her father's eye; Franz thought the world of his Kate. But sometime around 1875, when Kate was six, something occurred which changed the family dynamic forever.

At the time, Kate was attending St. Michael's School, about three blocks south and one block west of their home. It was an easy walk. Although Franz didn't seem to care much about attending church, Catharina attended St. Michael's Catholic Church regularly. Just as the Ganser family had done in Prüm, she visited St. Michael's nearly every day, attending Mass, lighting candles, and praying to Jesus and Mary for her loved ones.

Then, one day Kate came home from school crying. The nun had accused her of being naughty and spanked her with a ruler in front of the class. She was inconsolable. When her father asked if she was guilty of the deed, she insisted she was innocent. She had always been a polite and obedient child so he believed her, but aside from that, he didn't like the nun spanking his daughter.

Flashes of his childhood came back to Franz. Even after all these years, he was still angry for the punishment he had received at the hands of the San Salvatore priest. Now, the more he thought about his sweet little daughter being treated so badly, the angrier he became.

"That's it," he told Catharina. "The children will not attend St. Michael's School anymore."

Then, as if that wasn't bad enough, he added, "And the Deppe family will not enter the door of a Catholic church again. I forbid it!"

Catharina was horrified. The Church was very important to her. In her marriage vows, she had promised to bring her children up in the faith, yet nothing she said could persuaded Franz to change his mind. She was shocked and broken hearted.

This story is further explained in a letter, written many years later by Kate Deppe's daughter, Isabel Lockwood Ochsner, to her younger sister, Charlotte:

> "The Deppes were Catholic, but grandpa was really a nature lover and not very interested in religious orders. A nun spanked mother with a ruler when she was about six years old. Grandpa thought the punishment was undeserved and thereafter his family were not allowed to go to the catholic church."

While there is some question as to the date these events took place, at some point Kate was taken out of St. Michael's and sent to a small German school nearby. A year or two later, when Sophia joined her, the two studied German, music, and painting. The girls were quite happy with their father's decision, having no idea of the anguish it caused their mother until much later. In addition, it seems the family was not completely barred from attending church at that point (unless Catharina snuck the children there), because, until 1880, all of the children were baptized at St. Michael's within weeks of birth.

Whatever date this event occurred, in later years, Catharina, being a dutiful wife, followed her husband's orders. When Frank, Jr. was born, he was not taken to St. Michael's to be baptized. This was a sad and terrible thing for Catharina. God had blessed them with a son, yet Franz had turned his back on the church. What occurred after this is unknown. Did Catharina baptize the boy

Catharina Ganser Deppe

herself, or secretly take him to another church?

Two years later, on May 24, 1882, Catharina gave birth to a second son. The Deppes named him "Hermann," in honor of Hermann Kirchstein, but during the next two and a half months, it became evident the baby was not well. On August 9th, Hermann suffered from a series of spasms and died. Franz and Catharina were filled with sorrow and, possibly, guilt. Catharina may have seen Herman's death as a punishment; the result of the family deserting the church.

Almost immediately after Herman's death, Catharina became pregnant again. On June 7th, 1883, she gave birth to her last child, another girl.

"Ah, she looks like my sister. Anna Marie," commented Catharina, as the midwife handed the baby to her. Then smiling, she said, "I think this one we will call Anna!"

Interestingly, while Frank, Jr. and Hermann do not appear on the baptismal rolls of St. Michael's, Anna does. Perhaps Franz had softened in his anger at the church by then, or perhaps he didn't care if the girls were baptized. In any case, whether he agreed or not, Anna was taken to St. Michael's on July 26th and baptized "Anna Ottillia"—a name honoring both Catharina's sister and her niece.

After this concession to Franz's rule, however, Catharina continued to follow her husband's wishes and did not attend the Catholic Church. Yet, as the weeks, months, and years passed, the empty space in Catharina's life created a large hole in her heart. She felt as if a wall had grown between her and Jesus and the Blessed Mother. She would not disobey her husband, but for many years, neither could she bring herself to attend another church, Catholic or otherwise.

The Deppe home was filled with fine furniture, upholstered sofas with flowered brocade, and a forest green velvet settee. There were lovely carved tables of mahogany and bookcases filled with gilded books.

Franz Deppe also had a fine collection of classic books by authors such as: Baudelaire, the Bronte Sisters, Charles Dickens, Goethe,

Dorothy Wright's living room with green velvet settee where Franz Deppe used to take his nap and sofa (to the right, barely visible) which belonged to the Deppes. Other items like bookcase and statues may have belonged to them as well.

Victor Hugo, Elizabeth Barrett Browning and Harriet Beecher Stowe. He signed his name in those books he considered his. The others belonged to the girls.

The Deppe children were taught early to cultivate a love for fine literature. They read stories and poetry in both English and German. Everyone in the family enjoyed books of inspiration with an appreciation for beauty in art and nature. In their spare time, the girls made some of the books even more beautiful by covering them with flowered paper.

The three eldest girls all loved fashion, especially Sophie, who was considered a special beauty by her family. When she was a teen, there was a wild fashion in style for young girls—cutting the hair very short like a boy. One day, Sophie came home with her beautiful blonde locks gone, much to her mother's consternation.

"Ach, meine Gott!" "Was ist das?" Mother Deppe asked.

"It's the latest style, Mamma."

"What will your father say?"

Sophie didn't care. She knew Papa wouldn't say anything to her. Besides, her hair would grow back. A few years later, she turned her now golden blonde hair into a mass of short curls. Her younger sister, Louise, did the same.

Wealthy business man Marshall Field had a grand store bearing his name in downtown Chicago since 1871. It was estimated that 90 percent of purchases on State Street, where all the stores were, were made by women. The Deppe women were certainly part of that interest. While Catharina may have had some interest in shopping, the younger generation, having never known want, were definitely interested. Kate and Sophie loved to shop at Marshall Fields. Still, the family kept its strong ethic. The children were taught to appreciate the benefits of hard work and to take care for those who had less than them.

North Town, still mainly populated by families from Southern Germany, was a hub of activity. The neighbors all knew one another, and were often more like family than acquaintances. People popped in and out of each other's stores and homes on whim.

The bakery was a special whirl of activity. The children and later the grandchildren were all very curious about the goings on there. They loved waiting around for treats like hard rolls with butter and jam, donuts and apple strudel. There were also tarts with fruit, little cakes, and fresh baked white bread, pumpernickel, rye, and sourdough. Wonderful aromas filled the building, wafting into the street outside, irresistibly drawing neighbors and passersby in through the front double doors. Many years later, a man who had lived in the neighborhood as a child recalled, "They made the best hard rolls I ever ate."

The Deppe children did not have to work, though they helped out now and then. Franz and Catharina worked because that is what they did. More often than not, they asked the children not to get underfoot. They were just happy that their children were going to be far better off than they had been when they started out.

Kate loved music, so Franz bought her a piano. She was quite talented, and happy that instead of having to work at the bakery, she could spend her time practicing. Kate learned all the beautiful tunes she could. In the future, her granddaughter, Kathryn

Lockwood Stitt, would recall that she liked to play the music of German and Austrian composers, in particular, the music of Franz Schubert. Kate was a rather proper girl, who stood straight and tall. Although she loved the classics, she also had a great sense of humor.

Kate's sister, Sophie, a petite, delicate blonde, who kept herself fastidiously dressed, was drawn to the visual arts. She was particularly interested in oil painting, and was quite good at it. Attending the German school, she learned to paint china, furniture, and, eventually, large canvases. Having an affinity to nature, Sophie loved to paint flowers and nature scenes.

As early as 1841, Chicago schools felt it was important to teach music, singing, and visual art. Among the things the girls learned at school was an art known as decoupage. Kate, Sophie, and Louise learned to take magazine clippings and glue them onto boxes, in new designs. When the work was completed, they shellacked the entire box, melding the design and the wood of the box into one. This was a nice art for decorating things at home or making gifts.

By the mid to late 1880s, the Deppes were moving up and everyone was expected to act appropriately. The Deppe children were taught to have a certain level of civility with every person they met. Catharina insisted on good manners, and the children learned to behave properly at all times. There were to be no raised voices, mean words or anger shown to one another or about anyone. A saying passed down in the family was: "If you don't have something nice to say, don't speak a word." Even late in life, Sophie Deppe displayed these manners, never raising her voice.

In addition to good manners, the children learned the importance of being thoughtful of others; it was important to share what you had with those less fortunate. Mother and Father taught this by example, providing for other family members and persons in need. Catharina had seen both sides of life during her early years—the beautiful home with fine things and the loss of it all. She knew not to judge others. Catharina wanted to live by the words of Jesus, "Judge not, lest you be judged."

Yet even as the young Deppes learned about the benefits of hard work and the grace of helping those in need, they were also expected to comport themselves with decorum. It was expected that they be perfectly dressed and coiffed at all times. The children were dressed in the latest fine styles, equal to any other wealthy family in Chicago. Sometimes the girls even made their own finery.

Anna Deppe

Little Anna was a sweet, contented baby, who never fussed. Yet as she grew older, Anna sometimes felt left behind. Her parents and siblings frequently seemed too busy to pay much attention to her, and she was too young to take part in her sisters' activities. As a result, she often had the freedom to do what she wanted in a way none of the other children had experienced. As a result, it seems she lived a rather singular life. As she grew older, Anna revealed a talent like that of her sister Sophie—painting. In time, her medium of choice, however, would be china.

While the Deppe children spent a good deal of time together. Young Frank, being the only boy, was the odd man out. It seems he found friends of his own, but as the heir apparent to the Deppe Baking Company, a certain amount of responsibility rested upon his shoulders. His father had come from a world of difficulty and want. There was never any consideration but that he was fortunate to be born into a world where he had a profession, and money awaited him.

In 1887, when Louise turned ten, she began to show her own unique talent—that of dressmaking. Louise, like her sisters, loved fashion, but in her case, she had a

Frank Deppe, Jr.

Louise Deppe

special touch, sewing clothing and creating fine needlework. Hers was a talent everyone in the family admired. She was truly gifted. This talent may have received an even greater push when Papa and Mama insisted that less money be spent at Marshall Fields. Instead of buying the latest fashions readymade, Louise created them with her needle.

Chapter 17

The Deppes in Indiana

AFTER THE LOSS OF HIS BROTHER, FRANZ REMAINED IN CLOSE communication with Joseph's widow, Lena, and their three children. Although things were not easy, Lena was determined to stay on the farm with the children, Josie, Kitty and Frank. She was able to find some help, and the family struggled along.

On April 8th, 1885, sixteen year-old Josie Deppe married a neighboring farmer, twenty-four year-old Edward Reissig of Hobart. Edward was the son of Frederick and Amelia Reissig. At the time he and Josephine met, Edward was living with his brother, Herman, sister-in-law, Frances and their four children. As little money as they had, Edward and Josephine found a way to earn enough money to pay for their own farm by weaving baskets with the reeds that grew along Turkey Creek. Edward and Josie's first child, Francis Edward Reissig, was born a year after their marriage, on February 5, 1886. Two years later, the couple had a second child, a daughter, on August 1, 1888, whom they named Laura. Laura would remain in Hobart her entire life and became an important figure in that community.

A year after Laura's birth, another girl was born. Frank named the little girl after his mother, Amelia, but only two months later, the baby died.

There were no more children in the Reissig family for another ten years. In the meantime, the couple worked hard, raising corn, wheat, and horses. In the spring of 1899, Josephine was once again pregnant. A little girl, Sena, was born on November 12, 1899. By now, Frank Reissig, who was thirteen, kept busy working on the farm when he wasn't in school. Laura, eleven, was a bright girl. Seeing the hardships of farm life, Josephine and Edward both encouraged their children to keep up their education.

During this time, Josie and Edward took joy in their new little girl. Then, in early fall of 1900, nine month-old Sena fell ill. She had caught the dreaded spinal meningitis, which quickly went to her brain. Sena died of convulsions on September 17, 1900, and was buried two days later at the Hobart Cemetery. Josephine, who had a weak heart, would only live another seven years.

Josie's sister, Kitty, stayed at home during these years, and took care of their mother. Kitty would not marry until 1914, when, at the age of thirty-six, she became engaged to Hobart blacksmith, Robert Scholler.

From the age of eight, Joseph's son, Frank, had been working in the fields, helping to support the family. He was a responsible boy, who did what needed to be done. When Frank was thirteen in 1893, having completing the 8th grade, he left school to work on

Turkey Creek

the farm full-time. The Deppe family's farm helper, fifty-four year-old Dan Watchis, continued to live on the farm, helping Frank to keep things going.

On Franz Deppe's farm, the family cleared the land in order to grow more crops. Along with the big house, the property included a small house and barn. Besides the fields, there were also orchards to care for. The Deppes also added a special piece of Chicago history to the place—a street light that had survived the Chicago fire.

The "Chicago Deppes," as they came to be known, were thrilled to have a place to go where they could escape the humid heat of summer, and they embraced country living fully. What joyous days those were, boarding the train, the girls dressed in light cotton summer dresses and hats, the men in light suits. They were a pretty and festive group as they journeyed on the train from Chicago, an hour spent talking and laughing.

Arriving at Hobart's diminutive station, a horse and wagon awaited them. Possibly two trips or wagons were needed to bring them all back to the farm. Half a mile out of town, they crossed over a little bridge into green farmland. After traveling along the S-shaped curve in the road, and crossing over another little bridge, there was "the farm," as they called it. The house stood on the right side of the road, its tall windows open, rooms aired, a wonderful fresh meal awaited them.

On arrival, the children ran off, eager to greet the farm lady, "Annie," and help her feed the chickens. It was fun for the children to see all the animals on the farm. There were horses, pigs, sheep, cows, and chickens. In the daytime, there were beautiful country walks for the ladies. Taking off shoes and stockings, they cooled their feet in Turkey Creek. So delightful!

At night, the adults sat at a long, outdoor table for their evening meals. The grown-ups always ate first, while the children ran and played. After they finished, the children were seated at small tables for their meal. At bedtime, the girls shared one room, while Frank, Jr. shared a room with his cousins. How different from city living to lie in bed and listen to the sounds of nature outside your window—crickets and frogs, and the occasional moo of a cow or whinny of a horse.

Mansard window in the Hobart house

For Franz, it was a pleasure to see Joseph's children mingling with his own. The loss of his brother was forever with him. Although he admired the courageous efforts of Lena to keep the farm going, he wished he could do more for them. He knew that would be something his brother wanted. Meanwhile, it was a joy just to be there.

Franz and Catharina Deppe's second decade together passed more quickly than they expected. They had a thriving business, a large healthy family, and much to look forward to, but the couple could

Hobart woods on the farm

not help but realize the passage of time—they were growing older. By the end of the decade, Kate was 20, Sophie, 17, Louise, 12, Frank, 9, and the baby, Anna, 6. She was just starting school.

In the late 1880s, Franz and Catharina decided to sell the old property at 570 Sedgwick Street, and they soon had a buyer—Joseph Munchen. The deed was signed over to him on November 11, 1887.

Two years later, Franz was able to make his final mortgage payment to Frank Montinger for the property at 449–451 Sedgwick. Completing the legal purchase on May 2, 1889, Lots 15 and 16 in C. Kinzer's Subdivision of Lot 12 of North's Addition to Chicago were now completely his.*

Franz Deppe was clearly a good business man. He had not only built a successful baking business, he knew how to invest in property; it seems he was always able to cover his expenses and come up with more money. Yet, as a sharp businessman, Franz realized at this point he didn't need all this property; there were other things he'd rather do with the money. So the day after completing this purchase, Franz sold one-half of one lot to Rosalia Meyer. These transactions were noted in the *Chicago Tribune* of May 5, 1889. The half lot purchased by Rosalia Meyer later became 553 Sedgwick. On August 1, 1889, Franz and Catharina "quit claimed" their right to this newly created lot, which lay on the north half of the N E corner of Sedgwick at Tell Court.

---

* Torrens book #587, Pgs. 154–155

Frank, Jr. and Anna Deppe in California

Chapter 18

The Early '90s:
A Trip, a Fair and Marriage

AS A NEW DECADE BEGAN, FRANZ WAS FEELING TIRED. FOR OVER twenty-five years, he'd nurtured his business, yet he'd never taken a vacation. Now, having reached the age of fifty, he not only needed one, he felt he deserved it.

By the year 1890, America's transcontinental railroad had been completed, stretching from the Atlantic Coast, thru Chicago, all the way to the Pacific Ocean. Prior to this time, the only way to travel west was on horseback or in a wagon train. Now that travel was easy and safe, many Midwesterners, especially wealthy Chicagoans were heading out west. Winter was the prime time to go. Eagar to escape the bitter Chicago winters, anyone with a bit of money could board a train for an easy escape. It took approximately two days for these powerful engines to whip passengers across half a continent. Upon arrival, men, women and children stepped into another world—a paradise of warmth and sunshine, far, far from the frozen, windy city they called home. Suddenly, this trip to the 'wild west' was all the rage.

One afternoon, Franz Deppe was busy reading the paper, when, he saw it—the advertisement for California. It was fascinating. They didn't need to go to Europe to experience something grand. California had it all: mountains like Switzerland, deserts like Palestine, and beaches comparable to the Mediterranean Coast in Italy, France, and Greece. Franz made up his mind. He was going to take the family out west. It would be a wonderful trip for everyone.

In addition to his desire for a vacation, it seems likely Franz had heard about the benefits of the dry desert air for those suffering from rheumatism. With age, his joints were beginning to bother him more intensely. The hot, dry climate, he was told, was bound to make him feel better and give his health a boost.

The number of Deppe family members who actually accompanied Franz out west is unknown. We may assume that a trip of this kind would probably have included his wife and all the children living at home, but, in truth, few facts exist about this trip. It is possible Catharina stayed home, though it seems unlikely she would have let the younger children go on such a trip without her. For certain, ten year-old Frank, Jr. and seven year-old Anna accompanied him.

To begin the great adventure, the Deppes boarded a train at Chicago's Grand Central Station. From that point, there were many hubs, where one could change trains to go out west. They may have traveled directly west to Sacramento and from there on to San Francisco, or they may have gone to Omaha, Nebraska or St. Louis, Missouri and then boarded a train for the southern route to Los Angeles.

What an exciting adventure it was to ride in a line of cars behind the huge steam engine. For two days, the Deppes lived full-time on the train. Rolling along on iron tracks, they covered ground at speeds previously unknown to them, passing through the hills of Missouri, the flat plains of Kansas, and the Rocky Mountains, whose peaks were taller and grander than anything they had ever seen. The children were fascinated, their faces pressed up against the glass windows. They even saw Native Americans in ceremonial dress. The days passed with conversation and laughter. It must have been nice for Franz to forget the business for a while and just enjoy life.

Morning, noon and night, seated in the fine dining car, Franz and family ate dinner on tables set with fine linen, china, silver, and crystal glasses; all the while, zipping across the plains. Finally, on the third day, they had arrived. Excitedly, they stepped off the train, the conductor, swinging little Anna down from her high perch, to experience new wonders. The air was warm and dry. Out on the plains, there were cactus gardens and warm sun every day.

Hotels for travelers in the late 19th century were grand affairs, summer palaces with wide verandas where visitors sat, taking in the site of mountain ranges and endless acres of undeveloped land. Inside there were large parlors with polished, mahogany furniture, where one could sit and watch other visitors from all over the world discovering new joys. There were also extravagant dining rooms of the kind few travelers had experienced. These vacation hotels were created for families to remain comfortably in place for months at a time. Most of the people who traveled during this time stayed much longer than a few weeks. And many who came for a month, decided to stay permanently. The wealthy built grand homes, to which they returned each winter.

Pasadena was a town largely founded by wealthy Chicagoans for this very purpose. In light of this, millionaires from Chicago built grand hotels and mansions there. Other visitors would return to fulfill the dream of farming land that never saw snow. If Franz had been younger, perhaps he might have started a new life in California. But for now, a vacation was sufficient.

After arriving on the west coast, the adventureous Franz may have suited himself in western jeans, cowboy boots, and hat. The sole surviving evidence of this trip lies in a photograph taken on barren land, backed by a rocky mountain terrain. Seen vaguely in the background is a body of water and little boats. It was once thought that the man in this picture was Franz, but on closer examination, he seems to be a native to the area, a rough cowboy without goatee. The two children riding the mules are Frank, Jr. and Anna. This was probably the children's biggest adventure of the trip, and they gaze at the camera quite seriously.

How long the Deppes remained in California is unknown. Following a month or more of sunshine and relaxation, the family boarded a train and returned home. After all, they had a bakery to run. So, with a month of sunshine and rest under his belt, Franz returned to Chicago feeling like a new man.

As the 1890s began, Chicago continued to push the edges of her reputation. Already her population had reached over a million people. Aiming to be the biggest and the best in all things, the city was now focused on culture. Not long before, Chicago architects had created a building seven stories high. Then, they pushed for taller buildings—ten stories. Finally, the Masonic Temple at State and Randolph, was built with an unheard of twenty stories.

These new buildings were called "skyscrapers," and Chicago was proud of this first. By 1892, the city also boasted an elevated train, which took passengers from Congress to 39th Avenue. The elevated lines, ran above the street, which meant that nothing had to be disturbed, neither buildings nor streets.

Chicago's City Hall interior, 1911, a style inspired by Louis Sullivan

But as Chicagoans were aware, buildings did not just need to be tall, they needed to be beautiful. And so a new goal was set—displaying art for appreciation. Architect Louis Sullivan, also known as the "father of the skyscraper," was among those who created the amazing metal floral designs, which graced many a building.

As far as education was concerned, the city aimed high in that too. When the Baptist University of Chicago closed, John D. Rockefeller agreed to donate the money needed to re-open it with new buildings, if the Baptists could raise $400,000. They did, and Marshall Field donated ten acres of land. The school opened officially in 1892, becoming the University of Chicago. The Newberry Library, one of the grandest research centers in the country, also was founded during this time.

Social causes in the year 1890 saw Jane Addams and Ellen Gates Starr open Hull House, a settlement house, whose purpose was to "provide social and educational opportunities for working class people." The majority of the people helped at Hull House were recent European immigrants. In the future, this settlement house would be of particular interest to some of the Deppes, who felt especially sympathetic to this cause.

With all the progress the city of Chicago made in the 1890s, there would be one glowing triumph which brought the greatest notoriety—the World's Exposition of 1893. The planning had begun in 1885, when the Intra-State Exposition Committee passed a resolution to create a world's fair celebrating the 400th Anniversary of Christopher Columbus' discovery of America. At that time, the event was to be known as "The Columbian Exposition." For several years, there was some debate about where the event would take place. At that time, it was clear the fair would have to be backed by the nation's capital. Washington, D.C. and St. Louis, Missouri were important contenders for the honor of hosting the event, but the competition was greatest between New York City and Chicago.

In 1889, Chicago, now determined to host this celebration, formed a corporation. In a push to be the chosen city, the group put out five million dollars' worth of bonds. On February 24, 1890, voting by the U.S. Senate and House of Representatives for the chosen city was finalized. Chicago had won! President Harrison signed the Exposition bill on April 25th, and a few months later, official invitations were issued to foreign exhibitors.

As can be imagined, the excitement in Chicago was great. Mayer Carter H. Harrison headed the planning commission, with bankers and top business officials all taking part. There was also a woman's committee.

A huge tract of land along the lake, just south of the city, was chosen as the site for the event, and the official name was changed to "The World's Columbian Exposition." As plans took form, it became clear that in order to do this correctly, they would have to wait until 1893 to open. It would be fine for other cities around the country to celebrate Columbus in their own way, but Chicago's celebration was going to be the grandest. In the end, forty-six foreign nations took part and nineteen countries erected government buildings on the site.

Up north of the city, approximately a mile from the Deppe Bakery, advancements of another kind were being made. In 1884, the Fullerton Avenue Presbyterian congregation, first organized in 1864, built a church on Fullerton Avenue. The congregation at that time consisted of 22 adults and 106 children. This area was then considered a separate city from Chicago—the city of Lake View. Still quite rural, the town had cows pastured on empty lots along Fullerton, from Clark to Halstead Streets.

On October 21st of that same year, Anna Kirchstein purchased a lot on the downtown side of Fullerton Avenue, the only side of the avenue able to receive water. Anna purchased Lot 7 from Lucy Buckingham, who owned a huge portion of the area. She borrowed the money for the property from Lyman Baird, and a mortgage was created, which she was able to pay off on April 22, 1887. According to records, Anna had multiple leases on her property. Eventually, Lot 7 was divided into two lots, and one of those lots was sold to Catharina Deppe on July 30, 1887.

By the time the Kirchsteins finished paying for their lot, the area, now known as Lincoln Park, was becoming quite popular, especially among Germans. As a result, it was soon clear that a much larger Presbyterian church would be needed. Under the direction of their new minister, Rev. Coyle, a committee was appointed, and a site at Fullerton and Larrabee was chosen. Fundraising began and, after several sets of plans were rejected, an architect was found in the church congregation, John S. Woollacott.

Mr. Woollacott, who was known for his work in creating many large buildings, including several churches and a hotel, drew up plans for a building costing approximately $37,000. This price included the estimated cost for pews, heating, and lighting. Church members were pleased with the plans and voted to go ahead with the building.

Construction was begun in the late spring of 1887. That summer, the foundation was laid, and on August 31st, with the entire congregation gathered, the cornerstone was laid. It was a big event, with speakers and singing. Two hundred and thirty items were placed inside the cornerstone after which, the architect himself, Mr. Woollacott laid it in place.

By mid-December, the church was nearly completed. The first services were held in the church on Christmas Day, a Sunday. Construction, however, would not be completely finished until April of 1888.

The Fullerton Avenue Presbyterian Church was considered Romanesque in style. It contained a rock-face of Michigan buff sandstone, a slate roof, and a 125-foot steeple. Laid out in the shape of a cross, the church was graced with beautiful stained glass windows. It was certainly a grand asset to the community. As a result, it is not surprising that, when planning their home, the Kirchstein's asked Mr. Woollacott to design it. Not only were they impressed by his work, they wanted a home that would be in keeping with the style and quality of the neighborhood. (This story was related by family members, but it is uncertain as to whether Mr. Woollacott designed their home.) Although the Kirchsteins were not Presbyterian, certainly every person in the area

The Fullerton Presbyterian Church

appreciated the beauty and uplifting spirit the church brought to the community.

The Kirchsteins moved into their new home sometime around 1890. This was to be an elegant new phase in their life. At the time, Anna may have already begun writing for the Chicago published *Illinois Staats-Zeitung*, the most widely read German-language newspaper in the United States (1848 to 1922).

Each year, the newspaper put out a yearly almanac "Calendar" with poetry, translations of literature, articles on famous men and illustrations. It was called *Deutschegesellschaft von Chicago* (The German Society of Chicago). Anna was featured in "The German American Poetry" section.

Due to her work on the paper, Anna Kirchstein would become quite well-known among the artistic and intellectual German society in Chicago. As a result of her work, she mingled with the best of that society, and was invited to be a part of many intellectual groups. She and Hermann decorated their home elegantly, and likely hosted their own salons, entertaining many

The Fullerton house parlor

Anna and Hermann Kirchstein's parlor

of the best-known German intellectuals and artists in Chicago as well.

Their home address was 623 Fullerton. Although not exceptionally large, the house was beautifully designed with stained glass windows over the parlor picture window and in the large front bedroom upstairs. In addition to the lovely front parlor, the downstairs contained a dining room and a kitchen. Upstairs, there were two bedrooms and a small room in the center, which could be used either as a nursery or a dressing room. There were also handsome fireplaces throughout the house. Although the back door opened on an alley, in the early days, the street was narrow and a handkerchief lawn lay before the home.

On June 4th, 1891, twenty-one year old Ottilie Reutlinger married twenty-five year old druggist Albert Miller. Her cousin, Kate Deppe, and friend, Annie Nicholas, stood with her for the wedding at St. Paul's Kirche, a Lutheran church on La Salle Avenue and Ohio Street. It was a lovely wedding.

Just south of downtown Chicago, hundreds of workers were busy erecting the Columbian Exposition Village. A streetcar was installed which took visitors, eager to see the progress at the fairgrounds. It was no doubt a popular outing for young people like Ottilie and Albert and the Deppes.

Meanwhile, at the Deppe Bakery, a flirtation between young Sophie Deppe and one of workers, Charles Wurster, was in progress. Charles was a dapper young man, full of high spirits, dreams, and fun. Nineteen year-old Sophie was charmed. She enjoyed his attention and began to dream of an ideal future. She had fallen in love.

Ottilie Reutlinger

In the fall of 1891, a terrible tragedy occurred at the new Deppe bakery building. By then, the Deppe family's residence was listed as 122 Wilton Ave (today 1849 Bissell or just north of it), approximately one block above North Avenue and ten blocks west of Sedgwick Street. The reason for this move is unknown. Wilton was a nice residential neighborhood. Perhaps the Deppes had the opportunity to live in a house and took it. Another aspect of this may have been the decline of Franz's health. Considering his condition, the elimination of stairs would have been important. In addition, having a quiet home away from the business was a wonderful change for everyone.

Whatever the reason, that year the bakery ovens were rented out to a Mr. Keafitz and two other bakers, Reaginstein and Rosefeld. The upstairs apartments were also rented out. Living in the apartments were a number of families not related to the Deppes in any way.

Then, early on the morning of September 19th, at approximately 4:00 a.m., an alarm was sounded. The building was on fire! It began with one of the ovens in the basement. From there, it spread to the rear shed, where hay and straw for the delivery horses were stored. According to the story, which appeared on the front page of *The Chicago Tribune* later that day, the fire "ran up" from the shed to the "rear stairway." When it reached the stairway, while not burning the building down because it was brick, it proceeded to fill the back second and third floor apartments with smoke. The sleeping tenants were unaware of the danger. Those living in the front of the building on the second floor, namely John Rondo, his wife, and their two children woke in time and were able to escape out the front door.

The fire was discovered by Officer De Leale, who was making the rounds on his Sedgwick Street beat. De Leale called the firehouse, but, unfortunately, by the time the men arrived and put their ladders up to the third floor, it was too late.

1849 Bissel, possibly 122 Wilton in the 1890s

The back of 549-551 Sedgwick—2nd, 3rd, and 4th floors. The top floor was an attic.

The loss of life was tragic and shocking. Five members of the Schalk family were found dead from smoke inhalation: Mr. and Mrs. John Schalk, ages 45 and 42, and three of their children: Annie, 15, John, 12, and James Henry, 8. The Schalk's daughter, Cynthia, who was still breathing, was taken to the German Hospital.

Among the others to die on this terrible morning were Robbie Burns, a fifteen year-old boy, and an unknown woman—likely an immigrant worker or servant of some kind. The newspaper noted that the strangest "feature of the fire" was the fact that no one in the neighborhood really knew who lived in the building. What was known was that the building was owned by "Mr. Deppe."

Three days later, the funeral for the Schalk family was held at St. Michael's Church. The report on the funeral also appeared on the front page of *The Chicago Tribune*.

All of the persons who died in the fire appear to have been staying in the rear apartments, where the smoke was the greatest. Those who survived included the baker, William Keafitz, and his family. They escaped from the second floor by climbing down ladders.

This terrible loss of life in the Deppe's ten year-old building must have haunted them. Meanwhile, repairs were needed to restore the building to working order. At a later time, the Deppe family moved back into the front second floor apartment. Various other apartments would be used by family members in the future. Many years later, rumors went out that the building was haunted.

In the months following the fire, Sophie's romance with Charles Wurster continued. Clearly, Mr. and Mrs. Deppe had many other things on their minds and were somewhat hesitant about their lovely, young daughter marrying Charles. But according to Sophie's niece, Kathryn Halstead Foxcroft, Sophie had a talent for getting what she wanted, and soon Mr. and Mrs. Deppe agreed to the marriage.

The pair were married on January 21, 1892. At the time, Sophie was twenty and Charles, twenty-one. Because Charles probably had very little money, the couple may have settled in one of the apartments above the bakery. Once the vows were said, and the couple settled, Sophie found that life with her new husband was not at all what she had expected.

Charles' sense of fun and the outgoing ways Sophie so enjoyed prior to marriage had an attachment—Charles was a gambler. It is not an easy addiction to give up. He loved to attend the horse races and other betting games. He was always waiting for "lady luck" to smile on him, but as all gamblers learn sooner or later, this is a losing game.

When Sophie realized the extent of her new husband's addiction, she had to face the fact he was not the man she thought he was. If she did not have the strength to end the marriage, her father certainly did. This was a marriage that could only spell disaster.

A few months after they were married, Charles and Sophie divorced. She had hoped for a home and children, along with the kind of stability and love she witnessed between her parents. Now the dream was over. Even as she knew the decision was right, Sophie was pained. Her unhappiness would last a long time.

Perhaps her one solace at this time was her good friend, Anna Strasser. The girls had been friends since childhood and Anna lived next door at 545 Sedgwick with her mother, Anna, and her brother, Julius. Also living with them was her grandmother,

Rosa Meyer, the same person Franz Deppe sold half a lot to in 1889. Both grandmother and mother were Swiss Germans. Anna was still single and would be for a number of years. Together, the two young women commiserated over love.

In the midst of all this, while keeping the bakery building as their official address, the Deppes moved north to 1161 N. Clark Street (now 2500 N. Clark), about two blocks above Fullerton. The reason for this move is not known. Perhaps the family found a home there and wished to be closer to the rest of the family in this neighborhood. At the time, it was considered, out in the country, peaceful and a more desireable location.

Anna Strasser

The year 1891 would end even more sadly than it had begun. For some time, Hermann Kirchstein had been suffering from headaches and peripheral vision problems. Anna encouraged him not to work so hard, but cutting back on work did no good.

Finally, in the summer, Hermann went to see a doctor and was diagnosed with a brain tumor. The swelling from the tumor was causing compression of the brain. By the autumn, Hermann was paralyzed. Anna dealt with this terrible situation as best she could, but it was unbearably sad for her. The family rallied around her, but in truth, nothing could be done. On December 10th, at the age of fifty years and eleven months, Hermann Kirchstein passed away. Because the ground was frozen, he would not buried until April 9, 1892, when he was laid to rest at Graceland Cemetery, next to Anna's first husband, Andrew Reutlinger.

Hermann was a good man, someone everyone loved. His and Anna's years together had been happy ones. Now, finally, together in their beautiful new home, they had dreamed of wonderful times, but it was not meant to be. Anna was devastated. This was the second time she had lost a husband, and her sorrow was great. Unable to stand living in the Fullerton house by herself, she moved in with Ottilie and Albert, as they awaited the arrival of their first child.

Albert and Ottile Miller

The Miller baby was born on March 1st, and immediately was named Ottilie, after her mother. Six weeks later, Anna returned home with Ottilie, Albert, and the newborn, "Ottie." From now on, they would live together.

The loss of Hermann Kirchstein was sad for Anna on a deeper level. She had found a kind man, someone who willingly adopted her daughter, and treated her as his own. As a husband, he not only supported her financially, but spiritually, giving her understanding and encouragement as a writer. No one could ever replace him in her life.

After Hermann's passing, Anna's life revolved around two things: her family and her writing. In a sense, she never fully recovered from his loss. From this time on, she devoted herself to her writing and working for *Ill Staats-Zeitung*. She wrote a weekly column with poems. Writing was something which both expressed and healed her soul. Later, she would publish two books of poetry: *Herzenstone* (Heartstone) in 1910 and *Lieder* in 1915. In time, she became well-respected and well-known in the Chicago's German community. Today, she is also well-known among her German countrymen in the Eifel.

Anna, like her sister, Catharina, would prove to be a smart and generous business woman. Eventually, according to the family, she owned not only her own house on Fullerton, but three other houses as well. All had hot running water and heat—a luxury at the time. In fact, the Fullerton area was now the place where prominent Germans wanted to live.

On October 26, 1892, thousands flocked to the site of the Columbian Exposition to view the dedication ceremony, yet not all of the buildings were completed. Still, it did not matter. The winter which followed was severe. This interfered with the work, yet by the end of April, the construction was finally completed. The fairgrounds opened officially on May 1, 1893, and would remain open until October 30th.

Never before or perhaps since has such a grand fairground been seen. All of the buildings were white, causing the site to be nicknamed "the white city." There were Grecian and Roman palaces, and a grand Venetian canal with gondolas. Entering the World's Columbian Exposition, visitors were able to witness the glories of the world from China to Africa, from Greece to California, all in the space of 690 acres. At night, the buildings were lit by a General Electric searchlight—a new innovation for most people who lived by gaslight. During the six months the Exposition was open, more than 27,300,000 visitors came to see its wonders.

By the end of October, Chicago stood in a blaze of glory. The event had been a huge success. But at the end of the Fair, there was great

tragedy. Two days before World's Columbian Exposition closed, while standing in the doorway of his home, Mayer Carter Harrison was shot dead. Chicago was stunned and broken-hearted.

Harrison had a long history with the city. During the Haymarket Riot in 1886, Mayor Harrison had walked unmolested through the crowd of protesters, asking the police to leave the people alone. After leaving office, he continued with his work as owner and editor of the *Chicago Times*. Then, in 1893, he was re-elected to the position of Mayor.

His assassin, Patrick Eugene Pendergast, was a crazed and angry office seeker. As a result of Mayer Harrison's assassination, the closing celebrations planned for the Columbian Exposition were cancelled and replaced with tributes to their beloved Mayor, the only man in Chicago history to hold that position for five terms.

Just before the end of the Fair, on September 17, 1893, Otillie Miller gave birth to a son. She and Albert named him Carl Theodore Miller. Carl was certainly a blessing in the midst of their sadness. The family regretted that Herman was not there to celebrate this birth as well. Then, in the midst of the celebration, the Gansers learned they had another reason to grieve.

Only days before Carl's birth, Barbara Ganser Evert had given birth to a child as well, a little boy whom she named Frank John Evert (possibly to honor his uncles). Childbirth was dangerous during these years, and Barbara caught the dreaded "puerperal fever"—an infection often caught by women after childbirth. One week later, on September 14, 1893, attended by Dr. Linster, Barbara passed away in her home at 1907 Clark Street. Her death certificate listed "blood poisoning" as a complication. Barbara was laid to rest at St. Henry's Catholic Cemetery.

"Frankie," as the family had been calling him, did not last long. Ten days after his mother passed away, on September 24, 1893, he followed her. The baby, only twenty-one days old, was also laid to rest with his mother at St. Henry's.

In addition to the baby, Barbara left behind three other children: Anna Katharina Evert, born March 13, 1884, age six; Martha, born in April of 1885, age five, and Margaretha, born June 14, 1890, age three.

Barbara's other siblings, John Ganser and Annie Essen, were still living up in Lake View. On October 3, 1891, two years after the birth of their second child, Eliesabeta and John saw the birth of Catherine Therese, whom everyone called "Kate."

The Von Essens also lost a child at the beginning of their marriage. The baby girl, born July 7, 1886, was named for Annie's mother, Katie Koch. Sadly, she died eight days after her birth. Annie's sister, Anna Kirchstein, gave them a grave next to her brother John's first child, in her plot at Graceland.

Following the loss of their first child, Annie and Christian had a number of children. A second Kate was born in November of 1889, followed by Mamie in June of 1891 and Louise in December of 1893.

By the early 1890s, there were many Ganser descendants. They all got together frequently, and all the children knew one another.

In 1890, thanks to intense lobbying by veterans of the Civil War, Congress passed the *Disability Act of June 27th 1890*, described as:

> *An Act granting pensions to soldiers and sailors who are incapacitated for the performance of manual labor, and providing for pensions to widows, minor children, and dependent children."*

In recent years, Franz Deppe (who by now was using the name "Frank" almost exclusively) found that he was less and less able to work. For more than a decade, he had suffered various aches and pains, the result of his time in the war, but now these problems, officially termed "rheumatism," were becoming debilitating. This inability to work seems to have affected the Deppe Bakery as well. As a result, Frank brought others, such as Nicholas Becker, into the business. In time, Becker was made a partner.

On his initial pension application, Frank listed his home address as 122 Wilton Avenue (now Bissel). He stated that he had been a Private in Company K, Regiment 23, Illinois Voluntary Infantry. The application was filed on April 16, 1892. Frank's application indicates that he had hired an attorney, Milo B. Stevens of M.B. Stevens & Co., to handle his case.

When his application was received, the War Department responded by stating that no "Frank Deppe" had been found in the Union Army rolls. Frank probably didn't remember fully what happened nearly thirty years earlier, but he did remember his company and the date he enrolled.

It would take some time for this confusion to be straightened out, but eventually the War Department responded, stating that they had found a "Francis Deppie" who enlisted on March 3rd, 1865, and had served in Richmond, Virginia. The rolls also showed that he had been released on July 24 that same year. This response was stamped July 2, 1892.

Once this matter had been straightened out, the Bureau of Pensions stated that Frank would be paid retro-active a "pension at the rate of six dollars per month, to commence on the sixteenth of April one thousand eight hundred and ninety-two."

Down at the bakery, Kate Deppe was being courted by a young bachelor, Ozro John Lockwood. Born on May 7, 1863, Ozro was the son of Charles and Mary Lockwood. His father, a Civil War Veteran, who served in the 81st Ohio Infantry for three years, named him for his commanding officer, Ozro John Dodds.

Louise (left) *and Kate* (right)

Although Ozro was born in Eaton, Ohio, by the time he was a teen, the family was living in Muncie, Illinois, where his father worked as a dealer in shoes and boots. There was one older boy, Charles, Jr., and three younger girls, Isabelle, Mary and Eleanor.

By the age of twenty-four, in 1887, Ozro was working as a clerk at 140 Market Street in Chicago and living at 117 Larrabee Street, approximately half a mile south of the Deppe Bakery.* By 1891, still at the same job, Ozro had moved to 78 Menomonee (now 334), right around the corner from the Deppe Bakery.

---

* This address is not listed in the Re-numbering Street Index, but today would be approximately 1002 Larrabee.

Although it is not known exactly how the couple met, it was probably at the Bakery, sometime during the three or more years Ozro lived at this location. It is also possible he met Franz Deppe through the business he was involved in. By 1893, thirty year-old Ozro Lockwood was mature and ready for marriage. He held a steady job at 140 Market Street, where the Chicago City Directories list him alternately as a clerk and bookkeeper.

By 1893, Ozro was busy courting twenty-six year old Kate, who by now might easily have been considered an old maid. Kate, however, was a beautiful woman with fair skin, dark hair, and blue eyes. She was also loads of fun to be with. The pair were somewhat opposites, but they seemed to balance each other out. Besides that, Frank had taken a liking to young Ozro. He thought he was a bright, personable, and a conscientious young man with a fine future. When Ozro asked Mr. Deppe for Kate's hand in marriage, he agreed.

Kate had been attending the Presbyterian Church for some years now. As a result, the couple were married by a Presbyterian minister on December 27, 1893.

Following their marriage, the Lockwoods moved to 41 St. James Place (now 435), a nice area just north of Fullerton and a block west of Lincoln Park. Ozro's job had been upgraded to commercial traveler, a position defined as a salesman trying to sell a company's products or services. Perhaps Ozro's new position gave them more money for their living expenses. If not, Frank Deppe likely contributed something to make sure his eldest daughter started her married life in style.

By 1895, however, Ozro had returned to his job as a clerk. The couple then moved to the Deppe address at 1165 N. Clark Street. While no record has been found verifying that Frank and Catharina Deppe owned this building, it appears they may have rented it for at least ten years, during which time it was used as a place for various members of the family to live, when they were in need.

It seems likely that Frank and Catharina were also living at this location part of the time.

The Lockwoods did not stay at the Clark Street residence for long, however. By 1897, they were living at 1228 Wrightwood, another address just north of Fullerton and west of Lincoln Avenue and the park.* The following year, however, the couple moved back to 1163 N. Clark.

---

* The change of address cannot be verified for this number. It would be somewhere between 1122 and 1238.

Sophie Deppe

Chapter 19

A Trip to Prüm

Sophie was unhappy. Friends and family were getting married and having babies, yet at barely twenty-two, she was a divorced woman. Her dream of love and marriage was ruined. There were suitors who came to call, but she wasn't interested. She didn't want to try marriage again. She had believed in this man and look what happened. Perhaps, she still mourned Charles. No one knows for sure.

There was one suitor, however, who continued to pursue her. His name was Victor Stein. The pair met after Sophie's father moved the family to 1161 N. Clark Street in 1892.* At the time, Victor's family was living at 1153 N. Clark, just down the block. Victor was a pleasant fellow, who liked to engage everyone he met in conversation. Sophie enjoyed his company, but she was reserved.

Besides the heartbreak over her marriage, there may have been another reason Sophie was not so eager to form a relationship with Victor. He was Jewish. Still, he was likeable fellow with an interest in sports, theatre, music, and just having fun. Once, Sophie even agreed to go with him to try the new fad, a bicycle built for two!

In the 1890s, women's styles were moving away from hooped skirts and bustles, allowing for much greater freedom among

---

* 1161 N. Clark = 2500 today; 1153 = 2478 today. The address, next door to the address previously listed may have been an added residence, or may be a mistake in the City Directory.

the female sex. Corsets were looser, blouses had pleats and full sleeves to allow for movement, and skirts were bell-shaped. While some women wore loose bloomers to ride bicycles, others had a way of pinning their skirts in order to ride this contraption. Sophie was known, on occasion, to be daring and quite modern, so there is no doubt she tried Victor's favorite sport. There was even a popular song during this time about the bicycle. Perhaps he sang it to her:

> *Daisy, Daisy, give me your answer do,*
> *I'm half crazy, all for the love of you.*
> *It won't be a stylish marriage,*
> *I can't afford a carriage,*
> *But you'd look sweet,*
> *Upon the seat*
> *Of a bicycle built for two.**

A parody of the song was written the same year. It was the woman's response. No doubt, Sophie and her sisters knew it and laughed about it.

> *Harry, Harry. Here is my answer true.*
> *You're half crazy if you think that will do.*
> *If you can't afford a carriage,*
> *There won't be any marriage,*
> *Cause I'll be switched*
> *If I'll be hitched*
> *On a bicycle built for two.*

Still, with all the goings on in her life, Sophie's unhappiness, possibly even depression, continued. Finally, after more than a year, Franz decided to send Sophie and her sister, Louise, to Germany. They would go to visit his half-brother, Edmund Deppe. For the last twenty-two years, Franz had kept in touch with the relatives in Prüm. Cards and pictures were exchanged regularly.

---

* "Daisy Bell" (Bicycle Built for Two) was a popular song, written in 1892 by Harry Dacre.

Edmund Deppe and son, Peter, in Prüm

Edmund, now forty, was married to Katharina Pennin, originally from Brussels. The couple were married on October 21, 1880 at St. Bartholomew's Church in Neiderprüm. They had had six children, though one had died in infancy. Like their American cousins, the German Deppes lived in an apartment over their bakery. Edmund was a Master Baker, and the bakery was doing quite well.

Over the years, Franz had received many invitations to visit Prüm, but never felt he could take a long trip. Now, a trip for his daughters was arranged. Sophie and Louise headed to New York, with a chaperone, possibly, their father, to escort them safely to New York Harbor, where they boarded a ship to Antwerp, Belgium. Traveling to Prüm, they would be retracing their parent's steps some thirty years earlier.

What an experience it must have been for these two young women, ages twenty-three and eighteen to leave the busy life of Chicago and travel to the old country. Franz and Catharina asked that their daughters write them often. Although they could not travel themselves, they were eager to know how the old country looked, and how the people they had once known were. That life all seemed so far away. How amazing that their daughters would be there, in the houses and on the streets where they spent their early years. Even though Franz and Catharina's lives were embedded in Chicago, somewhere deep inside were memories of the past.

The girls planned to stay several months –the way people in the 1800s did when taking a long-distance trip. They wrote home often. Their letters home were written half in English and half in German; the former for their siblings, the latter for their parents. The Deppe children were bilingual, and had no trouble communicating with their German relatives, but staying in Germany, most certainly improved their skills.

Arriving in Prüm, the girls were greeted by Uncle Edmund and Aunt Marie, who welcomed them with great joy. They also met their German cousins, who were all slightly younger than them.

The Deppe Bakery in Prüm, circa 1918. L. to r. (top) Louise, Christina; (bottom) Peter, Edmund, Anna Peters Deppe (Peter's wife), Marie Pennin Deppe (Edmund's wife), Maria (adopted girl), and Susanna

Louise Deppe

Peter, the eldest, was fourteen, Louise, thirteen, Christina, nine, and Susanna, eight. The girls were sad to learn there had been another boy, six year-old Friedrich, who died only months before the girls arrived.

The German Deppes were excited to meet their American relatives and learn about life in the United States. It was good they were keeping family connections in the old country alive. And it was certainly interesting for the girls to see how their German relatives lived.

It must have been some comfort to the Deppe parents, knowing that at least two of their children had been able to see where they had grown up and to spend time with the relatives. It seems everyone in the family was quite excited about this journey.

Sophie and Louise appreciated the intimacy of Prüm. It was far from the hustle and bustle of Chicago. Visiting Prüm with its cobblestone streets, unpaved roads, and the legendary San Salvatore was a true journey back in time. The people of the town still wore traditional, old-fashioned clothing, and lived with candle and kerosene lamps. Not even the wealthiest homes in Prüm could compare the Deppe family's lifestyle in America.

While Prüm was very small, the beauty of nature surrounding it was something to relish. For Sophie, who loved flowers and trees, this aspect was ideal. Here, far from prying eyes and all that had troubled her, she was able to heal. During her time in Prüm, she took walks up narrow wooded paths to the hillside where she contemplated her future and found healing for her soul.

During this time, Sophie wrote a letter in English to her sister, Kate. Recently, the transcription notes for this letter were found.

> *I am glad that Victor spends his evenings and Sundays with you. What do you generally do? I do not think you can be very lonesome there are so many of you.*

Tell grandma we send our love and will have a great deal to tell her about her relatives when we get back.

Re the sewing lady . . . she charges 7½ cents to put on binding.

You are right in supposing that we found people and things very different here from what they are at home. We are constantly being surprised . . .

Sophie and Louise likely stayed in Prüm somewhere between two to four months. Then, it was time to go home. While the girls may have become attached to Edmund's family, they were ready to return home. The German Deppes and their friends gave the girls a big sendoff before they left for America, for the warmth of the southern Germans is well-known.

Back to Antwerp Louise and Sophie traveled, feeling quite relaxed and at ease. Now they could say they were world travelers. They boarded the *Southwark* in Antwerp and headed home. The ship was quite elegant with delightful dinners and entertainment. The two beautiful young girls, who were stylish dressers and clever conversationalists soon found themselves in the company of a wealthy family from Philadelphia.

Mrs. H and her daughters bonded with Sophie and Louise right away. After many days aboard ship, one day Mrs. H said, "Why don't you two come and stay with my family before you return to Chicago?"

Mrs. H had two sons and couldn't help boasting about how wonderful they were and how the girls should meet them. The sisters glanced at one another, thinking what a great adventure Philadelphia might be! A totally new life might be in store for them as a result of this trans-Atlantic trip! The family seemed very well-connected to old Philadelphia society.

Sophie made the decision and told Mrs. H that they would be happy to visit. Of course, she would have to contact their father once the boat docked, but she didn't think that would be a problem. They would take the train from New York down to Philadelphia, a mere two hour ride. They'd have a delightful time and meet Mrs. H's sons. From Philadelphia, they could easily catch a train back to Chicago. The girls were quite excited about the prospect, as was Mrs. H. In hindsight, it seems Louise may have been the most excited. Later, she would later look back on this moment as a lost opportunity for her life.

The boat docked in New York Harbor on July 8, 1896. It was a great affair. A band was playing, and scores of people were there to meet the ship. How exciting! As the girls stood watching the fanfare on the dock and preparing to disembark, they scanned the crowd. Suddenly, Louise cried, "Oh! Look who's there! It's Victor Stein!" Sophie looked, and there he was—Victor, in a white suit and straw boater, was on the dock, smiling and madly waving at them.

While they were abroad, Sophie had thought less and less of him. She was not attached, but now, after he had traveled all that way (probably with the permission of their father), they simply couldn't tell him they weren't coming back. No, they would have to return to Chicago with Victor.

So that was that. The courtship had begun in earnest.

Ludwig Stein

Chapter 20

The Steins

Victor was energetic and charming, which certainly was attractive, but more than that, he had missed Sophie a great deal while she was gone. He could not forget her. Indeed, he had traveled one thousand miles to come and bring her home.

Sophie admitted to herself, she liked him. Most everyone who met Victor liked him, but there was a lot more to consider in getting married. On weekends now, they went out riding together on the fashionable bicycle built for two, or strolling through Lincoln Park together. He also took her to the theater.

But Sophie was none too fond of Victor's family, and she never would be. She found his father, Ludwig, unpleasant to be around, his brother, Hugo, not that social or educated, and his twelve year old baby sister, Iddel or "Etta," as they called her, a rather rude child. Etta was not sweet and mannerly in the way Sophie's family was. The only members of Victor's family she liked at all were his mother, Julia, a sweet and gentle lady, and his middle sister, Laura, age fourteen, who also seemed very much a lady.

Victor Stein

Sophie knew that the Stein family had come to America from Vienna, and that they appreciated art and literature. In time she would learn much more. But for her, Victor was the real attraction, He was someone who exemplified all the best traits a man could have.

Vienna was a grand city, the home of Mozart, Beethoven, and Austrian royalty. Situated in the midst of the Alps, and bordered by the Danube River, it is a city of tremendous palaces, wide streets and amazing vistas. During the time the Steins lived in Vienna, Johann Strauss II was writing his glorious waltzes, romanticizing Vienna and garnering world attention. Besides royalty and musicians, the city also had a large Jewish presence.

Jews had been living in Austria's capital city as far back as 1194. Many more came in 1348–1349 to avoid the Black Death. Vienna had been spared that plague and was seen as a refuge. Of course, there was much anti-Jewish feeling among the towns people. From 1512 to 1624, the Emperor Ferdinand confined the Jewish people to ghettos. Only wealthy Jews were allowed to live in Vienna, with prayer services confined to private homes alone. Some of these Jews eventually became prominent in the royal court. Poorer Jews were expelled from Vienna during this time, but after the city suffered financial losses, it was proposed that they be re-admitted.

The Steins were likely among the poorer Jews, because according to public records, they lived in a place known as Boheme. Once a part of the Hapsburg lands, today this area is a part of the Czech Republic.

Boheme, where the Steins lived, is a land of coal and timber, a place for raising crops and livestock. It is also a place of enchantment. Boheme's flat plateau is surrounded by mountains, forests and rivers; it is a place where artists are inspired by the fairytale-like beauty that surrounds them. The river Vltava runs through the middle of the state, an area where Prague, the capital, lies.

For many years it was thought that Ludwig Stein was born in Vienna. However, a record of his birth in that city—a place which kept precise records—has yet to be found. Later Vienna records state that Ludwig was from Boheme, born there in April of 1841. It is thought that Ludwig had a brother and two sisters, but not much more than that is presently known about the family.

Ludwig's wife was Julia Sondek (sometimes spelled Saudek). Although U.S. Federal census records state that she was born in Austria, according to the family, she was born in Prague on March 23, 1842. At the time, Prague was considered a part of Austria and the Germanic states.

Ludwig and Julia were married in a synagogue in 1867. Though it was once believed they married in Vienna, no records to this effect have been found. It seems more likely the couple met and were married in Boheme, amidst their relatives. Theirs was a traditional Jewish ceremony. On that day, Julia wore a beautiful white silk wedding shawl with tassels. The shawl was very precious to her. After the wedding, she kept it carefully packed away. Through the years, it would be handed down in pristine condition, traveling from her children to grandchildren and great grandchildren.

On February 21, 1871, Julia gave birth to a healthy boy child. No records for the baby have been found in Vienna, so it seems likely the child was born in Boheme.

At the time of the baby's birth, Ludwig was a great admirer of the author, Victor Hugo. Perhaps he had read Hugo's great novel, *Les Miserables*. To honor him, Ludwig named his first son Victor. A year later, when Julia gave birth to a second son, Ludwig gave him the name "Hugo." Thus, his tribute to Victor Hugo was complete! Two years later, in 1873, a baby girl arrived whom they named Bertha.

In the late 1700s and early 1800s, the Congress of Vienna promoted Jewish wealth, and over the next 100 years the Jewish population in Vienna grew rapidly. In 1826, there were 59 synagogues in the city, with large sources of historic research materials.

Julia Stein's Silk Wedding Shawl

During the first half of the 19th century, however, there were still many restrictions for those called Jewish or Hebrew. In fact, there were two sets of laws: one for Christians and one for Jews. If a Jew were to loan a Christian money and the Christian—not paying it back—later denied that he owed the Jew anything, he would win. Jews were definitely considered lower in society. The attitude toward Jews seems to have been what Shakespeare illustrated in his play *The Merchant of Venice*.

Leopoldstadt was the center of Jewish life in Vienna. Though crowded, it was a busy and prosperous place, and many were excited to have the opportunity to prosper and grow in the midst of this grand city.

By the time the Stein children were four, three, and two, Ludwig was bent on making a change in all their lives. He moved the family to Vienna—"Wien 2," Kleine Stadtgutgasse 10, where he opened a grocery store with spices. It seems he was doing fairly well, because he advertised the store in *Lehmann's Home Advertisement*.

One year later, a fourth child was born. The birth register of the Israelite Community states that Oskar Stein, legitimate son of Ludwig Stein and Julia Sondek, was born on June 17, 1875. This record also notes that the father of the child is a merchant from the political district Horowitz, Boheme. Two years later, the Stein family moved to Wein 2, Kaiser Joseph Strasse 22 (today Heinestrasse).

By the time the Steins moved to Vienna, the ghettos were overcrowded. In fact, they were so crowded with buildings on the narrow streets, both streets and apartments had limited light. As a result, many of the residents became depressed. For this and other reasons we may not know, when opportunity came, it is not surprising Ludwig Stein considered moving to America.

Shortly before Ludwig and Julia were married, a gentleman named Emanuel H. Stein moved to the New World, settling first in New Orleans and then in Chicago. Ludwig and Emanuel were related, but how they were related is still uncertain. It seems Emanuel was either an uncle or possibly even Ludwig's father. Emanuel first appeared in the *Chicago City Directory* in 1866 under the name E.H. Stein. His business was listed as a "Gold Gift Sale Store." By 1869, he was listed under the title "Fancy Goods and Toys." Apparently, Mr. Stein was learning the market in Chicago and doing fairly well. In 1867, he was living at 70 Clark Street. From 1869 to 1870, Stein's business and residence were located at 83 Clark Street.* Addresses since this time changed twice (after the Chicago Fire and again in 1909), but it is assumed these businesses and homes were just north of the Chicago River.

Then, in 1871, shortly before the Chicago Fire, Emanuel Stein passed away suddenly, leaving behind a son, Louis. Louis had his own business with "Stein, Wright & Company, located at 202 Madison. His home, at 189 Dearborn Avenue, suggests that he was doing fairly well.†

Although not much is known about E.H. Stein, one thing confirms his wealth and connection to the Ludwig Stein family—his cemetery plot. In 1871, Emanuel Stein purchased a large cemetery plot in Rose Hill, a cemetery of grand monuments which would one day contain the graves of many of Chicago's leaders. The Stein plot eventually held a number of monuments, including two ghostly figures (which no longer exist) and two seated greyhounds, one at either end of his grave. The pillars on which the ghostly figures stood also contained Masonic square and compass emblems, representing Freemasonry.

At some point, events in Vienna and/or the success of Emanuel and Louis encouraged Ludwig to make the journey to Chicago to try his hand in business there.

The 1878 *Chicago City Directory* contains a listing for a jeweler, working at 93 Clark Street, named Ludwig Stein.‡ Ludwig's shop

---

* 70 = 443 No. Clark; 83 (87) = 500 N. Clark (just north of the Chicago River), however, these are before the Chicago fire, which likely changes the numbering.

† 202 = 821 W. Madison; 189 = 719 Dearborn

‡ 93 = 508 N. Clark

The Stein Plot at Rosehill Cemetery as it appeared in 1954.

was quite close to the address where E.H. Stein once had his shop. This listing, however, did not remain for long. Because of this, it seems possible Ludwig may have returned to Vienna for a time. The Vienna directory listed him as having a business on Kaiser Joseph Strasse until 1882.

While all the facts regarding Ludwig may be somewhat murky, what is certain is this. According to family stories, it was not Ludwig who brought his wife and children to America, it was his "brother," who made the arrangements and paid for their passage. Since we have no name for this brother, this information may point to the fact that Louis was his brother. And having experienced first-hand the horrors of traveling in steerage, the brother made certain that the family had a cabin in which to travel.

So it was that in 1878, Julia and three of the four Stein children: Victor, 8, Hugo, 7, and Bertha, 6, all boarded a train in Vienna and set off on a journey for the United States. Why Oskar was not with them is unknown. Not only is there no mention of him on the ship, he does not appear in the 1880 census, nor any other records in Chicago until the 1890s. Possibly, three year-old Oskar was sick at the time the Steins left, and they knew he would not be accepted into the country. In addition, they may have felt it was simply too risky for a tiny child to travel halfway across two continents and an ocean. We can only guess that little Oskar was left behind with relatives, who raised him until he could safely join his family. It must have been very difficult for Julia to leave her youngest child behind.

Boarding the train, Julia and the three children traveled north to the port of Hamburg, where they were to board their ocean liner. It was a journey of over 600 miles. Descending out of the mountains, the train stopped in Prague, and then continued on through the countryside of Germany. The children spent their time chatting and looking out at the grand sites with little villages so different from the city they had known most of their lives. They were going to America, where their father awaited them.

On September 11th, having arrived in Hamburg, the Stein family boarded a German ship, the *Suevia*, which traveled south to the picturesque French port of Le Havre, and then across the huge Atlantic Ocean. Except for possible rough seas, with their own cabin, Julia and the children were quite comfortable as they crossed the Atlantic. What an adventure!

Upon their arrival in the port of New York, the immigrants disembarked on the tip of Manhattan's Battery Park, where they entered a fort built in 1626, known as Castle Garden. The place had been used as an emigration center since 1855. Julia, Victor, Hugo, and Bertha all waited in one of many caged sections for the inspectors to show up. After that, they stood in long lines, amidst the babble of foreign tongues, so that they could fill out papers and receive health exams to enter the country. At last, they passed!

From there, the Stein family traveled to the middle of Manhattan Island where they boarded a train for Chicago. That night, they

The Suevia, *1870s*

slept on the train. They arrived early the next day, and were met Ludwig at the station.

Their new home was a small, brick apartment at 198 Clark Street, near Superior Street.* Victor, Hugo, and Bertha had to learn English so they could attend school, but it did not take them long. All were bright, especially Victor, who was full of energy and practical jokes. With his winning smile and ready humor, he was able to make people like him almost instantaneously. He was also quick to learn, absorbing new subjects readily.

Meanwhile, Julia set about making a home of their new abode. No doubt, she found Ludwig somewhat changed. It had been at least three years since they had seen one another, perhaps longer.

Ludwig was eager to be part of this new world and to succeed. He wanted to be liked, and to show himself an equal with those on a higher monetary level. These qualities often made him seem

---

* 198 = 707 N. Clark would be at Huron, just south of the Chicago River. This change of numbers and location is uncertain.

boastful. And although he loved his wife and children, he was not always considerate of their feelings. In fact, it seems he felt a kind of importance in showing how he could boss Julia around. Perhaps, this was the way he grew up, but it was something noticed by those who knew him. As a loving and kind wife, Julia never complained, but bore his treatment like one accepting her fate. Ludwig was definitely the master of the house.

In the beginning, Ludwig dreamed of having his own business. When his family arrived, he still had his jewelry business at 93 Clark Street.* It would not be long, however, before he came to the conclusion that he could not support his family selling jewelry. By 1881, when Victor and Hugo were ten and nine, respectively, Ludwig had found himself a good job working as a clerk with a company at 121 Superior Street.† Although the name of this company has not been found, likely Ludwig was working with a wholesale grocer of some type.

Julia, it seems, may not have been in the best of health when she first arrived in Chicago. Possibly, the change of location affected her. In any case, a year and a half after their arrival, she suddenly found herself with child again. The baby, born on the 6th of February 1880, was named Laura.

Two years later, on February 22, 1882, when another baby girl arrived, they called her Idelle. It would not be a name the girl liked or wanted to keep in this world so foreign to her parents. She was an American, a modern American. Eventually, she changed her name to Edith.

In 1883, by the time Idelle was a year old, Ludwig had found himself a better position, working as a salesman for a large wholesale grocery company, E. A. Robinson, located at 239 So. Water Street. As a result of Ludwig's increased income, and possibly the family's growth, the Stein family moved to 636 Sedgwick (now 1934),

---

* 93 = 508 N. Clark

† 121 = 326 E. Superior St.

a much nicer neighborhood, one block north of the F. Deppe Company. The following year, the Steins moved again, this time to 964 No. Clark Street (now 2151).

During these early years, Julia was quite busy at home. By 1884, the children had grown a great deal. Victor was now thirteen, Hugo, twelve, Bertha, ten, Laura, four, and Idelle, two. In addition, it seems possible that around this time Oskar, now nine, arrived from Vienna. Soon after his arrival, his name was changed to the more American spelling "Oscar."

Then, on July 17, 1884, Julia gave birth to another baby, a boy, whom they named Henry. But Henry, it seems, was not a well-baby. Weak at birth, or easily susceptible, Henry soon became ill. One month after his birth, on August 9, 1884, he died.

In later years, when asked by the census taker how many children she'd had, Julia Stein stated that she'd had "eight." During this period, Chicago Illinois Cook County records list the birth of two additional Stein babies: January 14, 1881—Female, Stein; and November 1883—Male, Stein. Either or both of these children could belong to Ludwig and Julia. If these were their children, it would mean that Julia was pregnant almost continuously between 1879 and 1884—five years—something not too unusual at the time.

Perhaps because of grief over the loss of the babies, or the need for cheaper rent and larger, nicer living quarters, the Steins moved once again in 1885. This time the address of their residence was only a few doors away—966 No. Clark (today 2153). This listing, however, may have been a misprint because in 1887, the family is found once again at 964 No. Clark (2151).

The Stein family of Vienna favored education and study of the arts. Although it would seem unlikely that Victor Stein attended school much longer than six years (the average time for most young people then), according to a biography found in *The Western Bowlers Journal*, Victor states that he completed the first eight years of grammar school at the Franklin School, a facility at 225 West Evergreen Avenue, near Wells Street in Old Town, which stands today.

From Franklin School, Victor continued on to a high school on the North side. At this time, he worked part-time. Whether his brother, Hugo, continued in school after 6th grade is unknown.

As the mother of a Jewish family, Julia kept the faith. On Fridays, she cleaned the house and prepared the Sabbath meals early in the day. Then, just before dusk, came the moment when the candles were lit and the blessing was said. This solemn moment is a privilege that belongs to the mother of a Jewish home. Moving her hands in a circular inward to outward motion over the lit candles, she prayed:

> Thanks to God who sanctified us by His commandments and commanded us to kindle the Sabbath lights.

Following in tradition, the family may then have attended a short service at the local synagogue and afterwards returned home to hear Ludwig recite the Kiddush, blessing the wine and challah bread. He would then have blessed his sons, Victor and Hugo, saying, "God make thee as Ephrain and Manasseh." Over his daughter Bertha, he would have prayed, "God make thee as Sarah, Rebekah, Rachel and Leah." Following a "Priestly Benediction," the family would sing, "Shalom alechem"—"Peace be with you, ye angels of peace."

According to the Jewish religion, two angels accompany each man coming from the synagogue, a good angel and an evil one. When entering the home, the good angel, finding the table set and the lights lit says a blessing, which forces the evil angel to say, "Amen." Thus, the family is blessed and protected.

It is thought that the Ludwig Stein family was not very religious, and a search has found that they were not listed as members of

any synagoge in Chicago. Coming from Vienna, however, the family brought with them two seven-branched candlesticks. These were looked on as treasured and holy items; items which were passed down through the generations. Eventually, they would be passed on Victor Stein and then, to his children.

Shabbat was a day of joyous thankfulness to God, a day setting aside earthly work and worries to concentrate on spiritual goals. While it cannot be said what life was truly like in the Stein family, Shabbat and other holy days in the Jewish religion are lovely moments, which make an everlasting impression on the children of Jewish faith throughout their lives.

In time, these religious customs may have been followed less and less. But in the beginning, certainly, the family prayed their thanks to God for allowing them to begin new lives in this free nation.

The 1886 City Directory reveals that fifteen year-old Victor Stein had moved out of his parents' home and was boarding at 964 N. Clark, a building where his family once lived.* Perhaps he was unhappy with his family or there simply was not enough room for him. Meanwhile, Victor continued with his education, while

---

* It also seems possible this listing was a mistake. Victor's family had lived at this address a year earlier in 1885 and was listed there again in 1887. It may also have been a joint address, i.e., 964–966.

holding on to a job. He definitely saw himself moving up in the world. Victor was not far from his parents; their residence was only one door away at 966 No. Clark, so he likely came home for dinner!

At that time, Victor was working as a clerk at 393 Wabash. The business was *A. E. Robinson*, a large grocery company with plenty of opportunity. This was the same company his father worked for, although a different location. While he was there, Victor advanced from clerk to cashier, which meant a pay increase. Extremely bright and personable, Victor was confident in his success. Brother Hugo, who was also working there, held the position of clerk.

In 1888, Ludwig and thirteen year-old Oscar went down and applied for citizenship. According to the law, an applicant was required to live in the United States for at least five years in order to apply. The process to become a citizen, which includes the right to vote, would take four years after the application. That meant Ludwig and Oscar would be able to become American citizens in 1892.

Meanwhile, Victor was now determined to move ahead in business. In 1888, at the age of seventeen, he found a new position as a clerk at 295 Wabash (412). One year later, he was working at 239 Water Street, where his father had a job. Victor was still residing at 964 No. Clark. He would remain at the same business and residence for the next two years. Then, in 1890, as a high school graduate, Victor went on to work for an even bigger firm, in a much grander building. His new job was with the illustrious Wm. M. Hoyt Company at 1 River Street.

Born in 1837, William Melancthon Hoyt, had come to Chicago from Vermont at the age of eighteen. Hoyt was a tenth generation American farm boy, who grew up learning to barter. After applying for a number of jobs and being turned down, he was hired by Mr. Bevans, a grocer, who paid him $10 a month plus room and board to be a clerk in his store. William worked hard on this job,

W. M. Hoyt Company.

W. M. Hoyt & Co. from Commercial and Architechtural Chicago *by W.W. Orear, 1887, courtesy of The Newberry Library*

and the following year, opened his own fruit stand at the prime location of State and Lake Streets.

During the Civil War, William Hoyt did well, so well, in fact, that at the conclusion of the war, he began buying up other produce companies. By 1871, he was one of the most successful wholesale grocers in Chicago, however, like many other Chicago businessmen, he lost everything in the Great Chicago Fire that year. By the mid-1870s, W. M. Hoyt & Co. was bringing in close to a million dollars a year. The company's earnings would grow to nearly $5 million by the 1890s, becoming one of the mid-west region's leading food distributors.

Victor Stein took to the wholesale grocery business and learned a great deal while he was there. As someone who put himself through college and made a great success, William Hoyt was a great inspiration to young Victor. Hoyt's philosophy was that if someone buys something they can't use, they waste money. It is better, he said, to pay more for something of quality that you can use—that is money saved.

Among the goods W.M. Hoyt & Co. sold were: Fort Dearborn Canned Goods, Yellow Crawford Peaches, Adena White Cheese, Snow Flake Gloss Starch, Fort Dearborn Mills spices, roasted coffee, and German preserves. There were also Tins of Smyrna Figs, and French prepared prunes, all considered delicacies. Another specialty were chocolate creams.

Around this time, Ludwig Stein moved the family further north, to an area in North Town considered much nicer. The 1891 Chicago Directory shows the family living at 1153 No. Clark (2478). The building, which no longer exists, was probably similar to other buildings there; a walk-up brick row house styled apartment. It was probably somewhat elegant and spacious, with more room for everyone. During this time, Victor Stein moved back in with the family.

Around this same period, Ludwig Stein also changed his employment, moving to the Wm. M. Hoyt & Company at 1 River Street, where Victor was working. Ludwig's new position was that of salesman, likely a position that would bring more income.

It seems Ludwig was not doing so well. Possibly the level of work for an older man—he was now fifty—was too much for him. It was said that William Hoyt was a demanding boss. In any case, by 1895, he was either fired or decided to change jobs. From Wm. M. Hoyt, he moved to Sprague, Warner & Company, located at 7 Randolph Street, just south of the Chicago River, not far from State Street.*

---

* This address no longer existed in 1909, but would translater to approximately 20 West Randolph Street now.

Most of the jobs Ludwig, Victor, and Hugo held were all in wholesale food distribution. Because Chicago was a great center for food packaging and distribution, these jobs were plentiful and paid a fair wage with opportunity for advancement. Possibly there was also less prejudice against Jews in this industry.

Sprague, Warner & Company was founded by Albert A. Sprague and Ezra J. Warner. It was one of the biggest and most important companies in its field in the entire United States. Albert Arnold Sprague was known as "an eminent merchant of Chicago." Like William Hoyt, he was born in Vermont. In 1863, he moved to Chicago, where he decided that a profession in groceries would be the best.

Mr. Sprague was an unusual boss. Although quite successful, he was not a boss with a high and mighty attitude. Sprague attended the Second Presbyterian Church and liked to spend his time doing religious work. He was a man who remembered "with pleasure" that in 1860, he cast his first vote for Abraham Lincoln. Because he didn't want to spend all his time thinking about his large financial holdings, Sprague spent a good deal of leisure on his farm and in reading books. His biography of the time stated that he had one of the best libraries of rare books and letters. He was also director of the Pullman Palace Car Company. He had five children and three grandchildren.

Originally located at 22 Canal Street, the Sprague, Warner & Company building moved to Michigan and Randolph in 1875. The business, which started as a grocery store on State Street, grew quickly. Mr. Sprague, as a traveling salesman, once drove his goods around both day and night over impassable roads. Like most businessmen in Chicago, he lost everything in the Chicago fire. Sprague sold roasting coffee, baking soda, refined syrups, cigars and tobaccos, as well as German preserves and pickles.

The second owner of the company, Mr. Ezra Warner, joined the firm in 1864, just before the end of the Civil War. It was said that neither Sprague nor Warner were men who liked to think about making money.

By the 1890s, the Stein family was doing fairly well. Although living with Ludwig may not have been the easiest, he did try to make his wife and children happy. The girls were given nice clothes to wear and toys with which to play. The only problem was, Ludwig wanted to make everyone happy, not just his family. In short, he wanted to impress others with his generosity.

Idelle had a doll named Elsie, which she cherished dearly. Elsie was a beautiful doll, and Idelle spent hours playing with her and talking to her; Elsie was her best friend.

As the story goes, one day, one of Ludwig's bosses came to visit, and seeing Idelle's doll seated on a chair in the parlor, commented,

"What a lovely doll. I would like to find such a doll for my little girl, Elizabeth."

"Here," said Ludwig, handing him the doll. "She's yours."

"Oh, no, I couldn't take her," said the gentleman. "That's your little girl's doll."

"Oh, Idelle getting too big for dolls. She hardly plays with her at all. Take her! I insist."

When Idelle returned from school that day, she ran to look for Elsie. The doll was not where she had left her, and Mother knew nothing about her disappearance.

That night, when Idelle learned that her father had given Elsie away, she was heartbroken. Nothing she could say or do, would bring back her best friend. This was one of several things Ludwig did that she she could not forgive. Her resentment of her father and his actions was not unfounded. There were deep troubles in the Stein family, and Idelle blamed Ludwig for most of them.

Family heirloom dishes, possibly having belonged to the Steins.

Bellevue Place

Chapter 21

Bertha

The following chapter is based on public record, as well as information discovered privately and at the locations where the events took place.

For many years, Julia had dreamed of going home to Vienna. She was homesick. As time passed, she had greater reason for this trip; she wanted Laura and Idelle to see the land of their heritage. Finally, in 1894, the voyage was a financial possibility. There was only one difficulty—Bertha was not well.

By 1894, for at least several years, nineteen year-old Bertha had shown evidence of mental and emotional problems. Although the details of her illness are not known, the evidence that exists suggests she may have been bi-polar.

The previous year, when her behavior reached a point of worry, the Steins sent her to Rochester Park Hospital. After a stay of five weeks, she showed great improvement and returned home. For a time, life continued with some normalcy. However, in the late spring of 1894, her previous symptoms returned.

Having already purchased tickets for Julia, Laura, and Idelle to go to Vienna, Ludwig now mentioned the concern about his daughter to a boss at Wm. M. Hoyt. This person—whoever he may have been—suggested that Ludwig look into Bellevue Place, a sanitarium in a small town outside Chicago called Batavia.

Originally constructed in 1854 for use as a boarding school, Bellevue Place included a three-story building with basement and two two-story wings, all fronted by cut stone. In 1867, Dr. R. J. Patterson had purchased the Bellevue estate with plans to turn it into a sanitarium for the "treatment of nervous and mental disease in women."* Dr. Patterson's purchase also included a sixteen acre estate with gardens and greenhouses; a place where patients could spend time with nature and find peace and well-being.

It was Dr. Patterson's belief that a peaceful atmosphere away from city living with plenty of fresh air, good food and relaxation, were all that was needed to cure mental problems. As a result (unlike most mental institutions of the time, which employed restraints and cruel treatments), Dr. Patterson's institution offered guests who were not seriously ill, a restful time and rooms that were furnished in a manner befitting a wealthy home.

At Bellevue Place, the buildings were quite modern for their time. They featured running water and electric lights on all floors. An advertisement for the place described the rooms as "large, light, airy," with a "homelike impression."

From the front of the building, there were views all the way down to the valley and the Fox River. In a booklet of the period advertising the home, the grounds were described as "private, quiet, and pleasantly shaded with evergreens and elms." In addition, there were greenhouses, wide walks with flowers, and places to sit, both outdoors in the sun, or indoors, protected from cold in the winter. The booklet even sported a picture of a woman reading a book in a hammock. It sounded like a place anyone would feel fortunate to visit.

In another portion of the booklet advertising Bellevue Place, it was clearly stated that those who were habitually "noisy, violent or destructive" would not be admitted. Clearly, Bellevue was a

---

* Early booklet on Bellevue Place Sanitarium, Batavia Depot Museum.

place for those who could be cured, and Bertha was considered eligible.

It should be mentioned that Bellevue Place also held some historic importance for it was here in 1875 that Robert Lincoln brought his mother, Mary Todd Lincoln, widow of President Abraham Lincoln, to rest and recover from, what seemed to him, a severe mental disturbance. Mrs. Lincoln remained at Bellevue Place for four months. Today, the bed where she slept may be viewed at the Batavia Historical Society Museum.

Eighteen years after Mary Lincoln left, the best people in Chicago were sending their wives and daughters to this facility for treatment. The majority found that after a few weeks or months, their loved ones were better and readily able to return home to live normal lives.

By 1894, the founder, Dr. Patterson, had passed on, and the institution was in the hands of Dr. Frederick H. Daniels. Raised in Maine, Daniels was a thirty-nine year old doctor who had served ten years at the Worcester Lunatic Hospital in Massachusetts. Accompanying him in his work at Bellevue was Lena Stimpson, his wife's sister. A short time after their arrival, Miss Stimpson become the Superintendent of Nurses at Bellevue.

Learning about the fine work at Bellevue took a weight off the Steins. Julia felt free to set off for Europe, and Ludwig made arrangements for Bertha to go on a "vacation" of her own.

Julia and her two youngest children, Laura, fourteen, and Etta, twelve, boarded the train in Chicago and headed for New York. Upon arrival, they traveled across town to the west side docks on the Hudson River, where they boarded a huge ship. Perhaps Victor or Hugo went to see them off. The ship left port with great fanfare. Traveling down the Hudson River toward the harbor, Julia and the girls gazed with amazement at the Statue of Liberty, a gift from France, erected eight years earlier in 1886. It had not been there when Julia arrived in America.

As the journey across the Atlantic progressed, memories of home and excitement about seeing her relatives flooded her thoughts. Yet Bertha was never far from those thoughts. It was sad that she had not been well enough to travel with them. Meanwhile, the girls were kept busy on the ship, and in their free moments, Julia told them about the wonderful sights they would see and the people they would meet.

After the ship docked in Hamburg, the family took a train to Vienna. Julia was anxious to see her family and to show the Laura and Idelle where their family had lived before they came America. It was going to be a wonderful vacation.

At home with Bertha, Ludwig was not having an easy time. Now that her mother and sisters were gone, Bertha quickly regressed to the state she had been in the previous year. Ludwig was often impatient, which didn't help. The situation was not one he could handle.

> Written on the property site, the following account has attempted to blend fact and imagination in a way that will bring the reader closer to the true story.

On, Saturday, June 9th, Ludwig and Bertha Stein boarded the *Chicago, Burlington & Quincy Railroad* for Batavia, a small town approximately 35 miles southwest of Chicago. It was a pleasant ride, a journey from city to country, but it was also a trip filled with hope and sadness. Was Bertha silent and depressed, or restless and talkative on the journey? The memory of that day has not been recorded.

At the station, the pair were met by the Bellevue Place carriage. They traveled through a neighborhood of stately homes and

tree-lined streets, then turned down a long drive of oak trees. At the end of the drive sat a somewhat forbidding, large stone mansion, with a circular drive before it. Now, the moment had come.

Bertha remained silent as her father looked out hopefully. The driver opened the carriage door, and they climbed out. Ludwig pulled the bell on the large front door. A few seconds later the door was opened by a rather stern looking woman with greying hair. Dressed in a dark gown with a white ruffle at her neck, the lady paused. Ludwig introduced himself. "Yes," the woman said, "you are expected."

Upon entering the front door, Ludwig and Bertha were met by the sight of two curving staircases lining the circular entrance hall, one to the right, and one to the left. The effect was rather overwhelming. Bertha seemed a bit lost and hesitant. Was she scared? They were informed that Dr. Daniels would be with them directly. The woman then escorted them into a rather cluttered office with bright windows.

"Sit, Bertha, sit," Ludwig told his daughter. She did, but rather than sitting still, began tapping her fingers nervously on the wood

of the chairs and the edge of the desk.

"I don't want to stay here, Papa," she said. "Please take me home."

"Now Bertha, you know there has been trouble. Stay here a few weeks and all will be better. You know I cannot leave you alone while Mother and the girls are in Vienna. When they return, I will come and get you. I promise. Cheer up, little one," he said in the endearing way he had spoken to her as a child.

Bertha sat staring at her hands. Why had they not taken her to Vienna? She wanted to go. It made her feel terrible that she had been left behind. She didn't know why she did the things she did.

Quite suddenly, the door opened, and a man appeared—a man so tall and gaunt, he made her gasp. His cheeks were sunken in, his face pale, his eyes piercing.

Ludwig rose from his seat.

In a kindly voice, the man said, "How do you do. I am Dr. Daniels." Then, turning to Bertha, "Hello Miss Stein. I understand you are in need of a rest and have come to stay with us awhile. I hope you will enjoy your time here."

Bertha sank into herself. She could not stay here. She must not. She grasped her father's arm, but he seemed to pay no attention. As he spoke to the doctor, she found she was distracted by the sight of some women walking outside. While the conversation was polite, she couldn't help feeling ashamed and embarrassed. She wanted to go home.

"And now Miss Stein," said Dr. Daniels, "Miss Stimpson will come to get you settled in and feeling at home for your stay. We are very relaxed and everyone is kind here. No need to fear."

Bertha felt as if her heart were stopping in horror.

"No, Papa. Please. I want to go home. I'll be fine."

She was holding Ludwig's hand, but he quickly took it away.

"You know we spoke about this."

Dr. Fredrick Daniels, Batavia Historical Society

Just then, Dr. Daniels opened the door with a swift movement, and a nurse wearing a pink dress with a white apron entered.

"Now dear," she said, reaching out to Bertha, "there is nothing to fret over. We will make you quite comfortable in your room, and you'll soon feel much better."

Something about the woman made it impossible for Bertha to resist. Without glancing back, Bertha walked through the door with the nurse. At that moment, Ludwig attempted to move toward his daughter to say goodbye, but Dr. Daniels stopped him. "Mr. Stein, it is better that you don't."

Ludwig had merely meant to give her a kiss on the cheek as was the family custom, but he found that even he was intimidated by the doctor.

"I will come to visit soon, daughter," he called to Bertha, as the door closed behind her.

Ludwig and Dr. Daniels spoke for a few moments about Bertha's condition. Then, the lady in the black gown offered him tea before he left on his long journey home, but staying was too painful.

He was escorted back to the front door. The carriage was waiting outside. Then, before he knew it, he was on his way back to the railway station. The sky was blue and the sound of birds singing filled the air, but it was a terrible trip home without Bertha, probably the worst trip he had known. On the way back to Chicago, though Ludwig hated to admit it, he was relieved. Yet, all the while, he kept thinking, "I did not even kiss Bertha goodbye. What will I tell Mother?"

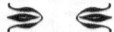

Bertha was given a small room on the second floor by herself. It was June. The air was filled with wet heat and only a slight breeze. The room was nice enough, with wall paper, a mahogany bed and dresser. The window looked out at the garden. Sounds of birds singing and insects buzzing filled the air. With the help of the nurse, Bertha opened her case and, at her suggestion, changed into a much cooler summer dress and soft slippers. She was to walk the grounds and see the doctor every day. She did not feel like going out, however. She was too sad.

Thinking of Papa leaving, she felt a kind of despair. She dug her fingers into her arm as she thought of how bad she was; she must be bad to be here. She had failed. Maybe if she punished herself, she would be good. She felt so alone now.

Bertha's first days at Bellevue were uneventful. Most patients were in bed by 9:00 or 9:30 p.m., with a night nurse watching to see how they were. In the daytime, Bertha seemed well rested. Dr. Daniels asked her what was troubling her, but his face frightened her. "I want to go home," she told him. Later, when the matron came to see her, she said, "If you continue this way, you will not go home."

At home, Ludwig received a letter from Julia telling him they had arrived in Vienna. After speaking about their trip, she inquired about Bertha. Should they write to her? Her little sisters wanted to send her a note, but in these kind of cases, you never knew what you should do. Sometimes the doctors didn't want the patients to have communication with their families.

A week after Bertha's entrance into Bellevue, Ludwig decided to write a letter to Dr. Daniels from his job at W. M. Hoyt. It was Saturday the 16th of June. He had not been able to visit Batavia, and had heard nothing from Bertha. He told the doctor that he had letters from Bertha's mother and sisters, and he wondered if she wanted to read them. He also asked that Bertha be made to write to her mother. There was a bill to pay for her stay as well. He sent Dr. Daniels $20 in the form of a check. That would cover the first week. After signing "L. Stein," Ludwig had an afterthought: "If there is anything she needs why let me know and I will get it."

While her first week at Bellevue had gone well, by the start of the second week, things began to change. She was becoming more restless, particularly at night. In fact, some nights she made quite a stir during the late hours. What this stir consisted of, no one said.

The night nurses were instructed to keep a record of patient behavior. They were also to write down any medication given, and how many times it was given. The night nurses were not especially well-educated. Often, it seems, they were foreign girls in need of work.

During this period, the medication given mental patients consisted of a tea, likely made of opiates. By drinking the tea, the patients became calm, even sedated to the point that they fell asleep. It was hoped that with proper rest patients would awaken, their spirits refreshed. Like his predecessor, Dr. Daniels believed that plenty of rest—along with peaceful scenery, fresh air and good food—was the real medication needed to heal a troubled spirit. For Bertha, this was not to be the case.

As the days passed, Bertha's condition was quickly deteriorating. During the second week at Bellevue, she had increasing difficulty at night. She would sleep a few hours, then awaken and become restless, at which point, the medication or tea would be given again. The night nurse found it necessary to give her repeated doses to calm her. One night, Bertha received three doses within three and a half hours. The following night, she was given medication at eight and eleven o'clock. Without realizing it, these applications were building up a dangerous level of opiates in her system.

By the 22nd of June, nearly two weeks after entering Bellevue, Bertha was not feeling well. Still the repeated ingestion of tea and medication several times a night continued. The nurses were pleased when she was able to sleep, but all was not well.

Then, in the early morning hours of June 25th, Bertha Stein died. When the coroner was called to sign her death certificate, under *Cause of Death,* he wrote simply: "acute insanity." For complication, the certificate stated: "prostration from heat." The duration of her disease was listed as "4 weeks." Dr. Daniels signed the death certificate.

People do not die of insanity. Had Bertha Stein driven herself to a state of collapse, and her heart stopped? Had she died by her own hand? If she had, possibly they might have written "suicide" as the cause. Without further description, one cause seems most likely, especially for a young girl, age nineteen.

For days, Bertha had been given "medicines" and "teas," all of which likely contained opiates for sleep and calming the nerves.

On the days when one treatment did not work, more doses had been given—with no regard for the fact that additional doses might be dangerous. It seems most likely that the cause of Bertha Stein's death was acute ingestion of opiates.

Her father had sent her to the finest sanitarium, in hopes that she would be cured, and return home shortly thereafter. Instead, seventeen days after she arrived at Bellevue Place, Ludwig was informed that his daughter was dead.

How the terrible news of her death reached him is unknown. Possibly it came by telegram. Bertha was laid to rest at Rose Hill on June 26th. They buried her, next to her baby brother Henry, who had died in infancy. The plot was E.H. Stein's cemetery plot. Whether "Uncle" Emanuel had willed half to the Ludwig Stein family, or Louis had simply given him a plot big enough for the family is unknown—as is the true relation of Emanuel and Louis Stein to the Ludwig Stein family.

Julia was having a grand time in Vienna. Although she thought often of Bertha, she was so happy to be home. Ah, the fresh air of the Alps and the glorious music. Sitting in the coffee house or park and enjoying the sights and sounds of this grand old city had no comparison. And there was nothing like the warm embrace of relatives.

It was fun, as well, to introduce the girls to her family and friends. Fourteen year-old Laura, though quiet, was a sweet and polite young lady. Twelve year-old Etta, however, was something else. She always had a comeback, even with complete strangers. When the relatives said to them—in the Viennese custom—"I kiss the hand," Etta came right back with, "I kissa the foot." Everyone laughed, but Julia didn't know whether to be embarrassed or laugh with them. "Edith was fresh," Dorothy Stein Wright, her niece recalled. "She was saucy."

Stein apartment window

Now, in the midst of this happy time for Julia and the girls, Ludwig had the necessity of telling her that their daughter was dead. How he dealt with this terrible responsibility is not known. In a sense, he must have felt he failed. Bertha had been left in his care. He'd done his best, yet it had not been good enough. He'd sent Julia and the two little girls off, believing that Bertha would be fine. Now she was gone forever. The pain of that moment must have been beyond imagination. Should he let Julia have her vacation and tell her when she returned? If that was the choice, how could he face her on her return? Yet learning in Vienna, knowing she would never see her child's face or touch her hand would be equally unbearable. Then, she must tell the two little girls, who loved their big sister.

A week after Bertha's burial, Ludwig responded to a letter from Dr. Daniels. His response on July 5th contained one sentence; he wanted his daughter's clothing "kindly" returned. Once the clothing was returned, he would pay the bill. Two days later, all of Bertha's belongings were returned.

Bertha's death was the first of two terrible events in the Stein family; events that were a blight upon the family. From this time on, Bertha would not be spoken of, but she was never far from their minds.

Sophie Deppe

Chapter 22

Joys and Sorrows in the 1890s

On November 8, 1896, Frank and Catharina Deppe saw the arrival of their first grandchild, Isabella Katherine Lockwood, named for Ozro's sister and Kate's mother.

Two months later, on the 9th of January 1897, Victor Stein and Sophie Deppe were united in matrimony. The marriage was witnessed by Ozro Lockwood and Martha Kendall, the minister's wife. Whether any other members of the family were present is unknown, but it seems to have been a small wedding. [see Notes]

It may not have been easy for the couple to find a minister who would marry them. The groom was Jewish and the bride had been born Catholic. The minister who agreed to marry them (possibly with the help of Ozro Lockwood) was the former pastor of the Fullerton Avenue Presbyterian Church, John Rusk. By 1897, however, this minister had something of a notorious reputation.

When Rev. John Rusk left Columbus, Ohio to serve as pastor for the Fullerton Avenue Presbyterian Church in 1892, he came to them with a fine reputation. For nearly two years, the Church had searched to find a good replacement for the much loved Dr. Coyle. At the time, Rusk was thirty-eight, and those who hired him had high expectations as to his ability to continue the work his predecessor had begun.

John Rusk was certainly not an average minister. He was indeed a dynamic speaker. Under his leadership the church congregation more than doubled in two years, growing to approximately

500 members. There was only one problem—Rev. Rusk was a radical.

As members of the church were soon to learn, John Rusk believed the role of the church was not only to follow Christ's example, but to enforce it. In the summer of 1895, after serving nearly three years at the Fullerton church, Rusk stated that he was unhappy with the Presbyterian Church's philosophy; it seemed too laid-back to him. Subsequently, he resigned his position and led as many church members out of the Church as would follow him. Then, he created his own church—the Church Militant.

Rusk's church held as its goal, the fighting of political corruption and crime. In 1895 and 1896, Rev. Rusk demanded that the police inspect certain homes and buildings—places where he believed criminal acts were being committed. (In many of these cases, he suspected prostitution.) When law enforcement was lax about his demands, Rusk called them "enablers of crime."

The intensity of this situation grew until finally John Rusk was arrested and put on trial for his actions. He remained in jail for a time. Then the court found that none of his actions justified imprisonment. In the future, Rev. Rusk would settle down to a life of writing books about historic personages. Meanwhile, his intense demands and actions provided material for numerous stories in the local press, including *The Chicago Tribune*, which covered the events surrounding the trial in detail.

After all this, it is interesting that Rusk was the minister Victor and Sophie chose to marry them. At the same time, as previously stated, it was probably not easy for them to find someone to marry them. They needed an open-minded minister and, it seems, Rusk was the perfect choice. After leaving the Fullerton Avenue Presbyterian Church, Rusk said he had changed his 'theological outlook," and, from now on, would welcome anyone who was "committed" to "bettering the condition of mankind, regardless of creed or lack of it."*

---

* "The Life and Death of the Radical Historical Jesus" by David Burns.

Although Victor Stein likely was not a practicing Jew at the time, there is no evidence at present that he converted to Christianity. Sophie, it seems, had begun attending the Presbyterian Church in her youth, and would continue to attend the Presbyterian Church for the rest of her life.

There was much happiness at the beginning of the Stein marriage. Victor was loving and attentive when it came to Sophie, and it was clear he would provide her with a good home. He loved children as well, and the couple was eager to start a family. Where the Steins set up housekeeping this first year is uncertain. It is possible they lived with one or the other's parents; either in Ludwig Stein's building, a brick townhouse apartment at 1153 No. Clark Street* or the bakery building at 551 Sedgwick. It is also possible they went to live in the Deppe family residence at 1163 N. Clark. Victor Stein does not appear in the 1897 City Directory. While no verification has been found on this, in keeping with the Deppe family history, it seems most likely the couple lived at the later for at least the first two years of their marriage.

Less than a month after Victor and Sophie were married, sorrow struck the family with the death of Sophie's forty year-old uncle, John Ganser. All these years, John had been a hard worker, running his bakery at 582 Racine Avenue (now 2837), but, increasingly, he had been having serious problems with his heart.

The doctor at Alexian Bros. Hospital stated on his death certificate that John Ganser died of Myocarditis Endocarditis, which is defined as inflammatory cells or infections on the surface of the heart. Also listed as a contributing cause was an inflammation of the kidneys.

John Ganser's death on February 19, 1897 was a terrible tragedy for his wife, Lizzie Wolf, and their four children: Jerry, 10, Julia Anna, 8, Kate, 5, and the youngest child, Carrie Laura, who was

---

* 1153 would be 2478 today, but is no longer in existence.

born on April 16, 1894, and baptized on September 9th of that year. Almost three, sadly she would never get to know her father.

Following John Ganser's death, the Deppe family supported Lizzie and the children in whatever way they could. They also offered her their plot at St. Boniface Cemetery, the same plot where their baby daughters, Maria and Barbara were buried. Although the plot was never officially signed over to Lizzie, it was understood that it was there for the family's use. John Ganser was buried there and Lizzie would later be buried by his side.

According to probate records, John Ganser left $1800 for his wife and children.* Frank Deppe served as the executor of his will, and signed all papers. The Ganser home may have been paid for by then, or possibly, Lizzie used the money John left them to pay off the mortgage. Lizzie and the children would continue to live in the rear of the bakery building on Racine many years. Running John's bakery was probably more than they could handle.

---

* $18,000 = $49,996 in 2017—http://www.in2013dollars.com

According to family memories, after John's death, "Lizzie," went to work cleaning houses. And almost immediately after his father died, ten year-old Jerry got a job to help his mother. Every penny was needed to support him and his sisters. As a result of John's early death, none of the children would stay in school past the 8th grade. In fact, the youngest child, Carrie, left school as soon as she finished the fifth grade. To support herself and her children, Lizzie cleaned houses for the next forty years.

For some time, fifty-two year-old Frank Deppe had been feeling the effects of "old age." This was not considered unusual at the time. In 1897, a fifty-two year old man was considered old. In fact, life expectancy for the average American male in 1900 was only forty-six years.

When Frank applied for his Civil War pension back in 1892, due to the confusion about his name, it took a while for the Board of Pensions to approve it. Now that his health had declined, he applied again. This time there were many more papers to fill out and send to The Department of the Interior, Bureau of Pensions. In his second application, Frank stated that the reason for his new pension request was the fact that he could no longer earn a living doing "manual labor by reason of Rheumatism, affection of the heart, and piles."

On September 8, 1897, a third set of papers for this application were sent to the United States Bureau of Pensions. On these papers, Frank wrote: "I have rheumatism in the legs, mostly in the winter time. It keeps me from work. I have a little asthma. I have no piles."

During his examination by the first doctor, Frank's height was noted as 5'5" and his weight, 158 pounds. Medical notations stated that he had no swollen joints, but that his heart was enlarged with a distinct "mitral murmur." More serious was the fact that his heart disease was rated at ten-eighteenths, possibly meaning that his arteries were more than half blocked, or that his heart was functioning slightly under half of its capacity.

During an examination by a second doctor, it was noted that Frank Deppe had had rheumatism since 1888, disease of the heart since 1890, and a disease of the rectum (piles) for ten years.

Today, heart disease of the kind Frank had—at least in part a blockage of arteries—would be treatable, but in 1897, this prognosis was accepted by Frank and his family as part of the aging process. He was now in the latter part of his life.

Along with the forms he filled out, Frank was required to submit three character references from people who knew him well. One reference came from his brother-in-law, Math Evert, husband of Barbara Ganser, who wrote that he had "known the claimant" since 1881, and that Frank had always been "a man of good moral character, sober and peaceful." Regarding his health, Math wrote that since 1894, Frank had often been sick, and had gone to his house, "unable to work."

In another reference, Frank's son-in-law, Ozro J. Lockwood, wrote that he had known Frank for eight years (since 1889), and "during this period he has been in poor health from general weakness." Ozro also attested to Frank's good character, stating that he had no bad habits or addictions. These references shine a light, both on Frank's character and the degree of his illness.

Finally, on November 5, 1897, Frank Deppe received an official certificate from the Department of Interior, stating that he had been due six dollars per month from the 16th of April, 1892.* Now, beginning on October 11, 1897, the letter said, he was to receive eight dollars a month.† The certificate was signed by Cornelius A. Theis, Secretary of the Interior.

---

* $6 = $153.32 in 2017; http://www.in2013dollars.com

† $8 = $222.20 in 2017; http://www.in2013dollars.com

Since the due dates had passed, that year Frank must have received a large retroactive check. It would seem that the Deppes had enough money, but since it was necessary to hire people to take his place in overseeing the business, these funds were no doubt welcome. Perhaps the pension payment was some reparation for his pain, and the depression over his inability to work.

In 1897, Frank Deppe's home address was listed as 1163 N. Clark Street. During this period, the differences of address between the City Directories, legal listings, and family memories make it difficult to say exactly where Frank and Catharina were living at any one time.

As a result of Frank's ill health and inability to work. he took on various business partners, persons who might help manage the bakery. In 1896, Frank joined in such a partnership with a widow, Mrs. Anna Simon, and Appoliner Biewer. According to Dorothy Stein Wright, the Biewers were related to the Deppes in some way. The

The Biewers

following year, Mrs. Simon and Mr. Biewer got married, with the City Directory listing the Bakery partners as Anna and Appoliner Biewar. It is uncertain what happened, but by 1898, the partnership was over. Appoliner had three boys: William, John, and Frank, and they opened their own bakery, A. Biewer & Sons at 62 Eugenie Street (now 425), literally just around the corner from the Deppe Bakery. In the meantime, Frank Deppe had two new partners in mind.

By the latter part of 1898, Victor and Sophie had been waiting many months for the arrival of their first child. On October 10th, the wait was over. Victor stayed home from work, and the midwife was sent for, as well as Sophie's sister, Kate Lockwood. That morning, Victor waited anxiously in the front parlor, while the women fluttered in and out of the bedroom. Finally, a cry was heard.

"It's a girl," Kate announced to the anxious Victor.

It is said that every man hopes for a son, but when Victor saw the tiny bundle wrapped in swaddling clothes, he fell completely in love. There, in a tiny, round face were the bluest eyes and the sweetest little mouth. It amazed him to think she was his—his and Sophie's. What a wonder.

"Why she looks just like a little rosebud!" he exclaimed, as he bent over the very tired, but pleasantly flushed Sophie to give her a kiss. "We'll call her Rose! Rose Stein." (As a side note, Victor may have been thinking of his mother's maiden name as well—Rosen.) Sophie agreed. It turned out that Rose Stein was a very Jewish name, but the name seemed to suit the little girl.

Sophie and Rose

In the beginning, a nurse was hired to help care for mother and baby. Later, Sophie found that she was kept quite busy taking care of little Rose. Still, it was all a joy. Catharina often came by to look in on her new grandchild. And Victor, busy with work at W.M. Hoyt & Co., was all the more inspired to be successful. The couple so loved their first baby that during her first two years, they took her to the photography shop every few months for a new picture.

After Rose's arrival, a large group of relatives came to see her. The number of visitors revealed that the family was indeed growing.

There were Frank and Catharina with the children still at home, twenty-one year old, Louise, seventeen year-old Frank, Jr., and fourteen year-old Anna. Ludwig and Julia Stein brought their family: Hugo, twenty-six, Oscar, twenty-three, eighteen year-old Laura and sixteen year-old Etta. Then, there was Sophie's sister, Kate, with husband Ozro Lockwood and their two year-old daughter, Isabel. If all the Ganser cousins did not make it, certainly Ottilie and husband, Albert Miller, were there with five year-old Ottie, two year-old Carl, and, of course, Aunt Anna Kirchstein.

Carl and Ottie Miller

About this time, Victor and Sophie had another exciting new development in their lives. Sophie's father, Frank, asked Victor if he would like to become a partner at the F. Deppe Company. Victor was delighted, but said he would have to think about it. He was very much invested in his job at the W.M. Hoyt & Company. At the same time, having worked in the wholesale grocery business all those years, he had a great deal to offer—ideas and connections, which would be useful in helping the bakery business grow even more. He was also energetic and good-natured; a person who got along with everyone he met. After some consideration, Victor decided to accept Frank Deppe's offer.

Sophie was extremely happy about her husband's new position. Victor had certainly proved himself in the field of business and trustworthiness, and she knew it pleased Papa to have her husband on board. Now, her two worlds were truly joined.

During this time, Frank Deppe brought another partner into the bakery, twenty-seven year-old Nicholas Becker. The Beckers were relatives of the Deppes, possibly through Nicholas' mother, Anna. John Becker, the father, and the eldest son, Tony, had

Rose Stein

earned a living for the family as musicians, but John had passed away some years earlier. Now, Anna and her two youngest sons, Nicholas and Charles, moved into one of the bakery's upstairs apartments.

Up in Lake View, Annie Ganser and Christian von Essen's family was continuing to grow. There were now five Essen children: Kate, 10, Mamie, 7, and Louise, called "Lulu, 5. The Essens had two more children in the late 1890s: a little girl named Maude, born April of 1895, who was now three, and a little boy named Frederick, born in February of 1897. "Freddie" was a cute baby, who surprised them all with his bright red hair—the only red hair in the family.

The Essens were living in a small, white two-story house, on a nice little street at 249 Cuyler. The house had a big front yard for the children to play in. Christian planted a couple of fruit trees, and Annie grew vegetables. Each day, Christian went to work in his bake shop, while Annie stayed home and took care of the children. Theirs seemed an ideal life.

Then, one day in December of 1898, Christian was not feeling well. He had an excruciating headache, and could not bear the light, so, he took to his bed. Annie was terribly worried. She tried to nurse him, but his fever was too high. A short time later, he no longer responded to her. One of the children was sent to fetch the doctor.

When the doctor arrived, after a quick examination, he stated that Christian had contracted Cerebro-spinal Meningitis, an illness that is extremely contagious. Of late, there had been quite a few cases of this illness in the area. An ambulance was ordered, and, despite Annie's declaration that they could not afford it, Christian was taken to the hospital. Above all else, the doctor said, the children must not be exposed to Christian, nor should she. And if there was to be any hope, Christian had to stay in the hospital.

The Von Essen home at 245 Cuyler

What terrible shock and desperation Annie must have felt as she realized she might soon lose her dear husband, and the children, their beloved "papa."

Christian remained in the hospital for eleven days, while everyone hoped and prayed for his recovery. Then, on December 20th, 1898 at 12:30 in the afternoon, Christian von Essen died. He was thirty-eight years old.

It seems apparent that no one else in the family contracted this dreaded disease. Out of necessity, soon after his passing, Annie went to work as a laundress. Now, only two years after her brother, John Ganser's early death, she was walking in the same path as her sister-in-law, Elizabeth Wolfe. Fortunately for Annie and her five children, Christian had bought and paid for their home on Cuyler Street. They would continue to live in that house for the next 40 years.

In 1899, Albert Miller had the good fortune to obtain a lease for the downstairs portion of Augustana Hospital at 1161 Lincoln Ave (now 649). The triangular building took the entire block on Garfield (now Dickens), from Sedgwick to Cleveland. Albert had the

The Miller Pharmacy, cira 1899

front section of the triangle. A sign painter was hired to paint "MILLER'S PHARMACY" in large letters across the front curve of the building. Besides the fortunate location—a hospital—for his place of business, it was not far from the house on Fullerton, which meant that he could easily walk back and forth. Albert would remain at this location for the rest of his career. Later, he would pass the business on to his son, Carl.

Left to right: Clerk (unknown), Albert Miller, Ottilie, Carl, and Ottie

In celebration of the grand opening, Albert hired a photographer to take pictures of the pharmacy, with the Miller family serving as model customers. Along with he and his wife, Ottilie, and the drug store clerk (whose name has since been forgotten), were the Miller children, Ottie and Carl. The numerous photos taken at that time reveal shelves with hundreds of bottles and jars containing medications. Inside the glass front cases were cigars, perfumes and other items. The drug store also contained a soda fountain, with tables and chairs where customers could sit and enjoy a strawberry, pineapple, peach or grape soda. There were eight flavors all together. A wooden donkey stood nearby, with little Ottie demonstrating how children could ride him. One of the popular products sold in the pharmacy was "Miller's Chilblain Cure," a product Albert Miller created to stop frostbite.

Ottie, an unknown child, and Carl playing across the street from the Kirchstein home

After the photographer finished at the pharmacy, he went down to the Miller house with Ottilie, Ottie and Carl, and took a few more pictures on the street in front of their home. The photographs taken on this day preserved the grand history of both the Miller Family and Lincoln Park.

Down at 449–551 Sedgwick, the F. Deppe Baking Company was quite busy. In 1899, with Nicholas Becker gone, Frank Deppe had asked Ozro Lockwood if he would become a partner in the company. Since Frank, Jr. had little interest in taking over the business, the idea of bringing in his sons-in-law meant that the F. Deppe Company would stay in the family.

Officially, Ozro's title would be "manager," and he was happy to accept. He liked Frank and he liked Victor as well. Now they would truly be one happy family. Frank Deppe was not well, and clearly could no longer manager the business. His two young and energetic sons-in-law with a good sense of how to treat the customer and attract business took over.

During this time, Victor Stein, who was always full of energy and eager for amusement, helped to organize the Commercial Bowling Club with E.B. Hull. In 1899, they played at Albert Schulhof's alley in Lake View. Though only their first season, the club was able to enter the North End League. Victor came in third for those "with an average of 177 for 60 games." Bowling was now his new passion.

Chapter 23

Oscar and Etta

During the early 1890s, according to the *Chicago City Directory*, Oscar Stein was living with his parents at 1853 N. Clark and working for Sprague, Warner & Company at 7 Randolph, a job he no doubt procured with the help of his father.

By 1898, however, Oscar had moved into his own apartment (or room) at 1175 N. Clark. For all appearances, he was like most young men, attempting to make his way in the world, but appearances were just that. Underneath, Oscar was an insecure and deeply unhappy young man.

In recent months, Oscar had fallen in love with a neighbor named Lillian Burkhardt, a beautiful young woman of twenty-six.* It is thought that she lived at 940 N. Clark Street, not far from the Steins. Whatever friendship or relation was had between Oscar and this young woman, one thing is clear—Lillian's feelings for him were not the same as his toward her. It was an unrequited love and, as a result, he was angry and depressed.

At some point, Oscar went out and bought a gun. Later, after making a delivery at the corner of 110th Street and Western Avenue, he took out the gun and shot himself in the head. He was discovered by a passerby, lying on the sidewalk unconscious. The witness called the police. Oscar was taken to Englewood Union Hospital.

---

* Although we have no proof that this is "the" Lillian Burkhardt, no other girl by this name and age is found in the directory or census.

*Location where Oscar Stein shot himself in 1899.
Photographed, 1986.*

After regaining consciousness, the doctors questioned him on how he had received his injury, but he refused to answer. The strange thing was, while a number of bullets were found in his pockets, the gun he used to shoot himself was nowhere to be found.

Because he had been driving the Warner, Sprague delivery wagon, the Company was quickly notified by the police, who then notified his family. For his parents, the shock must have been terrible. It is uncertain as to whether they went to the hospital.

As soon as the newspapers heard about Oscar's story, they showed up at the hospital. It was their investigation which revealed the story of Oscar's unrequited love. An article, appearing under the title *Was Tired of Life*, appeared in the *Chicago Daily Sun* on March 2nd, 1899.

The youngest male in the Stein family languished in the hospital for three days. Although the bullet itself had not killed him or destroyed his ability to think and speak, ultimately, the infection from the bullet took his life. Oscar Stein's death certificate states that he died from "cerebre spinal meningitis due to a bullet wound above the right eye." At the time of his death on March 1st, 1899, he was twenty-three years old.

Oscar Stein was laid to rest next to his sister, Bertha, on March 8th. Perhaps the unusual length of time between his death and burial was due to an investigation into the cause of his death. Oscar's suicide was the second great tragedy bringing sorrow and shame to the Stein family. After Oscar's death, Ludwig fell into a state of deep depression. In the past, he had enjoyed taking a drink after work. Now, his drinking began to spiral out of control.

Iddel Stein or "Etta" as she preferred to be called, was a very talented violinist. How Ludwig loved to hear her play. She had been studying violin since childhood, and by her teen years, it became clear that she was truly gifted.

One day, someone, perhaps her teacher, got her the opportunity to play for the great composer and band leader John Phillip Souza, who was visiting Chicago with his orchestra.

Born in 1854, Sousa, grew up on Capitol Hill in Washington, D.C. He began his career playing violin, and by the age of thirteen, had begun an apprenticeship with the Marine Band. For twenty-four years, he remained with the United States Marine Band, conducting and writing such great marches as *The Stars and Stripes Forever, Semper Fidelis,* and *The Washington Post.* Today, his work represents American patriotism. It is a standard no one has surpassed.

In 1892, when John Philip Sousa retired from the Marine Band, he went on to form The Sousa Band, which would continue to tour the world for the next 39 years. Between 1896 and 1904,

Idelle (Edith) Stein

Souza and his band came to Chicago at least once every year. The year in which Etta Stein met him can only be guessed as sometime between 1899 and 1902.

After playing for John Philip Sousa and others in the band, Etta was asked her to join them. How thrilled she was. What an honor to be invited by this great composer and band leader to join the Sousa Band and travel the world!

When she approached her father with the news, she was in a great state of excitement, but his response fell on her like a knife.

"Absolutely not."

She wanted to go; she was determined to go, yet nothing she said could change her father's mind. This would be the greatest opportunity she could ever have. Finally, with great resolve, Etta told her father, "If you don't let me go with Sousa, I will never play the violin again."

Ludwig would not budge. A young woman traveling with an orchestra? What sort of things would she be exposed to? What sort of life would she have? His only thought was that she should be satisfied to live under her father's roof and obey him. He knew what was best for her.

For whatever reason—perhaps she was underage and needed his permission—Etta remained at home.

Time passed, and Ludwig no longer heard the sounds of beautiful music wafting through the apartment. At first, he thought she was angry, and it would pass.

"Come Iddel," he said, "Play me a little tune. I am blue and I need to hear some music. Play 'On the Beautiful Blue Danube.' Please?"

Perhaps she did not even answer. It did not matter what he said, she would not play. He had ruined her future. She was as stubborn as her father, and she kept to her promise. The violin was put in its case and packed away in the basement storage. She was finished. It was a decision she did not go back on, but one she would speak of the rest of her life.

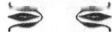

On February 19, 1902, Hugo Stein married Mary A. Beck, a twenty year-old German-American girl from Illinois. After the marriage, the couple moved into their own apartment. Hugo was 30, and Mary, 28. Like many other Jewish immigrants in this new country and like his own brother, Hugo did not marry a Jewish girl.

At the very least, the Stein family could look upon their two eldest sons as stable. Left at home now were Ludwig and Julia with their two youngest daughters, Laura, 22, and Etta, 20.

647 and 649 Fullerton Avenue

Chapter 24
A New Century

In early 1900, Anna Kirchstein had a suggestion. The house next to her was going to be available. Would Victor and Sophie like to rent it? The couple thought living there would be a dream come true. By spring of 1900, Victor, Sophie and two year-old Rose were happily settled at 647 Fullerton, right next door to the Anna Kirchstein and the Millers at 649.

Memories of the neighborhood from this time recall red roses growing in front yard of the Kirchstein-Miller house, and a large poplar tree as well. There was a small lawn and paved sidewalk, as well as a grassy curb. The trees planted in the curb had grown quickly, turning the avenue into a lovely tree-lined street with gracious homes and neat lawns.

By now, Victor Stein appeared to be doing quite well financially. A German girl, Marie Fell, was hired as a servant to help with the housework and take care of little Rose while Sophie went out. She had come to the United States five years earlier and was now twenty-one. When the census taker came to call on June 5, 1900, Marie was the one who answered the door and attempted to answer the questions. She did not know the months or years that Victor and Sophie had been born, so these spaces were left blank. Marie called Rose "Rosa," mistakenly stating that she had been born in September of 1896, and was presently three years old, a date corrected ten years later. Rose was then 20 months.

The Steins were quite comfortable in their new home and found it very convenient. Recently the Union Loop had been completed with a stop at Sedgwick Street. Victor was able to hop on the train and be at the bakery (only four blocks from the station) in a in a matter of minutes.* Sophie began attending the Presbyterian Church across the street, a church her sister, Kate Lockwood, attended as well.

The Federal Census of 1900 reveals a great deal about the Sedgwick Street neighborhood. That year Ozro, Kate, and Isabel, age four, were living upstairs on the third floor. Like Sophie, Kate also had a German servant, Emilie Piotroske. Emilie was 26, and had come to the United States only two years earlier. There were also four male bakers from Germany living on their floor: Otto Bloch, 27; Michael Schelennert, 35, Otto Reith, 21, and Nick Huber, 23. With the exception of Schelennert, who had been in the country since 1881, all of the men had emigrated within the last ten years. These men were probably piled in the smaller back apartments.

Downstairs, in the grand apartment on the second floor were Kate's parents and siblings: Frank, now 60, Catharina, 52, Frank, Jr., 20, and Anna, 16. Living in the back apartments on that floor were: Catharine Dobrulska, 21, a servant from Germany, and Bettie Chandler, 20, who served as the bakery clerk. Bettie had come to Chicago from Indiana. In addition, there were also four more bakers on this floor: John Ubia, 21, from Pennsylvania, Jacob Knesly, 27, from Switzerland, John A. Cophanouir, 49, from Germany, and Frank Folz, 27, also from Germany. Frank

---

* It should be noted that Catharina Ganser owned this house at one time. It is uncertain whether she or her sister, Anna Kirchstein, owned it at this time.

F. Deppe Company, third building to the right, circa 1900

was working as the hostler, taking care of and grooming the horses stabled behind the bakery.

On the top floor, were Peter Simonis, age 56, who had been in the country since 1872, and his wife, Catherin, 56. Their son, Peter, age 15, worked as a bundle boy, packaging and carrying baked goods for the bakery customers.

Among other persons living in the bakery were the Becker family. They included: Nick J. Becker, Jr. age 29, a pressman, his brother, Charles A., 22, a traveling salesman, and their mother, Anna, age 63. According to the Census, Mrs. Becker had been in the country 32 years, arriving around 1868.

Although Nicholas was no longer a partner in the bakery, the families remained friendly. Perhaps the Deppes felt sorry for them, and as stated earlier, it seems the Beckers were relatives. The Deppes, including Sophie, often went up to visit old Mrs. Becker on the third floor. The Beckers were all very musical. The one thing the children would remember about "old Mrs. Becker" and the apartment were the many yellow canaries she owned. The apartment was filled with the sound of music by those canaries. In the future, Rose and all her cousins were fascinated by that.

Outside the Deppe Bakery, Sedgwick was a hub of activity. A few doors down at 545 Sedgwick, Anna Strasser, age fifty-five, was living with her children: twenty-seven year-old Anna and twenty-five year-old Julius, who was working as a clerk for the railroad. According to the Census, Anna was born the same year and month as her good friend, Sophie Deppe Stein. She was still unmarried, and would not "tie the knot" until 1905. At that time, fearing her new husband's reaction, on the marriage license, she took eight years off her age. Living with the Strassers was Anna's grandmother, Rosa Meyer, now seventy-nine. According to the census, Rosalia had come to America from Baden in 1854.

Local history states that there has always been a tavern across the street from the Deppe Bakery building. In 1900, Deppe neighbor,

Bernhard Malburg, twenty-five years of age, appears to have been the owner. Boarding with him was his bartender, George Waxweiler, age 36. Both men had emigrated from Germany and had lived in the country approximately eleven years. The professions of residents on Sedgwick were quite varied and included: bookkeepers, laborers, railroad personnel, tailors and a milliner.

Although Frank was no longer working at the bakery, he was still busy trying to make more money. During this time, he and Catharina used a new lot they had purchased as collateral to obtain a loan from "Phelps & Hoyt." The Trustee Deed was dated November 15, 1900, and was paid off on the 1st of July 1901.

During the late 1890s through 1903, trusting the Deppe children to take care of themselves, Frank and Catharina often stayed at the residence on North Clark Street, leaving them live on their own in the apartments over the bakery. They expected their younger children to be responsible in their behavior. They also expected Kate and Ozro, who were living in the building, to keep an eye on them. Naturally, the young couple was busy with their own lives, and didn't want to spend their time bossing the younger siblings around. By now, Louise was in her early twenties, Frank Jr., between nineteen and twenty-one, and Anna, between seventeen and twenty.

According to Louise Deppe's daughter, Kay Foxcroft, the young people had parties, and things went on not too different from what might go on among unchaperoned youth today. Later, Louise blamed her mother for how things turned out in her and her sister, Anna's life. "Grandpa and Grandma Deppe should have paid a more attention to their children, rather than running around the way they did," Kay said later, repeating her mother's words.

It seems doubtful that Frank, with his poor health, did much running. Nevertheless, the opinion expressed—that a lack of guidance resulted in bad choices when it came time for the Deppe girls to marry, is something to consider. Whether this was Louise's opinion or that of Kay (who was quite opinionated), is difficult to know.

Louise Deppe was getting married! Her new husband was a tall, handsome, dark-haired man, and she was truly excited. Albert Halstead was the son of James and Emma Halstead, who had a farm in Ross Township, not far from the Deppes' farm. The couple probably met at one of the dances the Deppes hosted every summer on the top floor of their Hobart house. Albert, born on November 21, 1878, had no interest in working on a farm. Instead, he was living in Chicago, pursuing a career in real estate. This made the courtship of Louise all the more easy. Alfred was probably a frequent attendee at the bakery building parties.

In 1900, Louise was a beautiful young woman with golden blonde hair, and a lovely face and figure. Not only that, she had style. Any man would have been happy to have her on their arm, but there was something else that may have attracted men to her, something she likely never thought about—her father had money. But Louise was in love with Albert. It was the beginning of a new century, and the beginning of a new life for her. Everyone, including her sisters, was thrilled. When the couple was married on February 17th, 1900, Alfred was twenty-one, and Louise, twenty-two.

The newly married Halsteads moved into the Deppe apartment at 1163 North Clark Street. Like other buildings in the neighborhood, it was likely a brick townhouse. There were five apartments. The Halsteads lived on the first floor. City Directories for the 1890s, also showed Frank and Catharina Deppe living there. The Federal Census for 1900, however, lists only Louise's twenty year-old brother, Frank Deppe, Jr., at this address with them.

By 1900, rather than following in his father's footsteps at the bakery, Frank, Jr. had chosen to go another route—a job with the City Press Association, where he was in charge of inspection. Frank, Sr. was probably very disappointed by this. After spending his life building a grand bakery business, he had hoped his son would carry on the business. Meanwhile, as we know, Frank's two sons-in-law were basically running the bakery.

During this time, the climate of Chicago, and even North Town had changed. On October 19th, 1900, seventeen year-old Anna Deppe was mugged on her way home. The incident was reported the next day in *The Chicago Tribune*. The article reported that Anna's home was at 1163 North Clark, between Arlington and St. James Streets (now 2478). Poor Anna, as well as her family, must have been quite shaken.

It should be noted that in 1901, Frank Deppe, Jr. was listed at two addresses: both 551 Sedgwick with his parents and younger sister, Anna, and 1163 N. Clark Street.* As stated, the number of addresses lived in by the Deppes during this time make it difficult to know where they were living when.

In late 1900, Louise, or "Lou" as everyone called her, found she was expecting her first child. Living in the apartment they shared with Frank, Jr. and others was not conducive for family living. When Aunt Anna Kirchstein learned that Lou was expecting, she invited the couple to rent the house next door. The Halsteads were happy to accept.†

---

* Now 1757–1759 Sedgwick

† Family states that at one time, Anna Kirchstein owned four houses in a row on Fullerton. Information in the public records showing this have yet to be found. The only evidence found states that Hermann and Anna Kirchstein purchased a lot that was later divided in two.

Louise and Albert had their first and only child on April 12, 1901. She was a beautiful baby with Louise's lovely features and Albert's dark hair and eyes. They called her Katharina.

Three months later, on July 7th, Sophie gave birth to her second child. It was one of the hottest days of the year, a July day where no breezes blew. Sophie lay in the big bed on the second floor front bedroom, gazing at the beautiful blue and green stained glass flower windows. They were lovely windows to concentrate on to bring her peace.

Katharina Halstead

When the midwife carefully placed the tiny bundle in her arms, Sophie learned that she had given birth to another girl. Victor had hoped for a son, but she was happy. They named the baby, Dorothy Ruth Stein. "Ruth" was a Biblical name, connecting the child to her Jewish ancestors. Since the baby was born at home, as with her sister, the family did not bother to obtain a birth certificate.*

Dorothy was a small baby, with dark hair, which soon turned a golden brown. Time would reveal she had inherited her father's brown eyes. Sophie was pleased with her little daughter, who was a much quieter and more serious baby than the lively Rose. Soon after Dorothy's birth, Sophie may have decided that two babies was enough. Whether by plan or fate, there would be no more

---

* This statement is based on a search as well as Dorothy Wright's statement on needing a birth certificate for travel.

babies. Unlike her mother's day, the twentieth century would be a time when women began to take charge of their lives.

Though each busy with their own families and interests, Sophie, Lou, and cousin Ottilie formed a neighborhood of support for one another. They also looked up to Aunt Anna Kirchstein for her wise advice and positive attitude.

Anna Kirchstein was a working woman and quite busy. Along with her weekly poetry column in the Illinois Staats-Zeitung, recently, she had been named editor of the *Frauen-Zeitung* (Ladies Journal), which was part of the Sunday newspaper, *Der Westen*. Her calling cards stated that she "was distinguished by recognition of H.I.M. William II of Germany." Anna had made quite a named for herself in the German community and the family was very proud.

Aunt Anna must have been earning a fairly good living because she furnished her home with the best décor, including fine German china. During these years, she would be invited to the finest homes and salons, where artists and intellectuals met. She would

Dorothy Stein

The early days of the twentieth century were a wonderful time for Sophie in many respects. She had a beautiful home next to family members she loved, a kind husband who was making plenty of money, and two beautiful daughters. Four year-old Rose was a bright little girl, who loved to sing and dance. Dorothy was a sweet and quiet soul, who loved to look at her picture books. Sophie kept quite busy, but she had always been a quiet soul herself, one who preferred the country to the city. The neighborhood around Lincoln Park in 1900 was still almost bucolic and extremely peaceful, so it suited her well.

Yet this wonderful life on Fullerton Avenue was not as happy for one member of the family. Not long after Katharina Halstead was born, Louise's marriage began to crumble. Albert was not making the living she had expected. In fact, he was making nothing at all. (It is possible that Frank Deppe was helping to support them, which would have been humiliating to Louise.)

In addition. Louse realized that her husband had a problem with alcohol. When Louise spoke to him about it, he said, "Why would I want to work when your father is rich?" That comment hurt. It also showed her that, like Sophie's first marriage, she had made a bad choice; likely, hers was a marriage that would not last.

Meanwhile, with a new baby a home, Louise did her best to hold on to the marriage. She was only twenty-five. She had expected to have a marriage like the one her parents and her sisters had, but it was not to be. Within a year or two, Albert and Louise were divorced, and Louise returned to Sedgwick, to live at the bakery.*

Victor Stein was making great strides as a bowler. By 1901 (the year Dorothy was born), Victor had joined the North Chicago League, and by 1902, he was one of the regular players, finishing fourth, with a high was 207. This sent him on to the National tournaments, where he was able to bring honors to Chicago.

That year, in Buffalo, New York, Victor finished 7th. In Indianapolis he did even better, finishing 4th with a total of 650. Obviously, he loved bowling. He also loved the camaraderie of being part of a team. In minor events, he played on the Wholesale Grocer's league with the Hoyt team.

In the *Bowling Encyclopedia* put out in 1904 by *The Western Bowlers Journal*, Victor Stein's biography states that he had been married for six years, had a "pleasant home on the North Side," and "a delightful" summer home in Hobart, Indiana.

Meanwhile, up in Lake View, Katharina Koch Ganser had moved in with her youngest daughter, Annie Essen, to help take care of the children, but also just as likely because she needed to be cared for herself. Although her whereabouts for the previous

---

* Probably by 1903.

thirty years is unknown, it seems she was not far, and had continued to be involved with her children and grandchildren over the years.

Isabel Lockwood would later recall meeting her great grandmother during the first eight years of her life. "Katie Koch," as she was known, was now in her eighties and becoming somewhat forgetful and debilitated. Still, the children enjoyed being around her.

During these later years, Katie had a photograph taken—a photograph now lost. Memories of it recall a thin woman with dark hair and a serious face. She was a woman who had known more hardships than smiles. Isabel Lockwood Ochsner would later write of her:

> "I remember our great grandmother when I was a little girl. She died when I was about eight or nine. She spoke French so that I never could converse with her."*

Katharina Koch Ganser passed away on January 17, 1903. She was eighty-one. Frank Deppe, in planning for the future, bought a large cemetery plot in Rosehill Cemetery, and it was there that Katharina Koch Ganser was laid to rest.

---

* Letter of Mrs. Alton Ochsner to her sister, Charlotte Lockwood, April 28, 1961

Chapter 25

Love and Scandal

IN 1900, TWENTY YEAR-OLD FRANK DEPPE, JR. MET A YOUNG GIRL with whom he was quickly smitten. She was only sixteen and her name was Florence Dreyer.

Florence was born in Chicago in September of 1883, and, like Frank, both of her parents were from Germany. The similarities between the two families, however, ends there. Florence's family was extremely rich. There was one other matter that separated them. By the time she met Frank, Jr., her father was in prison.

Florence's father, Edward, was born to August and Louise Schoettelndreyer on August 5, 1844. When he came to America, he changed his name to Edward S. Dreyer. Dreyer had a sister, Lottie, who had studied piano with Liszt, and a brother, Ned, who had died from diptheria. Edward Dreyer was well-known in Chicago, and during his early career, he received a great deal of attention in the news. In 1884, the papers noted that he would vote for Grover Cleveland. In 1888, he became the head of the Chicago Syndicate, and in 1891, Dreyer was the one to unveil the monument honoring President Ulysses S. Grant.

Florence's father was the owner of a bank in Chicago known as E.S. Dreyer & Co. It was an "old institution with a large German clientele."* (Likely this was not the bank Frank Deppe used.)

---

* "Financing an Empire/History of Banking in Illinois," pgs. 310–312

In 1896, Dreyer's bank had comparatively few assets to liabilities. The banking law stated that no bank could loan an excess of 1% of their capital. E.S. Dreyer & Co.'s liabilities were listed at $1,350,000,* far exceeding this law. Four years earlier, the panic of 1892 had left the bank in bad financial condition. As a result, at that time E.S. Dreyer & Company asked for help from a much larger bank, the National Bank of Illinois.

Then, in 1896, discrepancies at the National Bank of Illinois were caught, and the government decided that there had been a mishandling of funds. Although the National Bank of Illinois was closed then, the discovery of this problem caused the closure of three other banks, including E.S. Dreyer & Co. This was only the beginning of the trouble.

Edward S. Dreyer

According to newspaper reports, Dreyer's bank owed the National Bank of Illinois over $500,000.† Three clerks, with no financial standing at the Dreyer bank, had signed notes to the order of the National Bank of Illinois for amounts of $99,000, $97,000 and $67,000, which today would total more than seven million dollars.‡ Ultimately, all of this had been done to cover up the fact that the banking law had been broken. Both Dryer's bank and the National Bank of Illinois had broken the law. Meanwhile, many depositors had lost their money.

---

* = approximately $36,399,205.00 in 2017. http://www.in2013dollars.com

† $500,000 = $13,592,298.00 in 2017; http://www.in2013dollars.com

‡ $99,000 = $2,716,362 in 20017; $97,000 = $2,661,448; $67,000 = $1,838,347

For nearly three years (1896–1899), the story of the failed banks and the resulting trial appeared almost daily on the front pages of *The Chicago Tribune*. It was one of the most sensational legal trials in Chicago history. Chicagoans followed the details with avid interest, as the events surrounding the scandal became increasingly shocking.

The disclosures in the investigation led to the death of William A. Hammond, who was said to have "wrecked" the National Bank of Illinois through his allowance of large overdrafts from those he favored, and manipulation of the books. When faced with criminal prosecution, Hammond decided to drown himself. His body was found on the shore of Lake Michigan in Evanston. Another banker, Otto Wasmansdorff, shot himself in the head in his home at 549 Cleveland Avenue. Headlines in *The Chicago Tribune* hit the front pages with titles like: "Is An Ugly Tangle," "Ruined by Hammond," "Banker Ends It All," and "E.S. Dreyer in the Net."

Finally, in 1898, Edward Dreyer himself was accused of accepting money from a bank depositor in the amount of $300,000 at a time when he knew the bank was insolvent.* He claimed that he was merely a trustee and had not taken the money, but when the depositor asked for his money back, he was unable to get it. In addition, it was found that two years earlier Fred M. Blou had gone to court stating that Dreyer had "unlawfully, feloniously and willfully" refused to pay him back $319,000.† Again, Dreyer claimed that he was Treasurer of the Chicago West Park Commissioners and did not hold the money himself; *he* had not taken it. Legislation to protect of bank depositors had been passed in 1877. This legislation made it a criminal offense for a banker to receive a deposit after a bank was insolvent. Clearly, the law had been broken.

The case dragged on for four years, while Florence's father sat in the Cook County Jail. Finally, in 1897, Edward Dreyer was

---

* $300,000 = $8,332,670.00; Ibid.

† = to $8,860,405 in 2017.

Florence Dreyer

convicted and given a prison sentence. Meanwhile, his incarceration was put off another three years. At the close of the trial, he was able to go home, but he continued to fight the charges. In the spring of 1900, Edward Dryer was notified that he would be taken to prison. Still, the wait dragged on.

In the midst of all this, Frank Deppe, Jr. was courting Florence Dreyer. How Mr. and Mrs. Deppe reacted when they found out their son was dating Dreyer's daughter is not known, but at least one of the Deppes didn't think much of Mr. Dreyer. According to Kay Halstead Foxcroft, her mother, Louise Deppe, thought Dreyer was guilty, stating that he had robbed people and caused great suffering. According to Kay, people had killed themselves as a result of his actions, which caused the loss of their life savings. Other family members seemed to feel that Florence, who had grown up in a wealthy home, acted as if she was better than the Deppes, who had worked hard for their money.

In any case, Frank, Jr. was in love and had eyes for no one but Florence. Florence, who certainly had not had an easy time, clung to Frank, Jr. According to one family member, she was frequently among those attending parties that the Deppe children had at 551 Sedgwick. Around this time, the eighteen year-old found that she was pregnant. This, of course, changed everything.

In the meantime, the families had began planning a wedding for Frank and Florence, but the couple decided not to wait and eloped. On their way to get married, they left behind this note:

Dear Folks:
Don't make any more plans for the wedding.
It is all over and we are on our honeymoon.
Don't expect us home til we get there.
Frank and Florence

Frank and Florence were married in Chicago on March 25, 1902. The groom was twenty-two and the bride, eighteen. Eight months after their marriage, the couple celebrated the arrival of their first and only child, a boy. Born on November 21, 1902, the baby was given the somewhat ostentatious name of Francis E. Deppe III. Although neither Frank nor Frank Jr. had ever been a "Francis" or had an "E" as their middle name, Florence seemed to believe Francis E. Deppe III sounded much more impressive. The "E" stood for her father, Edward. Some months later, the baby was baptized at the grand St. Alphonsus Church at 1429 Wellington, on November 21, 1902 by James Oth.

Forty days after the birth of his grandson, on December 31, 1902, at 10:45 in the morning, Edward S. Dreyer was picked up and taken to the Federal Penitentiary at Joliet. After arriving at the prison, Dreyer was made to put on prison garb, and his mustache and goatee cut off. Then, he was taken to his cell. The *Chicago Tribune* quoted him as saying, "For five years I have lived with the dread of this moment."

One week after the incarceration began, Mrs. Dreyer and the Dreyer children received notice that they would be allowed to visit him. Although Edward Dreyer claimed his innocence and believed he would be out within the year, his time at Joliet Prison lasted more than two years. While many condemned him, a well-respected former man of the bench, Judge Moran, stated that he had known E.S. Dreyer many years, and "the man" had never done a thing wrong in his life.

Left behind at the Dreyer home were Dreyer's fifty-seven year-old wife, Augusta, her mother, eighty-nine year-old Charlotte Bilgman, and two children: Edward, Jr., 23, and Charlotte, 22. As can be imagined, all were devastated by this turn of events. The Dreyers had occupied a beautiful home at 352 Diversey Avenue, an exclusive neighborhood across from Lincoln Park and Lake Michigan. Now they were living in a rented apartment at 2116 Hudson.

During the next months, Florence would often be too ill to visit her father, so Frank, Jr. would take her place. All this, of course, was noted by *The Chicago Tribune*, which kept a close eye on the case and the persons involved.

Baby Francis was likely Florence's greatest comfort during this difficult time. Francis was an extremely handsome child, and his mother doted on him. Naturally, he grew up wealthier than any of the Deppe descendants. His cousins looked upon him as spoiled, and apparently, he was. Aside from his wealthy and scandalous Dreyer grandfather, Francis grew up expecting that he would be heir to the Deppe Baking Company. Besides taking care of her son, Florence Deppe kept busy as a member of the Germania Club and other social clubs.

The listings for Frank, Jr. and Florence's home addresses are somewhat confusing during their first years together. Initially, Frank, Jr. listed his home address as 1163 N. Clark Street. An additional listing shows that the newly married couple had moved to 645 Fullerton, next door to Victor and Sophie.

E.S. Dreyer's release from Joliet Penitentiary, was granted by the Board of Pardons in 1905. It was later contended by the State that the money in question had been unlawfully transferred to the account of E.S. Dreyer & Co. and invested in real estate, Dreyer always stated that he was an innocent victim in the midst of circumstances over which he had no control. His release, in part, was due to the fact that he had "made good" on all monies taken from the Park funds.*

---

* Chicago Tribune Obituary, June 22, 1918

Sophie's older sister, Kate, and her husband were doing well. By 1902, however, Kate wanted a real home away from the bakery. There was Isabel, now six, and the new baby, Ozro Charles (born July 29, 1900), to think of. Kate looked at her sisters, Sophie and Louise, living in houses on Fullerton, and felt a tinge of jealousy. After Frank married and moved out of 1163 N. Clark, it was agreed that Kate and Ozro could use that residence as their own, which they did for the next three years. Isabel was now eight, and Ozro, two. On November 1, 1903, Kate had her third child, another little girl, whom they named Charlotte.

Being away from the bakery, gave the Lockwoods some space and sense of quiet. They were also not far from Fullerton Avenue. Kate could easily visit Sophie and Louise, and they could visit her.

In 1902, the baby of the Deppe family, Anna, married Julius Heinemann. It was not an auspicious marriage. He was neither wealthy, nor did he have a profession, but he was one son-in-law who did not attempt to join the baking business, nor live off it. Not much more is known about him.

At the time of their marriage, on March 1, 1902, Anna was only eighteen, and, according to Kay, pregnant. No baby materialized, however. Julius, her husband, was also about the same age. Considering these facts, it is not surprising Anna's older sister, Louise, felt that her parents had failed to give Anna the guidance she needed to ensure a happy, secure future.

The Heinemann's moved to the south side of Chicago and remained together for at least eight years. Four years later, on July 9, 1906, Anna would give birth to a son, whom they named Edwin. In the end, Anna's marriage was no better than that of "Lou's" (as the family called her). She would spend the rest of her life working to support her son and herself.

One thing that can be said for the Deppe women—they had seen a good marriage and a good father in Frank Deppe. When they found—as did Sophie, Lou and Anna—that they were not being treated well, they didn't stand for it; they got out. And, thankfully, they had a family willing to help them.

Getting divorced in the early 1900s was looked on with shame; it was not an easy time for these sisters. When Louise divorced Alfred Halstead, her family did what they could to rally around her. Lou moved back to the bakery where she lived with her parents and where there was always someone around to watch little Katharine, while she worked to make a living. There was no living off her family. She worked in the bakery as a sales lady. And in her spare time, using her own unique talent—needlework—Louise built a clientele. This was a great asset for her. Women interested in fine clothing learned of her work by word of mouth, and ordered lovely gowns. Family members also hired her to sew for them.

Katharina Halstead

Lou, to her credit, never said anything against Alfred to Kay. She simply told her daughter that she had married too young. Later, Albert Halstead married a rich farmer's daughter. "Katharina" would remember her father's father, James Montgomery Halstead, as a kind old man. He was hit and killed one day, walking along the side of the road, by his farm, outside Hobart.

Growing up, "Katharina," who later spelled her name "Kathryn," would recall that throughout her childhood German thriftiness prevailed. They ate "rot"—red cabbage at the bakery many nights.

In addition, to save money, her mother made all her clothes, but they were lovely ones.

Although she was surrounded by a loving family, "Kay" (as the family came to call her) could help feeling the hurt, growing up without a father, and with a mother who had to work hard for everything she had. Kay felt her mother deserved much better. She said later that she felt sad during her childhood and wished that others had considered what it felt like to be in her position. As an adult, Kay became a sharp critic of others, sharp enough that people feared her opinion.

Dorothy Stein loved her cousin Kay. She couldn't imagine why Kay could be unhappy because she was so beautiful with her fair skin and dark hair. Dorothy thought Kay was the prettiest of all the Deppe grandchildren. She wished she could look that pretty.

Chapter 26

Golden Days

VICTOR STEIN WAS A VERY SOCIAL PERSON, SO SOPHIE HAD NO reason to be bored. He took her to plays and concerts, of which there were many in Chicago. He was especially fond of Yiddish theatre, and with his friendly personality, made many friends in the theatrical community.

It was with great sorrow in December of 1903 that the family and all of Chicago learned of the terrible tragedy at the Iroquois Theatre in downtown Chicago. On December 30th, the matinee of the musical, *Mr. Bluebeard,* was filled with women and children celebrating the holiday. Midway thru the performance, the curtains caught fire. In order to keep the audience from panicking, the management instructed the performers to continue performing, but the fire spread much more quickly than anyone had imagined it would.

By the time the people in the auditorium realized the danger, panic ensued. Tragically, as was customary, the theatre doors were locked. No one had thought to unlock them. As desparate theatre patrons rushed to the doors, there was no way out.

Six hundred people died that day, at least 150 of them children. All of Chicago was in shock. Any member of the Stein or Deppe family might have been there to see the play. It was with great sorrow that Victor learned his old boss, William Hoyt had lost his daughter, Emilie, along with three of his grandchildren, ages fifteen, twelve and nine.

In honor of his loved ones, Mr. Hoyt had a huge monument built at Graceland Cemetery in their memory. Still, nothing could take away the terrible pain. They had died in the fire, locked behind closed doors. Two months later, unable to recover from the pain and shock of it all, Emilie's husband died as well. All of Chicago grieved over these terrible losses for a very long time.*

In the early 1900s, there were at least three to four related Ganser family descendants living on Fullerton. Anna Kirchstein and the Millers, Louise and little Katharina, Sophie and Victor with Rose and Dorothy, and finally, Frank and Florence with their son, Francis. Photos taken during this time reveal four charming houses with quite a number of children standing in various places around the yard and porches. (See page 264.)

As the children grew older, Sophie found more ways to fill her time. Rose and Isabel, who were close in age, loved to play with one another. They both attended the Abraham Lincoln School, a big, brick building just around the corner on Kemper Place. A school had stood at this location since 1871. The new building had just been erected nine years earlier in 1894. This building still stands today.

Little Dorothy, the Stein's youngest, was a sweet but serious, docile child, who played quietly on her own. She liked to look at picture books, and listen as Sophie read to her.

When Sophie wanted a piano, her mother, Catharina, agreed to buy one for the family, purchasing Sophie's choice—a baby grand A.B. Chase, which had been used for concerts in Chicago. Sophie bought some pretty children's music books, so the little girls could have music and learn songs. In her quiet time, Sophie worked on her art, painting lovely flowers on china, furniture, and canvases. Always interested in social causes, she volunteered at

---

* Chicago History, Fall 2003, Inferno at the Iroquois, Anthony P. Hatch

Hull House, and donated many of her paintings to Hull House to raise money for the cause.

When "Lou" was living next door, the two sisters spent a good deal of time with one another, while their daughters, Dorothy and Kay played together. Victor, Sophie or "Lou" often took the children down to the bakery to visit Grandma and Grandpa.

Meanwhile, in 1906, Ozro Lockwood was able procure a place at 54 Grant Street (now 508). Originally thought to be a house, it appears they lived in a large apartment, halfway between the bakery and Fullerton. These northern neighborhoods, out of the hustle and bustle of the city, were considered more desirable. With Isabel, now ten, Ozro, five, and Charlotte, three, Kate wanted her own home with more room, and a place for the children to play.

After her divorce, Louise and Katharina moved into one of the apartments at the bakery to save money. Rose and Dorothy were thrilled to stay there with their cousin. How they loved the bakery with its odor of freshly baked bread and donuts filling the air. Their cousin, Charlotte Lockwood, later wrote of it:

> *I wish you could have known the bakery as I did. I spent all the time I could there when I was a little girl. It was a huge retail store then with about three wagons and horses for wholesale delivery. They made the most wonderful German baked goods. Hard rolls baked on the hearth, delicious bread, cookies, sweet rolls, all with that home-made taste. There were huge glass cases with those tall glass jars filled with real chocolate creams. . . .*
>
> *There was one little lady who did nothing but peel apples all day long. She looked like a little dried up apple herself. There were 2 kitchen girls who did nothing but cook for the family and "help" and what meals! My Grandma and Grandpa Deppe lived upstairs . . . and spoke a patois of German and English, but their mother [Katie Koch] spoke French.*

On their visits, the children would stand before the glass cases, filled with fresh breads and rolls, their mouths drooling for a wonderful piece of bread with butter or cheese.

In the building next door, there was a big shoot where the flour sifted down through a hole on the third floor. It looked like so much fun. The children watched expectantly as the donuts were put in a big vat and fried. The babies were kept in baskets behind the counter of the bakery, but the little ones were allowed to wander and explore.

Upstairs in the Deppe apartment, Dorothy watched her Grandpa Deppe taking a nap on the elegantly curved green velvet settee, the same settee which later sat in her own home. She recalled how his white goatee rested on his chest as he slept.

At night, the girls were put in the bathtub, a round affair that if they soaped, became extremely slippery. Dorothy and Kay loved sliding around the circle of the tub and splashing into the water while their laughter filled the room. Life was wonderful for the children.

Sometimes, Rose would later recall, they'd go to visit Grandpa and Grandma Stein. The Stein apartment held special treasures to look at, but never to touch. It wasn't as much fun to visit Grandpa and Grandma Stein as it was at the bakery. Grandpa Stein was quite stern, and Papa told them not to make a sound or romp about there, but to sit quietly, their hands folded in their laps. Grandma Stein was very sweet with white, wavy hair. Dorothy thought her hair was beautiful.

At the Stein's new apartment on Beldon Avenue, the children listened intently to Grandpa as he told stories of how he used to raise greyhounds, a breed of dog he loved. The stone apartment building where they lived then had a small yard in front, enclosed by a tall iron fence with sharp spikes at the top. It was here he kept his dogs during the day while he went to work.

Greyhounds love to run—they need to run. The children were horrified as their broken-hearted grandfather told of coming home to find his dogs impaled upon the iron points of the fence. The dogs had attempted to jump out, so they could run free, but had not made it.

As time passed, the children no longer went to the Stein home. Grandpa

446 Beldon Ave, now 538

Stein was not well. He could not handle the dark memories of the past that rose up to haunt him. By now, his drinking had increased, and he was unable to work or get along with anyone.

So many things preyed upon Ludwig: the death of Bertha, the suicide of Oscar, and Iddel giving up the violin. He had been drinking for years, but now it was out of control. His health was poor, and his memory fading. With all his success, Ludwig felt he had deeply failed in life.

Julia had been a patient wife. She had dealt with his moods, anger, and rudeness, but now she could no longer care for him or control him. Perhaps what needed to be done was decided by her sons, Victor and Hugo. They loved their mother and could not bear to see her in this position. In likelihood, the brothers learned as much from their sisters, Laura and Iddel, as they did from their mother. But then, they could see what was happening with their own eyes.

The family chose to send their father to a state hospital, the only place they could afford, and one that could handle his condition—the Kankakee State Hospital, otherwise known as the Illinois Eastern Hospital for the Insane.

In 1877, the General Assembly had voted to establish this institution at Kankakee. It opened to the public two years later. Built in classical Romanesque style, the estate consisted of one large, central building, which held 400–600 patients, along with various cottages around the grounds. Unlike the sanitarium Bertha entered some ten years earlier, most of the men and women who entered Kankakee remained there.

Julia Stein

By 1906, the State Hospital was not in the best of shape. To begin with, the place was running a $12,285.64 deficit.* In addition, after being open for more than twenty-five years, many of the buildings were run down, and there was trouble with the heat.

A newspaper article in 1906 stated that Kankakee held 1,264 male patients and 1,135 female, noting that a good percentage of the patients who were released returned within two years. This same news article revealed that there was a danger of polluted water in the place, and some people had caught meningitis.

---

* $12,285 = $323,334.75 in 2017

To try to make things better, the institution, which had a small budget, gave the patients jobs to do to improve the place. Some were employed in the garden, while others were given work like digging tunnels to run pipes through for heating, or for laying sewage disposal pipelines. Still others had jobs tearing out old brick furnaces or mowing the 90 acres of lawn. It was a big place, with 4 acres of streets.

It is doubtful Ludwig, who was now in his early to mid-sixties, could do much work, though he may have enjoyed taking a walk now and then, or sitting in the sun. There were many areas like this for patients to enjoy, but it also seems possible that he may have been among those confined.

How long he lived at the Kankakee State Hospital or whether his family ever visited him is unknown. Meanwhile, in the Stein family home, peace finally reigned.

Down in Hobart, by 1905, Joseph Deppe's daughter, Kate, was 29, and, son, Frank, was 26. In 1914, Kate would marry Hobart blacksmith Robert Scholler, taking her mother, Lena, to live with them in a little house in downtown Hobart. Robert's mother also lived with them.

The year 1906 saw one of the last grand Deppe-Ganser summer get-togethers on the old farm. There, a romance began between Joseph and Lena's son, Frank, and John and Lizzie Ganser's daughter, Catherine. Some years later, a marriage would take place between these two, a second Frank Deppe and Catharine Ganser, but that was all down the road.

That summer, the entire Deppe tribe, which now included a large group of little ones, boarded the train in Chicago and headed to Hobart. There they enjoyed the pure experience of country living with its green grass, fresh farm crops, blue skies, and the peace

The Lockwood children helping feed the chickens.

of Turkey Creek. During the day, the children played, spending their time chasing the geese and turkeys, and feeding the chickens with the old lady who helped take care of the farm. When they weren't running, they soaked there feet in the cool waters of the creek, and sat on the big shady veranda in the back of the house, rocking in a line of rocking chairs.

In the early evening, a huge spread of fresh vegetables and fruits, along with freshly cooked beef or chicken would be laid out. While the children continued to run and play in the fields, the grown-ups ate their meal. In those days, it was understood that the grown-ups came first. During this joyous gathering, the conversation often led to the past—stories of the old country in Prüm, the events of the Chicago fire, and how the bakery had been built. An old street light, a survivor of the Chicago fire, stood near the house, a memory of where it all began.

When it was time for the children to eat, they washed their hands and faces, and changed into fresh clothing before sitting down at a low, round table for a meal, which all the mothers helped to serve.

Isabel, Ozro and Charlotte Lockwood watch a farmhand at work.

Later, after the children had been put to bed, it was time for the adults to kick up their heels. The fiddlers and banjo players would arrive and everyone, including the neighbors, climbed up to the third floor. Then, the dancing began—square dancing and folk dancing, all to wonderful music and laughter lasting late into the night. These were halcyon days; days which everyone looked upon fondly as the ideal of living.

Probably more than anyone else, Sophie loved country living. She said she would gladly give up life in Chicago to live here year-round. She even expressed this wish to Victor.

In the afternoons and early evenings, just before dusk, Sophie set up her easel with canvas and laid out her oil paints. During these quiet times, she worked to capture the beauty of nature on canvas with peaceful farm scenes. One painting, which still exists, is that of the setting sun behind huge pines.

The summer of 1906, Frank and Catharina Deppe saw the gathering of eight beautiful grandchildren on the old farm: Isabel, 10, Rose, 8, and three five-year olds: Ozro, Katharina, and Dorothy. There were also two younger children, the Lockwood's daughter,

Rose Stein on the farm with her doll.

Charlotte, and Frank, Jr.'s Francis Deppe III, both three, and finally Anna's new baby, Edwin. It was quite a gathering, and the Deppes had every reason to be proud.

All of Frank's children were married now. Although two of the children, Sophie and Louise, had been divorced, only one, Louise, was alone with a child. This was a new and much more modern world that knew such things.

Life had slowed down greatly for Frank Deppe. He continued to suffer from rheumatism and the shortness of breath caused by his failing heart. He tired more easily and often huffed and puffed going up the stairs, having to rest along the way. He had to sit down for a while after doing things until he felt normal again, and in the midst of all this happy family activity, often fell alseep. But he enjoyed life and loved his grandchildren.

Chapter 27

No Goodbyes

JANUARY 9, 1907—IT WAS WARMER THAN USUAL FOR CHICAGO IN January, around thirty degrees, and the sun was out, so Frank decided to take a walk. It was a little after 7:30 in the morning when he left home, but he was used to being up early after all the years he'd gotten up in the middle of the night to bake bread, or at least, supervise it.

Frank headed to his eldest daughter, Kate Lockwood's home at 54 Grant Place (now 508), a spacious new apartment in a lovely neighborhood. He thought it might be nice to visit them. Seven year-old Ozro was not feel well, and Frank thought he might cheer his little grandson up. After all, what little boy likes to stay in bed? Kate said he had a sore throat and a fever, when he had called the night before on that newfangled contraption they had, the telephone.

Having set out, partway there, Frank found that he was tired. The walk seemed further than he remembered, but too late to turn back. He forged on, even though his breathing was labored. Along the way he had to stop again and lean against an iron fence post before continuing. Finally, he arrived.

He rang the bell, and was greeted by Kate, who bid him rest, while she ran to get him some water. She would be right back. Frank sat down heavily in the front hall chair. When Kate returned a few moments later, Papa appeared to be resting, but before a moment had passed, her heart stopped. Oh Papa!

Running to the next room, Kate called the doctor attending to Ozro. The doctor came quickly and confirmed what she already knew in her heart, but hoped was not so. Frank was dead. He had died of a heart attack.

Meanwhile, the doctor had just diagnosed seven year-old Ozro with Scarlett Fever. Along with his high fever, sore throat, and chills, the scarlet eruption on his body had begun to show. The house must be quarantined immediately, he said. For at least a week, no one would be allowed to enter or leave. Because Frank had been in the house when he died, he was considered contagious.

The undertakers arrived, placed him in a wooden coffin, and sealed it quickly. It could not be opened again. We can only imagine Catharina as she learned the news. Her husband had left that morning to visit their daughter. Now, after forty years together, she would never see his face again. There would be no goodbyes.

The newspaper announcements posted as to Frank Deppe's passing stated that only family members would be allowed at the funeral. Frank Deppe was sixty-six when he died.

Great sorrow prevailed. It was the end of an age, a pioneer who came to America with nothing and built a great business; the head of a family, a well-loved husband, father and grandfather, known and respected by the entire neighborhood. He was gone. No one had expected this.

In his will, Frank left everything to his widow, Catharina Ganser Deppe. A few years later, unable to deal with the business, Catharina would "sell" everything to her five children.

A little over two weeks after Frank's death, Joseph's daughter, Josephine Deppe Reissig, passed away from heart failure at age of thirty-nine.

On June 24th, 1907, six months after the passing of Frank Deppe, Ludwig Stein passed away at the Illinois Eastern Hospital for the Insane. He died twelve years and one day after Bertha. Ludwig was sixty-six years old. The cause  for his death was listed as a "Cerebral Hemorrhage." As listed in a doctor's reference book of the time, it states that rheumatism, gout, alcoholism and other diseases may predispose one to this. The coroner listed two other contributing factors in his death: Chronic Nephritis and Anti-Stenosis, which meant that Ludwig had both kidney disease and heart trouble. One day after his passing, according to Jewish custom, Ludwig Stein was buried in the family plot at Rosehill. Two days after his passing, on June 26th, Ludwig's daughter, Laura, married Charles Wendell.

Sophie Deppe and Victor Stein each lost their fathers in 1907; two men who came to America to follow their dreams, each historic in his own way. It was truly the end of an era.

The Deppe, Ganser and Stein families would stay in Chicago for many years. Today, there are still family members in the area. The F. Deppe Baking Company, managed by Frank, Jr., Ozro Lockwood and their children, would continue for two generations. When it closed in the 1960s, the Deppe Baking Company was the oldest wholesale bakery in Chicago.

To be continued . . .

Notes

Chapter 1
Based on the author's first trip to Prüm.

Chapter 2
From multiple sources, both online and German books. See Bibliography.
https://en.wikipedia.org/wiki/Pr%C3%BCm_Abbey

Chapter 3
Napoleon in Prüm information—The Museum of Prüm and a German book on Prüm history by Josef Faas (since lost).

Family facts came from the Prüm Standesamt, since moved to Kreisarchive Bitburg-Prüm.

Chapter 4
Information on Friedrich Carl Deppe, his marriage, and ancestors are taken from his marriage license, which detail two generations before him. Other elements based on the author's experience in Prüm. Imagination is used to fill out the facts.

Saarbrücken and Zweibrücken history was studied in online sites. https://en.wikipedia.org/wiki/Saarbr%C3%BCcken

https://en.wikipedia.org/wiki/Zweibr%C3%BCcken

Chapter 5

Deppe Children Birth Certificate information—Prüm Standesamt.

Franz Deppe—punished as an altar boy—Dorothy Stein Wright.

Dislike of church—Kay Halstead Foxcroft from her mother, Louise Deppe.

Children running in the hills—*Eifelvereinsblat* interview with Anna Kirchstein

Chapter 6

Based on books and articles with quotes by German immigrant. Visits to the sites Franz and Joseph lived and worked in Chicago added to the ability to comment.

"Follow your dreams" is an imagined statement but certainly represents the message would-be immigrants heard. Planning the journey also imagined.

Citizens forced to house soldiers- https://de.wikipedia.org/wiki/Victor_Schily

A book of records on emigrants from Prüm was discovered on Ancestry.com, revealing names, ports, dates and ships.

https://www.measuringworth.com The changes in the value of money from different times was taken mainly from this site.

Chapter 7

Chicago history: See Bibliography.

Tanner: online definition, Wikipedia.

Much of this chapter is imagined from basic information. No further information was found as to when or how Franz Deppe arrived in the USA or what his first job was. The information written provides some guidelines as to how he may have gotten his start as a baker in Chicago.

Franz Deppe—not wanting to be a soldier—Rose Stein Ubil and Dorothy Stein Wright. Clearly, something was different when Franz decided to enlist in the Civil War.

Chapter 8

In the 1980s, the author was able to view the original camp books for the Illinois Infantry, 23rd Regiment, Company K and take notes. Other notes taken from on-line archives/researchers. Later, copies of Franz Deppe's pension papers were acquired. See also *Bibliography*.

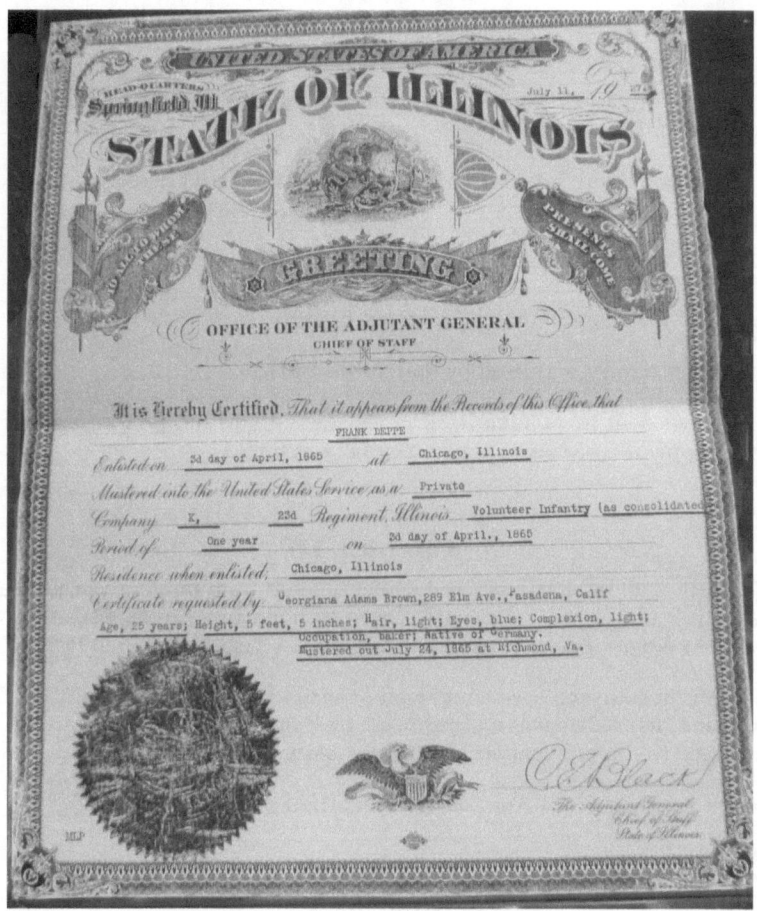

The exact amount of the bounty received by Franz Deppe is unknown. Offers of $300 and $400 can be found in numerous Chicago articles /recordings.

Careful research was conducted to follow Company K (a new company formed in 1865, as they traveled from place to place just days after the end of the war. While much of this journey is imagined, it is all built around actual historic facts and stories. Dates and descriptions are all from written documents, including Deppe's enlistment paper.

Unknown—in which camp the men trained in April 1865. The author visited Richmond, Virginia twice.

Description of uniform—http://www.visit-gettysburg.com/civil-war-union-uniforms.html

Food in the Civil War—http://www.pbs.org/food/the-history-kitchen/civil-war-cooking-what-the-union-soldiers-ate/

African-Americans with jewels and fine furniture—taken from first-hand accounts of those in Richmond—source uncertain.

Description of store taken from history book and eye witnesses.

Chapter 9

Date of Franz Deppe's return—pension papers.

Joseph's marriage—guessed by daughter's birth.

Prüm news sent by Monika Rolef in Germany and *Chicago City Directory* of 1865 supply the names of family members in town.

Chapter 10

Information on family members has been taken from public records/Standesamt in Prüm. Jerry Canine, great grandson of Anna Kirchstein, and Dorothy Stein Wright, spoke of Anna coming from a wealthy home in Prüm.

Anna Maria Ganser's early childhood—German Article: "Wie konnt ich Dein vergessen, Ich weiss, was Du mir bist!" by Edmund Dansen. The article was published in the publication, *Eifelvereinsblatt*, around 1900.

Poem—*Herzenstone* by Anna Kirchstein, 1910

Chapter 11

This chapter is based on the newly discovered case: Criminal Procedure Against Dr. S. Grün and 22 Companion s for High Treason resp. Looting the Armory at Prüm. This book maybe found online and downloaded, however, it is only in available in German.

https://de.wikipedia.org/wiki/Victor_Schily; further information found online, mainly German websites.

Ganser family—from Prüm vital records.

Death Certificate for Heinrich Ganser was procured from Landeshauptarchiv Koblenz/Landesarchivverwaltung Rheinland-Pfalz

Chapter 12

Andrew Reutlinger's—Chicago City Directories/post fire Directory, Gerald Canine's family history records.

The Ganser/Koch family history trip information comes from Ancestry.com.

Franz and Catharina's opinions, actions and family living is only guessed at from the way they led their lives and the ensuing years.

Kath Koch—ship information from Ancestry.com. Most exchange rates from www.measuringworth.com

Chapter 13

The story of the Great Chicago Fire has been taken from numerous books and visits to the Chicago Historical Society's exhibits.

The story of Anna Reutlinger came from her great grandson, Gerry Canine, a story passed down through the years. Numerous eye-witness accounts have been used to make the situation real. Joseph and Lena Deppe's whereabouts uncertain. Franz and Catharina Deppe's story—passed down by Rose and Dorothy Stein.

120- note quote

Chapter 14

Bakery site—*Chicago City Directory*/Census. Property records were found with the help of Memory Trail Research, Inc.

Birth of children—St. Michael's baptism records along with Cook County Death records and grave records.

Thomas Wright, who worked at the Deppe Bakery in the 1950s, revealed at that time some of the work done in baking bread. Several visits to the area filled in on streets and descriptions.

The Deppe farm in Hobart, Indiana has always been known by the author. Rose Stein Ubil and Dorothy Stein Wright often spoke of it. Copies of the deeds were obtained from the owner, Ray Hanley, in 1986. What is still uncertain is whether Joseph Deppe bought his own farm, or farmed a portion or all of his brother's property. Joseph's descendant never clarified this matter either.

Sophia Deppe: information found in the Federal Census, City Directory and ship records.

The story of Joseph Deppe's death was passed down from all the relatives. No death certificate seems to exist and no news article for this sad event has been found. Although his grave says he died in 1880, he was alive for a visit from the Census Taker. U.S. Census and visit to Crown Pointe also helped.

Chapter 15

Records of the Bakery were verified, not only by sale of property, which shows a later date, but buy a news article showing when the building was built (Chicago Tribune, April 3, 1881, p. 17), as well as the date on the building itself. City Directories also reveal that the family was living there in the early 1880s.

Stories by the author's great aunt Dorothy Wright, as well as several visits in the 1980s, along with an interior tour given by Owen Deutsch, then the owner, revealed how lovely and upscale the front apartment was. Later, the interior was reconfigured and cut up into small rooms. At present, the upstairs of the building has been completely gutted and made into million dollar condos.

Loan on Indiana Property—Lake County, Indiana Deed

Andrew Reutlinger's probate revealed that he owned his house on Sedgwick which appears in City Directory.

"Tillie" & Kate's poem—Gerry and Caroline Canine archive

Math Evert—U.S. Census Records and City Directory

John Ganser children—Ancestry.com

Anna Strasser and Family—Dorothy Stein Wright

Chapter 16

The story of Kate Deppe in school comes from her daughter, Isabel Lockwood Ochsner. The story of Franz Deppe's dislike of the Catholic Church and his history came from Dorothy Stein Wright (and possibly my mother, Marian Ubil, as well, who would have gotten it from her mother, Rose Stein, the daughter of Sophie Deppe Stein).

Some of the fine library of books of Franz Deppe were witnessed by the author. They contained Franz Deppe's signature and had been handed down from his daughter, Sophie, to his granddaughter, Dorothy Stein Wright, who grew up with a great love for books. Some of the books are those which were in the home of the Steins and Deppes. Photographed and shown here.

The stories of Dorothy Stein Wright and Kay Halstead Foxcroft supply the information for these pages, including pictures and items seen in their homes which came from the Deppes.

Extensive notes were taken in the 1980s when interviewing these relatives as to the character and history of the children of Franz and Catharina Deppe.

Chapter 17

The descendants of Josephine Reissig, including Josephine Gourley and Hoard Bracken supplied a great deal of information on Joseph and Lena Deppe's family when interviewed in the 1980s. Public records such as the census back up this information. Death records on Ancestry.com filled in cause of death.

According to family memories, Franz Deppe bought the farm to help support his brother's family. Later these descendants would buy their own land in the area of Hobart.

Photos, family stories from Dorothy Stein Wright and a news article in the Hobart paper from the 1950s or '60s (since lost) filled out the details.

Chicago probate records and property records are bases for end of chapter.

Chapter 18

The picture shown here supplies the greatest and only proof of the California trip. Dorothy Wright verified it was California. The historical facts have been filled in. Nothing more is known.

World's Columbian Exposition—See bibliography and the Wikipedia.

Hull House—hppts://en,wikipedia.org/wiki/Hull_House

Fullerton Avenue property—family stories from the Kirchstein/Miller/Canine archives are the basis of this story. Extensive property and history research were needed to fill in the dates and verify it. Katharina Deppe owned one lot in 1880s. When she sold it is unknown. The Canine family believed that Anna Kirchstein owned four lots in all.

Illinois *Staats-Zeitung*—https://en.wikipedia.org/wiki/_Sillinois_Staats -Zeitung

German Society Calendar—Gerry and Carolyn Canine

153- It should be noted that at some point, Carl Deppe changed his name to Charles.

Fullerton Avenue Presbyterian Church archives and anniversary books supplied the story of the church and the building of the neighborhood.

Kay Foxcroft first revealed to the author and her mother, Marian Prefontaine, that Sophie Deppe was married before her marriage to Victor Stein, that the man worked for Franz Deppe and that he was a gambler. Research revealed that this man was Charles Wurster. The date of their divorce is unknown but apparently they were not married long at all.

In the 1980, owner at the time, Owen Deutsch stated that it had been said the bakery building was haunted. woman.

Information from *Chicago Tribune,* 9/19/1891

Information on Ozro Lockwood came from the archives of Betsy Moen, Lockwood's granddaughter, and were verified by other persons, including Kathryn Lockwood Stitt, also a granddaughter.

Chapter 19

The trip to Prüm was first discovered in the archive of Dorothy Stein Wright in the form of a letter in German from Louise Deppe to her parents in Chicago. Ship records confirm Sophie and Louise traveled together. A family member (possibly Kay Foxcroft) later stated that Sophie's father sent her there because of her inability to recover from the failure of her marriage.

Christine Bierfert, niece of Mrs. Edmund Deppe, provided the photo of Edmund. Kathryn Foxcroft told the story of Louise and Sophie meeting the wealthy family from Philadelphia and Victor Stein meeting the ship. Louise wondered what might have happened had he not been there and they went to Philadelphia instead. Name of family not discovered.

Sophie's letter from Prüm was shared with the author in 1985 by Dorothy Stein Wright. She and her mother kept many old records and itmes, including a long golden blonde tail of hair, which Sophie had cut off in her youth. These items have since diappeared and it is doubtful the letters still exist and it is doubtful they exist. Luckily, the writer took some notes at the time. Half of the letter was written in German, the other half in English.

Chapter 20

Sophie not fond of Stein family—revealed by relative.

Victor Stein—stories of his youth told by Dorothy Stein Wright.

Jews—https://en.wikipedia.org/wiki/History_of_the_Jews_in_Vienna

Stories of Victor Stein and Julia Sondek: Dorothy Stein Wright

Stories of Ludwig Stein: Rose Stein Ubil and Marian Ubil Prefontaine

The wedding shawl: Louise Wright Ghidossi

Records of the Steins in Vienna: From Vienna, Austria

E. H. Stein—first discovered in Rose Hill plot, then *Chicago City Directory*. Further research leads to the question—how are they related. Possibly, he was Ludwig's father. More likely, he was an uncle.

Naming sons after Victor Hugo—Dorothy Stein Wright.

Records of the Steins aboard ship from Hamburg to New York City—Ancestry.com

*It is not known how religious the Stein family was.

Chicago City records show place of business for Steins. W.M. Hoyt was known by the Stein family.

Story of Etta's doll—told to the author by Etta (then Edith Schweitzer) 1962-63.

Hoyt—http://www.encyclopedia.chicagohistory.org/pages/2709.html

Chapter 21

Story of Bertha revealed to the author by Dorothy Stein Wright in 1986. Through Bertha's death certificate, the rest was discovered. The fact that Mary Lincoln had once stayed there, meant information on the history was better preserved. Visits to Bellevue and Batavia Historical Society followed.

Contacting authors and other records, some private, revealed the details over time. The conclusions are the author's. Some writing was done on the grounds of the old Bellevue site and immediately after a visit to the inside.

Julie and the girls in Vienna at the time was revealed when searching under travel on Ancestry.com .

Chapter 22

John Rusk's name appears on the marriage license of the Steins. Research on who he was revealed a totally surprising story. His story is detailed in *The Chicago Tribune* articles which reveal his history the year prior to Sophie and Victor's marriage. http://archives.chicagotribune.com/1896/04/23/page/3/article/more-trouble-for-rusk

John Ganser's told by his descendants, including LeRoy Schamper and Norm & Earl Ganser. Cook County Death Certificate revealed the details.

Franz Deppe health—Civil War Pension Papers

The Biewers and the Beckers spoken of by Dorothy Stein Wright, though she was uncertain of the relation. Mrs. Becker's canaries—notes from Dorothy Stein Wright interview, 1985. Craig Pfannkuche of Memory Trail Research

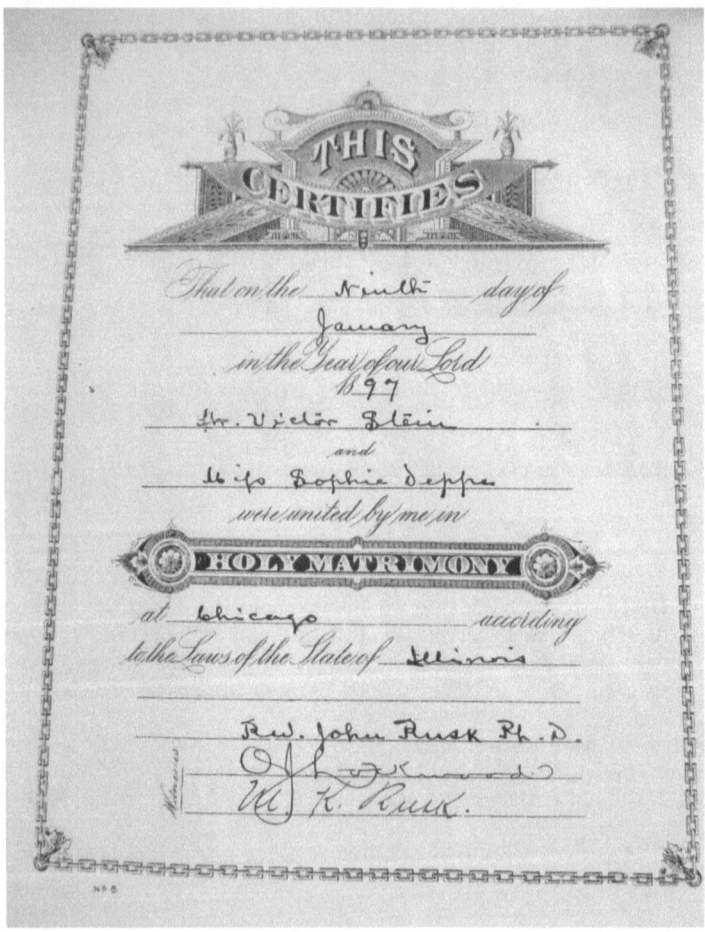

found that Nicholas Becker contested ownership of a property on Tell Court (now Willow) in 1912. The case could not be found.

Miller Drug Store—story told by Gerry Canine, further information from Canine archive. Photos contributed my Mrs. Caroline Canine.

Memories of Fullerton Avenue—red roses—taken from a tape recorded interview of Ottie Miller Canine.

Chapter 23

Oscar Stein—The creation of this chapter began with information given by Dorothy Stein Wright that there was another Stein child named Oscar who killed himself. His death certificate verified and gave further information.

The article found in March 2, 1899 *Chicago Daily Sun* revealed more. In the 1980s, the author visited the area where he was shot. The rest is only a guess, including Lillian Burkhardt, found in the 1900 Federal Census.

The story of Sousa was told numerous times by Edith Stein Schweitzer to our family. The Souza organization verified the dates John Philip Sousa and his band visited Chicago.

Hugo and Mary—Ancestry.com

Chapter 24

Louise & Albert Halstead—Kathryn Halstead Foxcroft answered the author's questions regarding her family history in the 1980s and 90s. Her cousin, Dorothy Stein Wright, also knew of these events, but Kay was a person with a sharp detail for memory, her own and others.

Further information was found in the Chicago City Directories and the Federal Census.

Thanks to invitation of the residents in Fullerton Parkway in the 1980s, the author had tea and pastry in the front parlor and was able to visit and see the interior of the home, which was still pretty much the way it looked when the Steins lived there. She also saw the room where Dorothy Stein Wright was born, with original stained glass windows intact. Dorothy had many stories regarding this home, as well as Anna Kirchstein, whom she greatly loved and admired.

Ozro Lockwood and the bakery comes from family records, the City Directory and the Federal Census.

Rose and Dorothy Stein knew the Essens quite well. The author visited their home in the 1980s, and met Mamie in California. Further information was gathered from the city directories and census. Christian von Essen's death certificate revealed the facts behind the story.

Chapter 25

The story of Edward S. Dreyer was first made known to the author by Kay Foxcroft. Francis Deppe IV had documentation in a family scrapbook, with his pictures. Further information is detailed in the *Chicago Tribune* papers from 1894–1908 or thereabouts.

The letter from Frank and Florence to their parents was copied from the Francis Deppe IV archives in the 1990s or 2003.

Rose and Dorothy Stein contributed the balance of the story about the bakery, Louise and Kay. The notes from Kay Foxcroft's interview contributed the balance.

Chapter 26

Iroquois Fire—Chicago History, Inferno at the Iroquois, by Anthony P. Hatch: Fall 2003, Volume XXXII, Number 2, p. 4.

The main portion of this chapter comes from the memories of Rose Stein Ubil and Dorothy Stein Wright, along with family items the author grew up with.

Stories of the Steins—Dorothy Stein Wright

Charlotte Lockwood Williams' letters are an invaluable source of information about the bakery. These were given to the author by Kathryn Stitt. On a further search, it seemed that the letter had been copied and each family member, Rose, Dorothy and Kay all had copies.

Ludwig Stein and Kankakee—stories of Ludwig came from the author's mother, Marian Prefontaine, handed down to her by her mother Rose Stein Ubil and Dorothy Wright. Ludwig's death certificate verified his problem. Further information has been obtained online: http://darkspire.org/asylums/Kankakee_il/

Descriptions of summer in Hobart: Rose Stein Ubil, Dorothy Stein Wright, along with a Hobart newspaper article from the 1960s which detailed life in the big farmhouse on Liverpool Road.

Franz Deppe's health—Ozro Lockwood and others who stated in the mid-1890s how he had gone downhill.

Chapter 27

The story of Franz Deppe's demise was passed down by all family members, in particular, Dorothy Stein Wright. They must have been deeply impressed by it. Although the paper states he died at home, families state he walked to Kate Lockwood's home—as the story tells.

There appear to be no existing records for Ludwig Stein at Kankakee. Information taken from his death certificate.

Bibliography

1679–1979 300 Jahre Pfarrkirche Niederprüm, Herausgegeben von der Pfarrgemeinde, 1979

Basilika St. Salvatore Prüm/Eifel, Verkag Scgbekk Steuberm 1985

Beleaguered City Richmond (The), Alfred & Bill Hoyt, Greenwood Press, 1946

Boys' War—Confederate and Union Soldiers Talk About the Civil War [The], Jim Murphy, Clarion Books, 1990

Challenging Chicago—Coping with Everyday Life. 1837–1920, Perry R. Duis, University of Illinois Press, 1998

Chicago: An Intimate Portrait of People, Pleasures, and Power, 1860–1919, Stephen Longstreet, David McKay Company, Inc., 1973

Chicago History 1972–1973, Vol. II Series, Chicago Historical Society

Chicago World's Fair of 1893 [The], Stanley Appelbaum, Dover Publications, Inc, 1980

Chicago Yesterday, Gingko Press, 1998

Chicago's Famous Buildings, Arthur Siegel, Editor, The University of Chicago Press, 1965

Chicago's Opulant Age 1870s–1940s In Vintage Postcards, Jim Edwards, Arcadia, 2001

City Comes of Age, Chicago in the 1890s [A], by Susan E. Hirsch and Robert I. Goler, Chicago Historical Society, 1990

City of the Century, The Epic of Chicago and The Making of America, Donald L. Miller, Touchstone—Simon & Schuster, 1996

Civil War Handbook, William H. Price, L. B. Prince Company, Inc. 1961

Deppe and Ganser Family 1790–1987 [The], Michelle Russell, 1987

Everyday Life in the 1800s, Marc McCutcheon, Writer's Digest Books, 1993

Experiment in Rebellion, Clifford Dowdey, Books for Libraries Press, NY, 1946, 1970

Gardner's Photographic Sketch Book of the Civil War, Alexander Gardner, Dover Publications, Inc., 1959

George Earle and Family of Hobart, Indiana, Hobart, Dorothy Dunning Ballantyne, Historical Society, 1972

German American Family Album [The], Dorothy and Thomas Hoobler, Oxford University Press, 1996

Germans to America, Vol. 12, Editors: Ira A. Glazier, P. William Filby

Germans of Chicago [The], Rudolf A. Hofmeister, Stipes Publishing Company, 1976

German Workers in Chicago, edited Hartmut Keil and John B. Jentz, University of Illinois Press, 1988

Good Old Days (The), *They Were Terrible*, Otto L. Bettmann, Random House, NY 1874

Great Chicago Fire [The], Robert Cromie, Rutledge Hill Press, 1958, 1994

Herzenstone, Anna Kirchstein, 1910

Historical Sketch of Graceland Cemetery Chicago, Graceland Cemetery Company, 1980s

History of Chicago, Alfred Theodore Andreas, Vol. 2, Arno

History of Germany 1780–1918, David Blackbourn, Blackwell Publishing, 1997

I Am a Union Soldier, Diana H. Loski, Thomas Publications, 1997

Insanity File, The case of Mary Todd Lincoln [The], Mark E. Neely, Jr. and R. Gerald McMurtry, Southern Illinois Press, 1986

Jewish American Family Album [The], Dorothy and Thomas Hoobler, Oxford University Press, 1995

Lieder aus Deutschlands erhebender Zeit, Anna Kirchstein, 1915

Lincoln Park Chicago—Images of America, Melanie Ann Apel in Association with the Chicago Historical Society, Arcadia Publishing, 2002

Medieval and Early Modern Times—The Age of Justinian to the Eighteenth Century, Carlton J.H. Hayes and Frederick F. Clark, The MacMillan Company, 1966

Manners and Morals of Long Ago, John E. Duncan, Chandler Press, 1993

Mrs. O'Leary's Comet! Cosmic Causes of the Great Chicago Fire, Mel Waskin, Academy Chicago Publishers, 1985

Napoleon, Emil Ludwig, Boni & Liveright, 1926

Napoleon A Biography, Frank McLynn, Arcade Publishing 1997

Napoleon The Last Phase, Lord Rosebery, Harper and Brothers, 1900

Old Town Triangle District, Commission on Chicago Historical and Architectural Landmarks, 1979

Our Old Town: The History of a Neighborhood, Shirley Baugher, Old Town Triangle Association, 2001& Company, Inc., 1967

Pictorial History of the Civil War Years, Paul M. Angle, Doubleday

Prümer Impressionen, Herausgegenben vom Eifelverein, 1972

Wanderung in die Vergangenheit, Prümer Landbote Zeitschrift des Geschichtsverein "Prümer Land" 28/91, AG Brauchtum / Denkmalpflege, 1987

Richmond During the War, Sallie B. Putnam, 1983

Short History of Chicago [A], Robert Cromie, Lexicos, 1984

Story of Chicago (The), Kirkland

Wanderung in die Vergangenheit 1, Georg Jakob Meyer; Rolf Dettmann, Matthias Weber, Gurgand Barret, 1985

Photo Credits

Batavia Historical Society, 235

Christine Bierfert, 201

Canine Family Collection: 104, 107 bottom, 131, 132, 134, 182, 183, 184, 185, 251, 255, 256, 257

Francis Deppe IV Collection: 278, 280

Louise Wright Ghidossi Collection: 79, 142, 149 (Sophie)

Diane Gonzalez: 186

Betsy Williams Moen Collection: 195

Newberry Library, 223

Kathryn Ringrose Collection: 87, 149 (Louise), 158, 204, 215, 284

Michelle Russell: 7-8, 10, 11, 16, 18, 23, 25, 36, 62, 71, 84, 91, 119, 121-122-123, 138, 146-147, 162, 163, 165, 170, 171-172, 178, 187, 212, 221, 227-228, 233-234, 241, 254, 260, 269, 273, 292, 298-299

Kathryn Lockwood Stitt Collection: 294, 295

Rose Stein Ubil Collection: 174, 198, 242, 246, 250, 252, 262, 264, 265, 272, 295

Dorothy Stein Wright Collection: 107 top, 129, 135, 149 (Frank, Jr.), 154, 161, 163, 166, 167, 189, 190, 203, 208, 209, 249, 259, 274, 292

Unknown: 27, 30, 93, 109, 190, 217, 192

Index

A

Aagaard, Frederik, 68
Aachen, 14
Abbey (Prüm), 9–10, 12–16, 23, 41
Abbot Assuerus, 12
Abbot Gerhard, 14
A.B. Chase baby grand, 288
A. Biewer & Sons, 249
Abraham Lincoln School, 288
Addams, Jane, 179
Adventures of Huckleberry Finn (The), 153
A.E. Robinson Company, 222
Aiken, Loton L., 68
Alexian Bros. Hospital, 245
Ameis, Johann Peter, 17, 89
Ameis, Maria Katharina, 86–87, 89 (photo)
Anton, Bernard, 97
Antwerp, 45–46, 103, 108, 135, 202, 206
Appomattox Courthouse, 70
Arthur, Chester A., 152
Austria, 15, 165, 210–211

B

Bach, Benedict, 96
Baird, Lyman 180
Baltimore, 69
Batavia, 229–235, 237
Batavia Historical Society Museum, 231, 235, 310
Baudelaire, Charles, 162
Beames, J., 78
Beck, Mary A. (Stein), 263
Becker, Anna, 251, 268, 311
Becker, Anthony (Tony), 251
Becker, Charles, 251, 268
Becker, John, 251
Becker, Nicholas, 194, 251, 257, 268, 309
Becker, Stephan, 98
Bellevue Place, 228–239
Bergweiler, 27, 32–33
Bertrada of Laon, 9–11
Bertrada of Prum, 9
Bevans, Mr., 222
Bierer, E.H., Lt., 74
Biewer, Anna (*see* Simon)
Biewer, Appoliner, 253, 249
Biewer, August, 144
Biewer, Frank, 249
Biewer, John, 249
Biewer, William, 249
Bilgman, Charlotte, 281
Billy the Kid, 153
Blessed Mother (Mary), 27, 91, 159, 162
Bloch, Otto, 266
Blou, Fred M., 279
Boheme, 15, 210–211, 213
Bonaparte, Napoleon, 17–24, 86, 94
Booth, John Wilkes, 74
Bowling Encyclopedia (*see* Western Bowlers' Journal)
Briss, Matthias, 97
Bronte Sisters, 162
Brooklyn Bridge, 153
Browning, Elizabeth Barrett, 163
Burkhardt, Lillian, 259
Burns, Robbie, 187

C

California, 174–178, 191
Camp Douglas, 63, 66–67
Camp Fry, 63–64, 66–68
Carolingian Dynasty, 12
Catholic Church, 14–15. 23–24, 112, 159–160, 162, 243
Chandler, Bettie, 266
Charibert (Count of Laon), 9
Charlemagne, 10–12, 13–14
Chemung, 68
Chicago Board of Trade, 58
Chicago, Burlington & Quincy Railroad, 232
Chicago Business Directory, 153
Chicago City Directory, 80, 106, 126, 132, 151, 155, 199, 214, 221, 245, 249, 259, 305–307, 309, 312
Chicago City Hall, 119, 126
Chicago Daily Sun, 260, 311
Chicago Fire (Great), 115–124, 129
Chicago River, 51. 58. 63, 113, 116–118, 214, 225; Chicago skyscrapers, 178
Chicago Syndicate, 277
Chicago Times (The), 192
Chicago Tribune (The), 145, 173, 186–187, 244, 271, 279, 281–282
Chicago West Park Commissioners, 279
Christian, 10–11, 211, 245
Christian Commission and Relief Association, 78
Christianson, Lars P., Sgt., 68
City of Limerick (The), 108
City Point, 73
City Press Association, 271
Civil War (the), 46, 60, 62–78, 153, 194–195, 223, 247
Clemens, Hubert, 97
Clemens, Jacob, 98
Cleveland, Grover, 277
Clotilde, 10
Clovis, 10
Collman, William Joseph, 97
Columbus, 243
Columbus, Christopher, 179–180
Commercial Bowling Club, 258
Company K, 66–68, 70, 72–75, 78, 194, 304–305
Confederates, 63, 69–71, 73, 76
Congress of Rhineland, 95
Cook County Jail, 279
Cook County Records, 103, 126–127, 219, 246
Cophanouir, John A., 266
Coyle, Dr. 181, 243
Crosby Opera House, 107–108, 119
Crown Point, 136–138, 309

D

Dacre. Harry, 200
Daisy Bell, 200
Daniel, Dr. Frederick H., 231, 233–235 (photo), 236–238, 240
Darimont, Anna Margaretha, 21
Darimont, Caspar, 20, 38
Darimont, Claudia, 21
Darimont, Johannes, 21
Darimont, Katharina, 38–41, 135
Darimont, Michel, 17
Darimont, Susanna, 21
Daubach, John, 98
Delahane, Adolph, 96
De Leale, Officer, 186
Department of the Interior, 247
Deppe Bakery (Chicago), 55, 57 65, 68, 72, 80–81, 103, 105–106, 111–113, 121–122, 125–127, 129, 136, 141–151, 164, 178, 185– 189, 194–196, 245, 249– 251, 266, 268–269, 2671, 284, 289–290, 301
Deppe Bakery (Prüm), 39, 41, 43, 45, 60, 201–203 (photos)
Deppe, Anna, 158 (photo), 161, 166–167, 173, 174 (Anna), 176–177 (photo), 245, 251, 266, 269–271, 283–284, 296
Deppe, Anna Marie (Germany), 38
Deppe, Barbara, 134
Deppe, Carl (son or Rudolf), 30–32, 40
Deppe, Carl (Chicago, unknown), 135–136, 153, 156
Deppe, Carl (son of Carl unknown), 135
Deppe, Carl (son of Friedrich), 38–41, 43–44, 58, 80, 111, 135, 152
Deppe, Catharina (*see* Ganser)
Catharina (wife of Carl – *see* Stich)
Deppe, Catharina Christina, 39–40, 45
Deppe, Christina (daughter of Edmund), 203, 205
Deppe, Edmund (Friedrich Edmund), 39–40, 43, 45, 200, 201 (photo), 202–203, 206

Deppe, Elise (daughter of Carl), 135
Deppe, Florence (see Dreyer)
Deppe, Francis, III, 279, 280, 286, 296
Deppe, Frank, Jr., 142 147, 149 (photo), 158, 160–161, 167 (photo), 172–174 (photo), 176–177, 251, 257, 266, 271, 277, 280–283, 296, 299
Deppe, Frank William (son of Joseph), 137, 169–170, 293
Deppe, Franz (Frank, Francis), 130, 137, 151, 153, 155–156, 164, 171, 196–197, 200, 202, 243, 246, 251, 266, 269, 271, 274, 276–277, 280–283, 288, 290, 295–296; childhood, 37–41, 91, 93; coming to America, 43–47; coming to Chicago, 52–60; Civil War, 63–78, building the bakery, 79 (photo), 80–81, 147–152, 253, 257–258 ; marriage, 82, 103, 105–106, 111–112; Chicago Fire, 115–116, 119–124; attitude to Catholic Church, 41, 112, 159–162, 307; property, 125–127, 129, 135–136, 144–145, 147–149, 173, 188, 249; home description, 147–148, 162–163; father's death, 133; brother's death, 140, 152, sister's death, 156; California trip, 175–178; health,194–195, 247–249, 270; death, 297–298
Deppe, Friedrich Carl, 27–28, 31–34, 36–41, 45, 59, 80, 133
Friedrich (son of Edmund), 205
Deppe, Frederick (son of unknown Carl), 135
Deppe, George, 122, 126
Deppe, Hermann, 161
Deppe, Johann (son of Carl), 135
Deppe, Joseph, 37–41, 43–47, 51–52, 56–60, 63–65, 79, 81, 108, 111, 118, 122, 125–127, 133, 135–140, 152, 169, 305
Deppe, Josephine, 108, 122, 137, 169–170, 298
Deppe, Katherine (Kate Lockwood), 108, 112, 120, 125, 147, 150, 159–160, 165, 173, 184, 193, 195 (photo), 196, 205, 243, 250–251, 266, 269, 283, 289, 297–298
Deppe, Katharina (Kitty), 136–137, 139, 169–170, 293

Deppe, Katharina Christina, 39–40, 45
Deppe, Lena (see Helena Weckman)
Deppe, Lena (daughter of Carl), 135
Deppe, Louise (daughter of Carl), 135
Deppe, Louise (Maria Louise, "Lou" Halstead), 133–134, 147, 149 & 158 (photos), 163, 165, 167 (photo), 168, 173, 193, 195, 200, 202, 204 (photo), 205–207, 251, 269–272, 274–275, 277, 280, 283–284, 288–289, 296
Louise (Lüschen), 203, 205
Deppe, Maria, 126, 133–134
Deppe, Moritz, 39–40, 45, 59, 80,–81, 135, 152
Deppe, Peter, 201 (photo), 203, 205
Deppe, Rudolph, 28, 40
Deppe, Sophia, 37–40, 45, 59, 124, 135 (photo), 136, 153, 155–156, 307
Deppe, Sophie, 124, 135, 147, 149 (photo), 160, 163–167, 173, 185, 188, 198 (photo), 199–201, 204, 206–207, 209, 242 (photo), 243, 245, 250–251, 265–266, 268, 272–275, 282–284, 287–289, 295–296, 299
Deppe, Susanna, 203, 205
Deuster, Heinrich Wilhelm, 97
Deutschegesellschaft von Chicago, 183
Dickens, Charles, 162
Diedenhofen, Gotthard, 97
Dieppe, 28
Dillenburg, John, 97
Dodds, Ozro John, 195
Dobrulska, Catharine, 266
Dorsey, Thomas, Pvt., 69
Dreyer, Augusta, 280–281
Dreyer, Charlotte, 281
Dreyer, Edward, Jr., 281
Dreyer, Edward S., 277–278 (photo), 279–282, 312
Dreyer, Florence (Deppe), 277, 279–281 (photo), 282, 288

E

Earle, George, 129
Eaton, 201
Eifel (The), 14, 17, 24, 32, 41, 55, 80, 90, 183
Eliel & Co., 51

Eliel, Gustav, 51
Eliel, Louis, 51
Emergency Cottage Relief Fund, 129–130
Engels, Friedrich, 99
England, 108
Erie Canal, 127
Esch, 33
E. S. Dreyer & Co., 277–278, 282
Essen, Annie (*see* Ganser)
Essen, Baby, 193
Essen (von), Christian, 155, 193, 253–254
Essen, Frederick (Freddie), 253
Essen, Katherine (Kate), 193, 253
Essen, Louise (Lulu), 193, 253
Essen, Maude, 253
Essen, May (Mamie), 193, 253, 312
Evanston, 279
Europe, 10–11, 31, 43–44, 56, 94, 156, 175, 179, 301
Evert, Anna Katharina, 193
Evert, Barbara (see Ganser)
Evert. Frank John, 193
Evert, Margaretha, 193
Evert, Martha, 193
Evert, J. Mathias (Math), 151–152, 248

F

F. Deppe Company, 144–145, 148, 219, 251, 257, 267 (photo), 289, 299
Federal Penitentiary at Joliet, 281–282
Fell, Marie, 265
Feverscheill, 15
Field, Marshall, 163, 179
Foehr, Matthias, 98
Folz, Frank, 266
Ford's Theatre, 73
Forster, Anton, 96
Fort Dearborn Canned Goods, 224
Foxcroft, Kay (*see* Katharina Halstead)
France, 17, 19, 22–24, 28–29, 31, 38, 94, 99, 153, 175, 232
Franklin School, 220
Franz, Magdalen, 101
Frauen-Zeitung, 273
French Revolution, 17, 31
French Troops, 17, 22–23, 31, 94
Fullerton Avenue Presbyterian Church, 180–181, 196, 243–244

G

Galena & Chicago Union, 58
Ganser, Anna Marie, 41, 81–82, 85, 87–92, 100, 102–103, 106–107 (photo), 108, 113, 116–118,129–133, 150, 154, 161, 180, 183–184, 189–191, 193, 251, 265, 271, 273, 288, 305–306, 310, 311
Ganser, Annie (Maria Anna Essen), 91–92, 101, 110, 132, 143, 154 (photo), 155, 171 193, 253–254, 275
Ganser Bakery, 249, 251
Ganser, Barbara (1st Barbara), 87–91
Ganser, Barbara (Evert), 91, 101, 111, 132, 134, 143, 151, 193
Ganser, Bernard, 154
Ganser, Carrie Laura, 245
Ganser, Catharina (Deppe), 41, 81–82, 85, 89—91, 100, 103–104 (photo), 105–106, 108, 111–112, 115, 119–120, 122, 124,–126, 129–130, 133–135, 140–143, 148, 159–161 (photo), 162, 164–166, 172–173, 176, 180, 191, 196–197, 202, 243, 249–251, 266, 269, 271, 280, 286, 289, 298
Ganser, Catherine Therese (Kate), 193, 245, 293
Ganser, Elizabeth (Lizzie) (see Eliesabeta Wolf)
Ganser, Eleanore, 154
Ganser, Heinrich, 24, 41, 85–89, 92, 94, 99–103, 110
Ganser, Henry, 154
Ganser, Gerard (Jerry), 155, 159, 245, 247
Ganser, Gerhard (John), 88–89, 100, 111, 132, 143, 154–155, 193, 245–247, 254
Ganser, Joannes, 89, 101, 110–111
Ganser, Johann Peter, 87–89, 9, 100–101
Ganser, Julia Anna, 155, 245
Ganser, Katharina (*see* Koch)
Ganser, Sherbart, 154
Garfield, James (President), 138, 152
Gebaur Hotel, 20, 22–23
Germania Club, 106, 282
Germany, 15, 31, 34, 45, 52, 57, 68, 81, 94–95, 102–103, 106, 110, 132–133, 135, 144, 146, 155, 164, 200, 202, 216, 266, 269, 273, 277

Gobel, Andreas, 97
Goethe, 162
Goldenstern Hotel, 20
Graceland Cemetery, 132, 154, 190, 193, 288
Gradel, Karolina Sophia, 40
Graf, Heinrich, 25
Grant, Ulysses S., 70, 153, 277
Greece, 173, 191
Green, Peter N., 68
Greyhounds, 214, 290
Grün, Carl, Dr., 93, 96, 98, 113
Guiteau, Charles, 152

H

Hadrian (Pope): 11
Hall, Christopher, 97
Halstead, Albert, 270-272, 274, 280, 283-284
Halstead, Emma, 270
Halstead, James, 270, 284
Halstead, Katharina (Kay Foxcroft), 272, 274, 280, 283-285, 288-290, 296
Halstead, Louise (see Deppe)
Hamburg, 132, 216, 232
Hamann, Peter, 97
Hammond, William A., 279
Hancock, Scott, 138
Harrison, Carter H. (Mayor), 179-180, 192
Haviland, William H., Sgt, 68
Heinemann, Anna (see Deppe)
Heinemann, Edwin, 296, 283
Heinemann, Julius, 283
Heintz, Michael, 97
Henry, Peter, 97
Hensch, Hugo, 96
Heribert (see Charibert)
Herzenstone, 197
Hiller, George, 128
Hilligonds, Cornelius, 127
Hobart, 128-129, 136, 169-172, 270, 275, 284, 293
Hoffmann, Hubert, 97
Holy Roman Empire, 10-12, 14, 29
Horowitz, 213
Horton, Lt., 78
Hoyt, William M., 222-225, 287-288 (see also W.M. Hoyt & Co.)
Huber, Nick, 266
Huckleberry Finn, 153

Hugo, Victor, 163, 211
Hull House, 189, 289

I

Illinois, 136, 195, 263
Illinois and Michigan Canal, 58
Illinois Eastern Hospital, 291, 298
Illinois Staats-Zeitung, 183, 191, 273
Illinois Volunteer Infantry, 63-64, 67, 69-70, 194
Imandt, Peter, 93, 96, 98-99
Indiana, 111, 122, 126-127, 129, 136, 144-145, 154, 169-172, 266, 275
Intra-State Exposition Committee, 179
Iroquois Theatre Fire, 287
Israelite Community, 213
Italy, 11, 28, 175

J

Jackson, Jacob H., Sgt., 68
James, Jesse, 155
Jesus Christ, 10, 13, 25, 91, 161, 164, 168, 246
Jewish, 201, 212-215, 222-223, 245, 252, 265, 274, 299
Johnson, Benjamin, Sgt., 68
Johnson, C., 78
Johnson, T., 78
Joliet (see Federal Peniteniary)

K

Kankakee State Hospital, 291-292
Kas, Franz Jacob, 97, 99
Kauffman, Maria Magdalena (Helena), 33-34, 40
Keafitz, Mr., 185
Keller, Anna Christina, 17, 89
Kelly, Charles, Sgt., 69
Kesker, Charles, 144
Kiesweiler, 32
Kinzer, C. 173
Kirschstein, Anna Marie (see Ganser)
Kirschstein, Hermann, 132 (photo)-133, 150, 161, 183, 189-191, 271
Kishner, F., 78
Klein, Andreas, 96
Knesly, Jacob, 266
Koch, Georg Anton, 21, 85-87, 89, 101

Koch, Johann Moritz, 17, 86, 89
Koch, Maria Katharina (Ganser), 85–89, 91, 100–101, 103, 108, 110–111, 132, 193, 275–276
Krieschel, Jacob, 98

L

Lacquinot, Martin, 96
Lacquinot, Nicolas, 96
Lake Michigan, 44, 53, 58–59, 80, 116, 279, 281
Lake View, 180, 193, 253, 258, 281
Lee, Robert E., General, 70
Lee, Robert E. (Mrs.), 69
Lehmann's Home Advertisement, 213
Les Miserables, 211
Letterman, Carrie, 149
Letterman, George, 149
Letterman, Louis, 148
Lieder, 191
Lincoln, Abraham (President), 63–64, 69–70, 73–74, 77–78, 152, 225, 231
Lincoln, Mary Todd, 231, 310
Lincoln Park, 180, 196, 209, 257, 274, 281
Lincoln, Robert, 231
Lincoln, Tad, 69
Linster, Dr., 193
Liszt Franz, 277
Lockwood, Charles, 195
Lockwood, Charles, Jr., 195
Lockwood, Charlotte, 283, 289, 293–296
Lockwood, Kate (see Deppe)
Lockwood, Isabella Katherine (Isabel Ochsner), 160, 243, 276, 283, 288–289, 293–296
Lockwood, Isabelle, 195
Lockwood, Mary, 195
Lockwood, Ozro, 195–196, 243, 248, 251, 257, 266, 269, 283, 289, 299
Lockwood, Ozro, Jr., 283, 289, 294–299
Loew, Johann Mathias, 31
Loew, Katharina, 31
Lombardy, 11
Louis Philippe (King), 94
Louis XIV, 29
Lothar I, 13
Ludwig Kirche, 30
Luxemburg, 7, 95, 151

M

McCormick, Cyrus, 58
Maine, 231
Manasseh, 220
Marx, Karl, 99, 102
Masonic (Temple), 178, (symbols), 214
Massachusetts, 231
Mediterranean Sea, 11, 175
Mehs, Gotthard, 98
Meyer, Rosalia (Rosa), 173, 188, 268
Midell, Christian, Sgt., 68
Miller Pharmacy, 255–257
Miller, Albert, 184, 190 (photo), 192, 251, 254, 256–257, 265, 288
Miller, Carl Theodore, 192, 251, (photo), 256–257
Miller, John, 107, 125
Miller, Ottilie, (see Reutlinger)
Miller, Ottilie (Ottie Canine), 190, 251 (photo), 256–257
Missouri, 176, 179
Montgomery, John A., Sgt, 68
Montinger, Frank. 173
Morgan, Daniel, 1st Lt., 68
Moselle River, 9, 102
Moselle Valley, 13, 17
Mr. Bluebeard, 287

N

Napoleon (see Bonaparte)
National Bank of Illinois, 278–279
Native Americans, 176
Nauert, Gotthard, 98
Nels, Joseph, 96
Neumann, Balthasar, 15
Neustadter, John, 97
Neptune (The), 46
New York, 45–47, 58, 110–111, 144, 152–153, 155, 179, 202, 216, 275; harbor, 153, 202, 207, 229
Niederprüm, 15–17, 21, 24, 85
Niles, Peter, 97
Normans, 13
North End League, 258

O

Ochsner, Isabel (see Lockwood)
Ohio, 69, 195, 243
Ogden, William, 58
O'Leary, Mrs., 116

Olson, Arrent, 68
Omaha, 176

P

Palatinate (see Rhineland)
Palatinate-Baden, 93
Palmer House, 119
Papal States: 11
Paris, 12, 17, 94, 99
Pavia, 11
Patterson, Dr. R. J., 230–231
Pendergast, Patrick Eugene, 192
Pennsylvania, 58, 266
Pepin the Hunchback, 13
Pepin the Short (see Pepin III), 9
Pepin III (King of the Franks), 9–13
Petersburg, 73–74, 76
Pfund, August H, 68
Phelps & Hoyt, 269
Philadelphia, 135, 206–207, 309
Piotroske, Emilie, 266
Pinten, Angelica, 15, 89
Pittsburgh (PA), 69
Poland, 94
Pope Hadrian, 11
Pope Leo III, 12
Porta Nigra, 102, 111
Prague, 210, 216
Prince Metternich, 97
Prussia, 31, 46, 94–95, 111, 132
Prüm, 7–31, 33–37, 39–45, 53, 59, 80–81, 84–102, 133, 144, 146, 159, 200–206, 292
Presbyterian Church, 181–182, 196, 225, 243–245, 266, 307
Pueperperal Fever, 193

R

Rascop, Barbara, 17, 86
Rascop, Margaretha, 17
Rascop, Peter, 17
Reaginstein, Mr., 185
Reissen, Bernhard, 97
Reissig, Amelia, 169
Reissig, Edward, 169–170
Reissig, Frances, 169
Reissig, Frank (Francis E), 169–170
Reissig, Frederick, 169
Reissig, Herman, 169
Reissig, Josephine (see Deppe)
Reissig, Laura, 169–170

Reissig, Sena, 170
Reith, Otto, 266
Reuland, Stephan Anton, 17
Reutlinger, Andrew, 106, 107 (photo), 108, 116–117, 129–133, 190
Reutlinger, Anna Marie (see Ganser)
Reutlinger, Ottilie, 108, 113, 116–117, 130, 133, 148, 184–185 (photo), 190, 251, 256, 257, 273, 288
Reutlinger Tavern, 106, 108, 117, 130
Rheinische Friedrich William Universistat, 95
Rhineland, 23, 31, 43, 94
Rhineland Palatinate, 17, 28
Richmond (VA), 62, 69–77, 194
River Prüm, 7
Rochester Park Hospital, 279
Rockefeller, John D., 179
Roe, Gus W., Sgt., 68
Roman: 11–12, 14
Romania, 11
Rondo, John, 186
Rocky Mountains, 174
Rome, 12–13, 102
Rosefeld, Mr., 185
Rosenfeld, F., 78
Rosehill Cemetery, 151–152, 215, 268, 276, 298–299
Rusk, Rev. John, 243–244, 310

S

Saarbrücken, 28–33
Saarland, 28–29, 31
San Francisco, 174
San Salvatore Basilica: 7–8, 10–13, 15–17, 19, 39, 41, 91, 159
Saxons, 11
Schalk, Annie, 185
Schalk, Cynthia, 185
Schalk, James Henry, 185
Schalk, John, 185
Schalk, John, Jr., 185
Schelennert, Michael, 264
Schillo, Peter, 128
Schily, Victor, 93, 95–96, 98, 99
Schlegel, 95
Schlossmacher, Gotthard, 97
Schlossmacher, Liborius, 97
Schneider, Nicholas, 97
Schoden, Anna Marie, 16, 21, 24, 85, 89
Schoden, Caspar, 16

Schoden, Gerard, 15, 24, 89
Schoden, Joseph Peter, 15, 89
Schoden, Magdalene, 15
Scholler, Robert, 170, 293
Schottelndreyer, August, 277
Schottelndreyer, John (see Dreyer)
Schottelndreyer, Lottie, 277
Schottelndreyer, Louise, 277
Schottelndreyer, Ned, 277
Schroder, August, 97
Schroeder, John, 128
Schroeder, Margareth, 128
Schubert, Franz, 165
Schulof, Albert, 258
Scotland, 108
Seibel, Sebastian, 97
Shenandoah Valley, 58
Siebert, Wilhelm Albert, 97
Siegel, Henry, Captain, 68
Simison, Samuel, Lt. Colonel, 63–64, 74
Simon, Anna (Biewer), 249
Simoni, Peter, 268
Simoni, Peter, Jr., 268
Simoni, Catherin, 268
Slaves (former), 69, 71
Slocum, Giles, 2nd Lt, 68
Smith of Glasgow, 108
Sondek, Julia (Stein), 209, 211–213, 215–220, 229, 231–232, 237, 239–240, 245, 251, 263, 290 (photo), 292
Souza Band (The), 261–262
Sousa, John Philip, 261–262, 311
South America, 108
Spain, 11
Spaniards, Augustin, 96
Sprague, Albert, 225–226
Sprague, Warner & Company, 224–226, 259–260
Sprinkling, Peter, 97
Stations of the Cross (Prüm), 25
Statue of Liberty, 153, 231
St. Alphonsus Church, 281
St. Bartholomew Church, 16, 202
St. Boniface Cemetery, 135, 156, 246
St. Henry's Catholic Cemetery, 193
St. James Docks, 69
St. James River, 69
St. Louis, 176
St. Michael's Church, 60, 112, 119–120, 122–124, 126, 133–134, 160–161, 187, 306

St. Michael's School, 159–160
St. Paul's Kirche, 184
Starr, Ellen Gates, 179
Statue of Liberty, 153, 231
Steilen, Peter, 101
Stein, Bertha, 229, 231–239, 299
Stein, Dorothy Ruth (Wright), 135, 160, 239, 249, 268, 272 (photo), 274–275, 288–290, 296
Stein, Emanuel H. (E.H.), 213–214, 237, 239
Stein, Henry, 219, 239
Stein, Hugo, 209, 211, 215–220, 222, 235, 231, 251, 263, 291
Stein Idelle (Etta, Edith), 209, 218–219, 226–227, 229, 231–232, 239, 251, 259, 261, 262 (photo), 263, 291
Stein, Julia (see Sondek)
Stein, Laura, 209, 218–219, 229, 231, 232, 239, 251, 263, 291, 299
Stein, Louis, 214–215, 239
Stein, Ludwig, 208 (photo), 209–211, 213–215, 217–220, 222, 224, 225–227, 229, 231, 327, 239, 240, 245, 251, 261–263, 291–293, 299
Stein, Oscar (Oskar), 213, 215–216, 219. 222, 225, 251, 259–261, 291
Stein, Rose, 250–252 (photo), 265–266, 268, 272, 274, 289–291, 296 (photo), 296
Stein, Victor, 199–200, 205, 207, 209 (photo), 210–220–222, 224–225, 231, 243–245, 250–251, 258, 265–266, 272, 275, 282, 289, 291, 295, 299
Stein, Wright & Company, 214
Stephens, John, Sgt., 68
Stich, Catharina (Deppe), 135, 144
Stich, Peter, 144
Stimpson, Lena, 231, 235
Stitt, Kathryn (see Lockwood), 165, 308, 312
Stoll, Michael, 198
Stowe, Harriet Beecher, 162
Strasser, Anna (mother), 188, 268
Strasser, Anna, 188, 189 (photo), 268
Strasser, Julius, 188, 268
Suevia, 216
Sullivan, Louis, 178
Switzerland, 68, 94, 101, 175, 266
Syvertson, Henry, Sgt., 68

T

Thiel, Nicholas, 97
Thubeauville, Christoph, 96
Trier, 14, 45, 92–103; Archbishop of, 14–15
Turkey Creek, 169–170, 172, 294
Twain, Mark, 153
Twenty-Third Regiment (*see* Illinois Volunteer Infantry)

U

Ubil, Rose Victoria (*see* Stein)
Union Army, 63–64, 69–74, 76, 151, 192
United States Bureau of Pensions, 194–195, 247
United States House of Representatives, 179
United States Marine Band, 261
United States Senate, 179
University of Chicago, 178–179

V

Vallat, Ludwig, 97
Varain, Bernhard, 96
Vienna, 94, 209–211, 213–215, 219, 221, 229, 232, 234, 237, 239–240
Vink, Alle Cornelsche, 129

W

Warner, Ezra, 225–226
Warweiler, Johann Baptist, 97
Washington, DC, 69, 152, 179, 261
Wasmansdorff, Otto, 279
Weckman, Barbara, 81
Weckman, Helena (Lena Deppe), 81, 108, 118, 122, 125–126, 136–137, 139–140, 169, 172, 293
Weiland, Maria Magdalena, 29–30, 40
Wellenstein, August, 97
Wellenstein, Johann, 20, 33–34, 40
Wellenstein, Katharina (Deppe), 32–34, 36–38
Wellenstein, Magdalena (*see* Kaufman)
Wellenstein, Susanna, 33
Wendell, Charles, 299
Wenzel, General, 77
Westen (Der), 271
Western Bowlers' Journal (The), 220, 275
William II of Germany (H.I. M.), 273
W.M. Hoyt & Co., 222–223 (photo), 224, 229, 237, 250–251, 275
Woollacott, John S., 181
Worcester Lunatic Hospital, 231
World's Columbian Exposition, 179–180, 184, 191–192
Wolfe, Eliesabeta (Lizzie Ganser), 154–155, 193, 245–247, 293
Wolf, Jacob, 154
Wright, Dorothy Ruth (*see* Stein)
Wurster, Charles, 183, 188, 309

Y

Yates, Governor, 64

Z

Zweibrücken, 29–30

www.ingramcontent.com/pod-product-compliance
Lightning Source LLC
Chambersburg PA
CBHW030228170426
43201CB00006B/149